British History in Perspective

General Editor: Jeremy Black

(*List continued overleaf*)

History of Ireland

D. G. Boyce *The Irish Question and British Politics, 1868–1996 (2nd edn)*
Seán Duffy *Ireland in the Middle Ages*
David Harkness *Ireland in the Twentieth Century: Divided Island*

History of Scotland

Keith M. Brown *Kingdom or Province? Scotland and the Regal Union, 1603–1715*
John F. McCaffrey *Scotland in the Nineteenth Century*
Bruce Webster *Medieval Scotland*

History of Wales

A. D. Carr *Medieval Wales*
J. Gwynfor Jones *Early Modern Wales, c.1525–1640*

Further titles are in preparation

Please note that a sister series, *Social History in Perspective*, is now available. It covers the key topics in social, cultural and religious history.

British History in Perspective
Series Standing Order
ISBN 0–333–71356–7 hardcover
ISBN 0–333–69331–0 paperback
(*outside North America only*)

You can receive future titles in this series as they are published by placing a standing order. Please contact your bookseller or, in case of difficulty, write to us at the address below with your name and address, the title of the series and the ISBN quoted above.

Customer Services Department, Macmillan Distribution Ltd
Houndmills, Basingstoke, Hampshire RG21 6XS, England

Anglo-American Relations in the Twentieth Century

Ritchie Ovendale
formerly Professsor of International Politics,
University of Wales, Aberystwyth

Published by
PALGRAVE MACMILLAN
Houndmills, Basingstoke, Hampshire RG21 6XS and
175 Fifth Avenue, New York, N. Y. 10010
Companies and representatives throughout the world

PALGRAVE MACMILLAN is the global academic imprint of the Palgrave Macmillan division of St. Martin's Press, LLC and of Palgrave Macmillan Ltd. Macmillan® is a registered trademark in the United States, United Kingdom and other countries. Palgrave is a registered trademark in the European Union and other countries.

Outside North America
ISBN 0–333–59612–9 hardback
ISBN 0–333–59613–7 paperback

Inside North America
ISBN 0–312–21454–5 paperback

This book is printed on paper suitable for recycling and made from fully managed and sustained forest sources.

A catalogue record for this book is available from the British Library.

A catalog record for this book is available from the Library of Congress.

Printed and bound in Great Britain by
Antony Rowe Ltd, Chippenham and Eastbourne

Contents

ACKNOWLEDGEMENTS

Part of the research of this book was made possible by grants from the Nuffield Foundation, and from the British Academy and its Small Grants Fund in the Humanities, and by a visiting research fellowship from the American Council of Learned Societies tenable at the University of Virginia, Charlottesville. The Australian National University, Canberra, kindly elected me a visiting research fellow in the Department of International Relations attached to the Research School of Pacific Studies.

I should like to thank the following for assistance: Professor Christopher Andrew, Sir Harold Beeley, Professor Inis Claude, Professor John Garnett, the late Professor Agnes Headlam-Morley, Professor Edward Ingram, Professor Ieuan John, Dr Clive Jones, James W. Leyerzapf, Professor Wm Roger Louis, the late Professor J. D. B. Miller, Professor Ian Nish, the late Professor F. S. Northedge, Dr Alistair Parker, Professor James Piscatori, Sir Frank K. Roberts, Professor Keith Robbins, Dr Len Scott, Professor Jack Spence, David Steeds, Professor Geoffrey Warner, and Professor D. Cameron Watt.

I am grateful to the library staffs of many institutions and archives for their expertise. In particular I should like to thank the following and, where appropriate, acknowledge permission to quote from collections in their custody: Churchill College, Cambridge, and the Earl Attlee for the Attlee Papers; the British Library for the Oliver Harvey Diaries; the British Library of Political and Economic Science for the Dalton Papers; the Western Manuscripts Department of the Bodleian Library, and the Master and Fellows of University College, Oxford, for the Attlee Papers; the Guy W. Bailey Library, the University of Vermont, for the Warren R. Austin and Ernest Gibson Jr papers; the Eisenhower Library, Abilene, Kansas; the Aldeman Library, University of Virginia; the George C. Marshall Library, Virginia Military Institute, for George C. Marshall's papers and other collections housed there; Princeton University Library; the Harry S. Truman Library, Independence, Missouri; the Franklin D. Roosevelt Library; Georgetown University Library for the Robert F. Wagner Papers;

the Library of Congress Manuscript Division; the National Archives in Washington together with the National Records Centre at Suitland, Maryland; the Australian Archives in Canberra; and the Australian National Library for the papers of Sir Percy Spender and Sir Robert Menzies. The staff of the Public Record Office, London, were always obliging and courteous; copyright material housed there appears by permission of Her Majesty's Stationery Office.

The *Explore* group, travelling on the Silk Road from Rawalpindi to Peking in August 1997, provided a welcome break from the writing of this book.

1

RAPPROCHEMENT

The relations between Britain and the United States have their roots in a war, the American War of Independence, initiated on 18 April 1775 with exchanges of fire at Lexington between the colonists and British forces, and concluded by the Peace of Paris on 3 September 1783, which left uncertain the boundaries with British North America. George III was reluctantly forced to accept 'the dismemberment of America from this Empire'. For the American colonists the separation from the mother country marked the birth of a new nation.[1]

Jay's Treaty of 1794 attempted to ameliorate difficulties between the two countries, but the provision of neutral rights allowed Britain during the Napoleonic Wars to violate American sovereignty by impressing American seamen into the British Navy often on the pretext that they were 'deserters', and to search American ships. Bradford Perkins, however, characterises the following decade as 'The First Rapprochement': there was peace on the frontier; both countries valued trading with one another; strife over impressment and ship searches lessened; and controversies with France forced the two English-speaking powers together.[2]

Against the background of the Napoleonic Wars and continued British impressment of American seamen, and Royal Navy violations of American territorial waters, the American Congress on 18 June 1812 declared war on Great Britain. Over fifty historians have offered explanations for this war for 'Free Trade and Sailors' Rights'. It involved the fledgling Canada. H. G. Nicholas observed of the peace at Ghent that ended the war in 1814 that it was 'the consequence of both sides recognizing that war was too costly a method of resolving their differences and that it had brought about certain lasting changes in their mutual relations'. It ushered in 'a period of Anglo-American pacification'.[3]

Trans-Atlantic commerce flourished. Between 1815 and 1826 around
2,877,000 immigrants came to the United States from Britain, adding to
the already considerable British population there, but 2 million of these
immigrants were Irish, forced out by famine, and not well inclined
towards England. Britain acceded to the American acquisition of
Florida from Spain, and suggested to Washington a joint Anglo-
American declaration recognising the independence of the former
Spanish colonies in Latin America, what Bradford Perkins has described
as a 'limited alliance', but although it was only British power that could
keep the European powers out of Latin America, Washington thought
that Britain and the United States were rivals in trade in Latin America.
In his message to Congress of 2 December 1823 President James
Monroe, mentioning the Old World and the New World as separate
spheres, stated: 'In the wars of the European powers, in matters relating
to themselves, we have never taken part, nor does it comport with our
policy so to do. *It is only when our rights are invaded, or seriously menaced* that we
resent injuries, or make preparations for our defense.' From 1852 this
became known as the Monroe Doctrine. It meant in effect that any
interference by Europe with the independence of American states would
be considered as unfriendly by the United States.

The Webster–Ashburton Treaty of 1842

Britain reserved to itself the right to colonise any 'unappropriated parts'
of America. A rebellion in Canada in 1837 precipitated a crisis in Anglo-
American relations, but Lord Durham, who had been sent by Britain to
report on conditions in Canada, thought that discontent in Canada
could result either in war between Britain and the United States, or in
some Canadians pressing to be annexed by the United States. He
recommended responsible government for some of the Canadian
provinces. The Webster–Ashburton Treaty of 1842 established the
boundary between Maine and Canada, and helped to settle most of
the North-Eastern boundary disputes. Some historians have interpreted
this as a considerable British diplomatic victory. British imperialism
and American manifest destiny also clashed over Oregon where the
American claims could have linked with those of Russia and stopped
Canada at the Rockies. Certain American diplomatic historians have
seen the subsequent Oregon Treaty as a triumph for American diplomacy, but Wilbur Devereux Jones insists that it was, rather, the

'accomplishment' of Lord Aberdeen, the British Foreign Secretary, who drew up the final items of the treaty himself. He considers that together with the settlement of the Maine boundary dispute, it was the most important product of the era, and that the signing of ambiguous agreements could be seen as 'one of the finest evidences of a mutual desire to keep the peace'.[4]

The Clayton–Bulwer Treaty of 1850

British influence in Central America actually increased between 1825 and 1848. In 1846, Washington, to shorten the routes from the Atlantic ports to the Far East, and to improve communications with the new territories on the Pacific, negotiated with Columbia rights to construct a canal over the Isthmus of Panama. A proposed alternative way through Lake Nicaragua stimulated British interest in its territory of Belize (British Honduras), and in 1848 Britain used its protectorate over the Mosquito Indians of Nicaragua to try to secure some control over the eastern end of the envisaged Nicaragua canal. Washington and London negotiated the Clayton–Bulwer Treaty in 1850, noted for its ambiguity and for the agreement that neither government would claim exclusive control over the proposed Isthmian canal. When in 1852 Britain made the Bay Islands, disputed with Honduras, a crown colony, the Americans invoked the non-colonisation principle of the Monroe Doctrine. But in 1869 Britain ceded the Bay Islands to Honduras, and relinquished its claims to the Mosquito coast of Nicaragua, and so ended 'a passage in British diplomatic history equalled in its tediousness only by some obscure aspects of the Eastern Question'.[5] The two decades before the outbreak of the American Civil War was a time when Britain had to accommodate to the emergence of the United States as its chief maritime rival, and a power of economic and military significance. As the commercial bond between the two countries strengthened in the 1850s, threats of war to settle disputes between them became less and less credible.

The American Civil War

With the secession of the slave states in the winter of 1860–1 Anglo-American understanding shattered. The preceding decade, in the view of

Michael Crawford, had been one in which 'cooperation and inter-dependence between Great Britain and the United States had never been greater'; 'for British political and economic leaders in particular the vision of an Anglo-American hegemony in the civilised world offered a powerful inducement for eradicating those differences which, it was assumed, prevented the consummation of a unique and irresistible partnership across the Atlantic divide'.[6] There has been a great deal of argument about the changing opinions of various sections of British and American societies towards each other during the Civil War. Several episodes left a legacy. A British ship, the *Trent*, carrying representatives of the South to London hoping for recognition of the Confederacy, was intercepted in the Bahama Channel by Captain Charles Wilkes of the United States Navy. National honour was saved on both sides by personal diplomacy conducted by officials who liked each other, and by unofficial representations, and the Southerners were released.

The South also acquired ships from Britain, and one, the *Alabama*, between 1862 and 1864 was armed and destroyed commerce between Britain and the United States by attacking trading vessels. After the war, against the background of demands for the cession of Canada as compensation, Britain accepted arbitration, and on 14 September 1871 agreed to pay $15,500,000, a gesture later viewed by a leading American historian as 'one of the most excellent investments the British Empire ever made': by this move Britain stopped the possibility of small naval enemies building fleets in neutral territory in future wars. Washington's sympathetic attitude to London during the Second Anglo-Boer War could be attributed to this resolution, and Britain, during the First World War, could also be seen as profiting 'beyond measure by her far-sighted decision not to protest the blockade during the Civil War in the United States'. The settlement of the *Alabama* claims was, as H. G. Nicholas has observed, 'followed by two decades of almost complete diplomatic inactivity between Washington and London, the longest period of amicable inanition that Anglo-American relations have ever known?', a period which saw marriages negotiated between the aristocracy of Britain and the industrial and financial houses of the United States.[7]

Imperialism and 'The Great Rapprochement'

It was, however, the era of imperialism that ushered in what Bradford Perkins has described as 'The Great Rapprochement' between Britain and the United States, a phenomenon which has been variously attributed to 'Anglo-Saxondom', an American realisation of the burden of imperialism, or as H. C. Allen has commented in gentler vein: 'The new friendship of the English-speaking peoples was an indispensable factor in determining the policy of each country and in ensuring that their paths ran on the whole parallel.'[8]

The two decades of diplomatic inactivity ended on 20 July 1895 when Richard Olney, the American Secretary of State, informed London that Britain should submit the dispute it had with Venezuela over the boundaries of British Guiana to arbitration. Invoking the Monroe Doctrine, he informed London that 'today the United States is practically sovereign on this continent'. There was talk of war. But against the background of the failure of the British-inspired Jameson Raid into the Transvaal in January 1896, aimed at undermining President Paul Kruger's Boer Republic, and the subsequent congratulatory telegram sent by the German Kaiser to Kruger, some authorities have argued that Britain felt isolated in Europe and could not afford to alienate the Americans. Britain agreed to a restricted arbitration, and, in any case, secured most of what it wanted when the board reported in October 1899, though Washington secured its objective in that Britain did not retain the entry to the Orinoco River, which was considered of economic value. Sometimes seen as the last threat of war between Britain and the United States, one author has observed of the settlement of this crisis: the British 'sacrificed their prestige to their belief that war with the United States was unthinkable'.[9]

Arthur Campbell Turner has pointed to the change of the American national experience at this time. He cites the address of 1893 by Frederick Jackson Turner on the passing of 'the Frontier', the availability of land for settlement in the West, and how shortly afterwards the United States itself became an imperial power in 1898 when it annexed the Hawaiian Islands, and following its victory in the Spanish-American War, acquired Puerto Rico, Guam, and the Philippines, and control of Cuba. Britain was the only European power which regarded this change in the American psychology in a friendly way. Lord Salisbury, the British Prime Minister, assured Washington in October 1897 that British interests in Cuba were commercial and that he would approve of measures to restore peace on Cuba. The British poet Rudyard Kipling, married to an American, wrote 'The White Man's Burden', urging the Americans to annex Cuba. British seapower was seen to have prevented intervention against the United States by Germany. In July 1898

London approved the American annexation of the Philippines and Hawaii. Britain became more popular in America than it had ever been, and enthusiasm for a common Anglo-Saxon heritage was evidenced. There was talk of an alliance, and even a reunion between the two countries.[10]

As a fellow imperial power, the United States indulged British colonial aspirations. During the Second Anglo-Boer War, 1899-1902, the United States reciprocated the friendly stand Britain had evidenced during the Spanish American War: in an election year the Republican administration ignored the Democrats' endorsement of the Boers.

In the Far East, Britain and the United States discovered a common interest in maintaining freedom of commerce for all nations. President William McKinley, during March 1898, refused a British proposal for joint action to preserve the 'Open Door' in China. But in September 1899 John Hay, the Secretary of State from September 1898 to July 1905, sent identical notes to London, Berlin, St Petersburg, Tokyo, Rome, and Paris proposing the nonintervention-with-commerce principles, known as the 'Open Door'. The other powers laid down conditions, but Britain approved. There was no real conflict of interest between Washington and London over China: both countries wanted to preserve China's territorial integrity, while maintaining its economic dependence and accessibility, and saw Russia and Germany as their opponents in this. When the West intervened in China with the Boxer Rebellion in 1900, both Britain and the United States were part of the rescue expedition but were anxious to prevent this from being an excuse to dismember China.

Britain did, however, experience difficulties with the United States on the American continent over the definition of the boundary between Alaska and Canada, and the revision of the Clayton–Bulwer Treaty of 1850 on the isthmian canal. Salisbury, feeling that the latter treaty placed Britain in an equal position to the United States on paper anyway, tried to negotiate over the two issues at the same time. But Washington proved to be inflexible over Alaska, and the acquisition of Hawaii and the Philippines made a canal between the Caribbean and the Pacific all the more urgent. On the canal issue the first treaty, signed on 5 February 1900 by Hay and the British ambassador, Sir Julian Pauncefote, by duplicating the provisions of the Suez Convention of 1888, retained the provision of neutralisation desired by the British. The American Senate objected. A second treaty of 1901, the Olney–Pauncefote Treaty, gave Washington the right to police the canal provided that it were open in peace and war to all ships. By this Britain effectively abrogated any pretensions to supremacy in the American hemisphere. President Theodore Roosevelt went ahead with the construction of the Panama Canal in 1904, and it was completed in 1914. On the Canadian boundary dispute Britain was conscious of Canadian sensibilities, and of the need not to concede too much to the Americans over this. But in 1902 Roosevelt sent American troops into Alaska. Britain had accepted the American proposal for adjudication by three American, two Canadian and one British judges. When the British judge aligned with his American counterparts, the Canadians in 1903 were forced to accept the American version of the boundary.

Perhaps by this time London saw its interests as being best served by ameliorating relations with Washington in the American hemisphere. Britain's policy of splendid isolation was increasingly challenged by Britain's diminishing industrial strength at a time when that of Germany and the United States was increasing significantly. With the coming into being of Admiral von Tirpitz's Navy Law in 1898 Germany decided to build an ocean navy: this resulted in a similar naval thinking in both London and Washington.

This emerging power alignment was tested with the Venezuelan crisis of 1902 when Britain, largely at Germany's instigation, sided with Berlin in mounting a naval demonstration to insist on the collection of foreign bondholders' debts: several Venezuelan ships were sunk. London did consult Washington in advance. The American public, however, was outraged, and many in Britain protested that this could jeopardise American friendship. The newly elected President Theodore Roosevelt, sensitive to European intrusions into the American hemisphere, wanted arbitration. Britain acceded, but Roosevelt had to put pressure on the Kaiser. This comparatively minor incident showed the extent to which London accepted Washington's newly found role as a world power, and was prepared to co-operate closely with its former colony on the basis of equal status.

At this time of Great Power realignment Britain's search for allies led, in the Far East, to the Anglo-Japanese alliance of 1902. This alliance established the principle of neutrality in any conflict with a third power, and committed both Britain and Japan to support the Open Door and the territorial integrity of China. To Washington this was a cost-free means of curtailing Russian expansion. During the Russo-Japanese War of 1904 it was Roosevelt who restrained the Japanese from securing an overwhelming victory. The American President was consulted about the revision of the Anglo-Japanese alliance in 1905. This showed that London was not prepared to commit itself to fight Washington. Under the revised alliance Japan and Britain bound themselves to maintain a force in the Far East superior to that of any European power, a change from the original 'outside' power, and neither state was obliged to go to war with any country with which it had a general treaty of arbitration. The alliance was constructed in such a way that it would not incite Anglo-American rivalry.

This decade of imperial expansion is often viewed as a bonding one in the Anglo-American relationship.[11] In a work published in 1964 Coral Bell observed: 'Perhaps 1896 can be regarded as the date of a firm decision by Britain that the normal sort of power competition between sovereign states must not be the mode of her relationship with the U.S.' It was then that Britain assumed 'that American and British interests would in the end prove complementary in the central conflicts of international politics'.[12] About the same time Max Beloff perceived that

ever since the 1890s the dominant element in the British 'establish-ment' has known in its heart that the world order dependent on British sea-power which was the key to the unparalleled growth of the western economy in the nineteenth century could no longer be sustained by British power alone. It was therefore the intended lot of the United States, perhaps its moral duty, to take over an increasing share of this burden and to use its new strength to further Britain's original purposes.[13]

Contemporary with these arguments was that in the monograph by R. G. Neale: 'The quality of Anglo-American friendship and the effect of the Spanish American War upon Anglo-American relations have both been greatly exaggerated.' Neale argues that the British took the initiative, and were always conscious of the continuing Anglophobia latent in American politics. The Americans always expected and re-ceived concessions from Britain: this showed 'the measure of Britain's need and of her determination to achieve an Anglo-American entente'.[14]

In 1981 Stuart Anderson, accepting that a diplomatic rapprochement was forged between Britain and the United States between 1895 and 1904, insisted that one of the most important contributing factors in the making of this friendship was the popular doctrine of 'Anglo-Saxonism', the doctrine that Britons and Americans were both racial and cultural kinsmen, and that as a 'race', the Anglo-Saxons were innately superior to other peoples. Anderson examines the extent to which Darwinism was a source of Anglo-Saxonism, and shows how British and American leaders, including Arthur Balfour and Joseph Chamberlain, and Theodore Roosevelt and John Hay, were influenced by Anglo-Saxonist ideas in their handling of diplomacy.[15] Turner had pointed out earlier that, at the time, Anglo-Saxondom was understood loosely, and embraced not only Americans generally, but the Afrikaners of South Africa and the French Canadians. Joseph Chamberlain extended the concept to the Germans, and this version of Anglo-Saxon was reflected in the original terms of the trust of the Rhodes scholarships, established by the great imperialist Cecil John Rhodes to educate the potential leaders of the Anglo-Saxon world at Oxford.[16]

Anne Orde, in her study published in 1996 of Britain's reaction to the assertion of American hegemony in the Western hemisphere between 1895 and 1914, points to a discussion of how the Anglo-Saxon navies could enforce the law of the sea against all the world, but shows that the omission of the United States from calculations of the British naval standard was hardly ever questioned, and that the Admiral of the Fleet from 1904 to 1910, Lord Fisher, never accepted that war with the United States was possible. Orde does emphasise, however, that on the American side the strategist Alfred Thayer Mahan, while never advocating challenging British naval mastery, only envisaged division of areas of interest. Suspicions of Germany and Japan meant that an American navy, originally anti-British, became more sensitive to the need to co-operate with the Royal Navy.[17]

Britain's Strategic Abandonment of the Western Hemisphere

Between 1904 and 1906 Britain withdrew its remaining garrisons from the West Indies and from Canada. This, in the words of Arthur Campbell Turner, meant 'a British strategic abandonment of the Western Hemisphere'. Precipitated by economic necessity the decision reflected a realisation that in the event of an unlikely American attack on either Canada or the West Indies, Britain would not be able to defend the territories. In 1909 the Committee of Imperial Defence concluded that attack by the United States need not be taken into consideration in determining the standard of defences of the ports of the Western Atlantic.[18] This was on the British side.

Bruce M. Russett argues that it was the lingering fear of war with

Britain, as well as the fear of being left alone in the world with a hostile Germany, that led to the American Navy's insistence on building many battleships throughout the first two decades of the twentieth century, and that this policy was not abandoned even with the desperate need for destroyers during the First World War. As late as June 1916 the Assistant Chief of Naval Operations measured American needs 'against all possible contingencies', including a war against Britain. It should be remembered, however, that the managers of the Anglo-American alliance took care to improve relations before the outbreak of the First World War. In 1912 the American Congress exempted American coastal shipping from paying tolls for using the Panama Canal when it opened. When, in 1913, President William Taft signed this into law, the British ambassador, James Bryce, protested that this contravened the Hay–Pauncefote Treaty that all tolls had to be levied equally. In 1914 Britain, supporting its oil interests in Mexico, supported a different faction from the Americans in the revolutionary situation. Britain and the United States achieved a compromise. The new American president, Woodrow Wilson, accepted the advice of his confidant, Colonel Edward M. House, that it was preferable to make concessions to Britain over Panama rather than risk losing its support for Washington's policy in Mexico, Central and South America. Wilson, a great moralist and convinced that Britain was right, asked Congress to repeal Taft's law. When Congress obliged, Britain withdrew its support from the Mexican dictator. On the eve of the First World War the two leading English-speaking nations could be seen to be capable of reaching an accommodation with each other, and to be moving closer together. In April 1914 the British Secretary of State for Foreign Affairs, Arthur Balfour, made the first official visit to the United States by a member of the British Cabinet.[19]

The First World War

In a recent study, Anne Orde points to the First World War as marking 'an important stage in the rise of American power, absolutely and in relation to that of Britain'. But she takes care to emphasise the limits of the newly acknowledged Great Power: Washington's economic and financial resources could not secure for President Woodrow Wilson the position of arbiter he wanted for himself and his country. She also shows that at the end of the war Britain's territory was not physically devastated, and that the financial dependence on the United States Britain had experienced in the closing period of the war was not expected to be permanent.[20] Throughout the period of the First World War financial dealings between London and Washington created difficulties. But the most obvious point of potential conflict was over maritime neutral rights, and this problem did not go away with the peace. At the outbreak of war Wilson asked the American people to be neutral 'in thought as well as in action'. But Wilson was surrounded and advised by men who favoured Britain and the Allied cause: his own counsellor, Colonel Edward M. House, believed in the Allied cause; the American ambassador in London, Walter Hines Page, has been described as 'extravagantly' pro-British. William James Bryan resigned as Secretary of State following the sinking of the *Lusitania* on 7 May 1915 rather than connive at Americans exposing themselves to being sucked into the war by allowing themselves to be exposed to danger. Robert Lansing, who succeeded him, believed that an Allied victory was essential for the United States. But perhaps, as H. G. Nicholas has argued, what swayed Wilson more 'was the pervasive awareness in London of the nature and grounds of American susceptibilities and the need for respecting them'.

It was evident from the outset of hostilities that a blockade would be a major weapon for Britain with its command of the seas, but that this would lead to clashes with the United States, the leading neutral trader in the world at that time. The British Foreign Secretary, Sir Edward (later Viscount) Grey, was determined that no Allied action should be taken that could break relations with Washington. For instance, to avoid disrupting American trade, cotton was not placed on the contraband list until August 1915. In any case, in many Americans' eyes, any infringement of neutral rights by blockade was overshadowed by German submarine warfare in the Atlantic.[21]

Many of the standard works explaining American intervention in the First World War concentrate on the period 1914–17.[22] John W. Coogan, however, has asserted that this periodisation has led to a distorted view of American neutrality, and that to comprehend it and the reasons why it broke down, it is essential to understand 'the legal as well as the strategic and political contexts in which British statesmen evolved the blockade of Germany and American leaders responded to the consequent curtailment of trade'. These maritime issues were not new: Washington and London had disputed doctrines of continuous voyage, visit and search, retaliation, contraband, and blockade for over a century, and in the fifteen years before 1914 two wars and three international conferences 'had emphasized the importance of maritime rights and shaped both the law and the perceptions of statesmen'. Coogan argues that a viable system of international law did exist in 1914, and that this system offered Washington a realistic opportunity to maintain effective neutrality; but 'this legal order crumbled, and the opportunities were missed, because Woodrow Wilson ultimately placed preservation of Anglo-American friendship above preservation of American neutrality under the rules of international law'. Coogan asserts that by April 1915 the United States was no longer entitled to the legal status of neutral.[23]

When Germany declared unrestricted submarine warfare, Wilson responded on 10 February 1915 that Germany would be held to 'strict accountability' for 'property endangered or lives lost'. On 7 May 1915 the Cunard liner the *Lusitania* was sunk off the coast of Ireland; 1,100 lives were lost including those of 128 American citizens. Germany justified its action in that the *Lusitania* was a 'semiwarship' which was carrying munitions and troops. Bryan, the Secretary of State, felt that Wilson's notes to Germany were close to an ultimatum, and he resigned arguing that Germany had a right to prevent contraband from going to the Allies. Following several other incidents Berlin agreed, on 4 May 1916, that no more merchant vessels would be sunk without warning. Wilson became determined to avoid American entry into the conflict by ending the war.

By this time Allied purchases were making significant contributions to the American economy. At the start of the war, Washington owed London money. Initially this helped Britain to pay for the goods it bought, and this was supplemented by British exports and the sale of British-owned securities in the United States. But loans became necessary, and the first in October 1915 came from the Anglophile House of Morgan. By the end of the war Britain had borrowed $3.7 billion. This American economic interest in an Allied victory, however, did not mean an enthusiasm for American military intervention.

Instead, in February, House suggested to Grey that Wilson was ready to propose a Conference to end the war. Should the Allies accept the proposal and Germany prove unreasonable, the United States would join the Allied cause. But Grey did not take the suggestion seriously, particularly as at that time Germany had the advantage militarily. With a presidential campaign in the offing Wilson, to pre-empt his

Republican opponents, strengthened the armed forces, and then campaigned for re-election under the slogan: 'He kept us out of war.' Frustrated in his efforts to negotiate peace, on 22 January 1917 Wilson outlined proposals for world peace which included freedom of the seas, a League to enforce the peace, the limitation of armaments, government by the consent of the governed, and 'peace without victory'. These were later elaborated in his Fourteen Points. Increasingly, it is argued, Wilson felt that America would have to fight before his ideas would be considered around the peace table.

Germany started unrestricted submarine warfare. In February 1917, Britain gave Wilson a copy of a telegram from Arthur Zimmermann, the German Foreign Secretary, to his minister in Mexico: Berlin proposed that if Washington declared war, Mexico should join forces with Germany and Japan and be rewarded with Texas, New Mexico and Arizona. When this was published on 1 March, opinion in the United States moved towards war. With the fall of the Tsar in Russia the Allied cause lost the taint of autocracy. In March five American ships were sunk by German submarines. On 6 April 1917 Congress endorsed Wilson's request for a declaration of war against the German Empire.[24]

In fighting the war at sea, Britain and the United States co-operated closely: there was a joint command under a British admiral. But on land the American Commander-in-Chief, John Pershing, insisted on maintaining the separate identity of his forces.

In a recent study of the politics of Anglo-American relations over the conduct of the land war in Europe between 1917 and 1918, David R. Woodward shows how the relationship between the British Prime Minister, David Lloyd George, and the American President, was poisoned by their mutual suspicion and hostility, which was encouraged by their disagreements over military strategy. Woodward argues that each country pursued its own interests: the Americans wanted, through their military effort in Western Europe, to achieve acceptance of Woodrow Wilson's 'new diplomacy' outlined in his Fourteen Points; the British worries about the threat the alliance between Turkey and Germany posed to Asia, and their worsening manpower situation, wanted to use American intervention for their own political and military purposes.

Woodward points particularly to the role of Pershing who, long before London considered the importance of American landpower, had 'developed plans that profoundly shaped America's participation in the anti-German coalition until the end of the war'. Pershing wanted an independent American army, and he was deaf to any British requests for assistance which impinged on his grand design. Pershing thought that a Western strategy would bring American victory in 1919.

Once the United States entered the war, Lloyd George became interested in negotiating a peace with Berlin, and began to equivocate over his policy of the 'knock-out blow': total victory might not be worth the price if Britain had to bear the brunt of the fighting on the Western Front in 1918. Wilson considered, and then rejected Lloyd George's proposal for the creation of a special Anglo-American relationship to achieve victory over Germany. This led to Lloyd George contemplating seriously peace negotiations with Berlin. Wilson thought Washington's interests were best served by concentrating on the Western Front. When Lloyd George tried to win American support for an extra-Continental role to further British interests, Wilson apparently agreed with House that the United States should not become involved in the expansion of the British Empire in the Middle East.

In delivering his Fourteen Points to Congress on 8 January 1918 Wilson, at the outset, insisted that all Russian territory should be evacuated by the Central Powers. In doing this he appeared, according to Woodward, to accept that only a crushing defeat of the German army could prevent Berlin dominating Europe. Lloyd George, however, was moving away from this concept, and the British Prime Minister said that a defeat of an impending German attack in France, Italy, or anywhere else would in itself constitute military victory. Wilson refused to allow American involvement to shore up Britain's deteriorating position in Asia. Effectively Lloyd George's plan 'of conserving British manpower by gradually shifting the burden of the fighting to the United States lay in ruins'.

German pressure on the British front in March and April 1918 did not forge close Anglo-American ties. The Americans wanted to build up an army capable of playing the leading role in defeating Germany in 1919, which would mean an American victory at the peace table as well. The British feared that without significant American assistance 'they would not have the means to secure both their position on the Continent and their imperial possessions against the Turko-German menace'.

In a chapter entitled 'Pax Americana' Woodward appositely concludes that 'despite America's and Britain's common struggle against Germany, Wilson's substitution of moral for traditional diplomacy and his self-appointed role as the peoples' spokesman militated against the future peace and stability of the world'.[25]

The Peace Negotiations

In January 1918 Wilson and Lloyd George separately made announcements of peace aims. Wilson outlined his Fourteen Points. London was worried that the first of these points appeared to exclude reparations from Germany, and that that would offend the French. The Point pledging freedom of the seas could also be seen as denying Britain the weapon of blockade. Germany asked for an armistice on the basis of the Fourteen Points, and against the background of Washington threatening to make a separate peace, negotiations started.

Wilson went to Paris for the conference which opened on 18 January 1918, faced by a newly elected Republican majority in the Senate with Henry Cabot Lodge, an opponent of Wilson's plans for an association of nations, as chairman of the Senate Foreign Relations Committee. In his so-called Khaki election of December 1918 Lloyd George had been seen as giving in to demands for soldiers' revenge and a punitive peace. Wilson's tour of Britain on the way to Paris showed that the American President had not understood the impact of war on the British public. The American President did not trust the British Prime Minister, and Lloyd George thought Wilson a hypocrite. John Maynard Keynes, a Treasury adviser to the British delegation at Paris, damned Wilson's lack of constructive ideas and moralistic idealism.

H. G. Nicholas, however, has observed that 'beneath these clashes of personality and national moods lay deeper long-range similarities of outlook and interests', and that this was most apparent in the shaping of the Covenant of the League of Nations, a body that in conception was as much British as American. The notion evolved from President Taft's 'League to Enforce Peace', and in Britain from the schemes of the Fabians and a group around Lord Bryce. At Paris there was a joint Anglo-American draft. At an early stage the main principles of the Covenant were agreed between Washington and London, with the emphasis being on the voluntary nature of the League, particularly with regard to powers of enforcement. There was also a large measure of agreement between Britain and the United States as to the terms of the peace: both wanted the elimination of Germany as a naval power but resisted French annexationist tendencies. Seth P. Tillman has shown that 'there was a natural harmony of interests between Britain and America in regard to the boundary settlements of Europe': both countries hoped that the boundary lines drawn would be durable because they were based on the self-determination of nationalities, or, in exceptional cases, on natural economic units.

There was conflict between Washington and the British Empire as a whole over the issue of colonies and mandates. Indeed, at a meeting of the War Cabinet on 30–1 December 1918, W. M. Hughes, the Prime Minister of Australia, objected to the American position and thought that the powerful British Empire had no need to co-operate with the United States. Lord Reading, who had acted as Lloyd George's emissary to Wilson, protested that Britain's 'main object was to bring about the closest cooperation hereafter between ourselves and the United States'. The Canadian Prime Minister, Robert Borden, however, thought that the greatest gain that the Empire could secure from the war was good relations with the United States. Lord Robert Cecil, the Minister of Blockade, explained that Britain's main interest was to secure a settled Peace: this could be best guaranteed by a good understanding with the United States. As well as Australia's demands for colonial territories to be taken from Germany, Britain had to take cognisance of the claims by the South African representative J. C. Smuts, made in the interests of South African security.

Hughes was also instrumental in securing a refusal of the Japanese request for a declaration of racial equality to be inserted into the Covenant of the League. In this he was supported by both London and Washington, and the Western powers were left in no position to resist the Japanese demands for the transfer to them of the German rights over Kiaochow and Shantung. Wilson's opponents in the Senate later used this transfer as a reason for rejecting the Versailles Treaty.

Washington and London differed on the matter of reparations from Germany. London's concern was to reduce the national debt, and to protect British trade from American competition. Washington was interested in the early revival of German trade, and in the general expansion of trade without restrictions.[26]

The provisions of the Treaty of Versailles went before the American Senate in the summer of 1919, and were rejected then, and again in March 1920. Arguably issues of Anglo-American relations had little to do with this rebuff. It is possible to single out the activities of the Irish-American lobby at a time when Britain was faced with demands for the partition of Ireland, and as Alan J. Ward has observed 'we know that the Irish in America were at the very heart of the American campaign to defeat the Peace Treaty'.[27] H. G. Nicholas has also argued that work by the economist John Maynard Keynes, *Economic Consequences of the Peace*, published in Britain in December 1919 and shortly afterwards in the United States, provided American liberals with the munition with which to reject Wilson's moralistic idealism.[28]

Recent scholarship has been inclined to consider Anglo-American relations during the first two decades of the twentieth century in terms of an enhancement of American power at a time when Britain could be seen to be in a state of relative economic decline. Britain's status as a world power rested partly on an Empire, which at the end of the First World War saw a huge increase in territorial suzerainty with the addition of much of the Middle East as a result of the Eastern campaign. Authorities have pointed to an emerging rapprochement between the former colony and the mother country during the nineteenth century, to similar outlooks in what has loosely been termed 'Anglo-Saxondom', and to the ability of individuals on both sides of the Atlantic to understand each other and co-operate. But most recent research has shown the extent to which the United States wanted victory during the First World War both on land and at the peace table, and that American leaders wanted to secure this in their own interests and at Britain's expense.

2

ISOLATIONISM AND APPEASEMENT

Studies of Anglo-American relations during the 1920s have emphasised the extent to which the United States increased its economic power in relation to that of Britain. These works have concentrated on the financial aspect of the relationship and have pointed to the extent to which Washington benefited at London's expense from the settlement of Britain's war debts to the United States in 1923, as well as the debt agreements Washington reached with the other Allies, the American role in restoring Germany's economy so that it could pay reparations, and the development by American financiers and industrialists of new markets abroad. Much of this work was by American scholars: it suggested that by the late 1920s Washington's world influence had, to an extent, superseded that of London.

In 1967 the Public Records Act of 1958 was revised: the fifty-year rule was changed to thirty years. Most of the documents of British policy which had been preserved for the record for the period 1914 to 1937 became available to researchers on 1 January 1968, and thereafter at the beginning of each year the records were available thirty-one years after they had been written – one year being allowed for their transfer to the Public Record Office. This vast new supply of documents changed the focus of the study of Anglo-American relations: it began to be viewed through the eyes of British policymakers; a new generation of historians, British or British-trained, together with a small group of American historians who enjoyed spending summers in London, began to produce a volume of literature inclined to question the assumptions of an earlier generation of pre-dominantly American historians. The newly available British account also included significant material on American policy the record of which either had not been preserved or was not available in Washington.

There is now a body of literature inclining to the argument that in the 1920s Washington's emerging economic strength merely meant that the power it exercised on the international scene was 'more potential than real'. Britain's power, however, was 'real': Britain still had a relatively strong economy, overseas wealth, and a stable currency; the size of the Royal Navy was considerable, and there were the strategic benefits of the Empire; Britain's participation in the League of Nations and the role it played on the European continent all helped to sustain its international status as a Great Power. Relative to Washington, London was in a weaker position than it had been at the outbreak of the First World War, but in 1929, with the Wall Street crash and the Great Depression, B. J. C. McKercher argues that Britain had yet to be surpassed by the United States: 'The struggle for supremacy in the 1920s had not been lost by Britain.'[1]

At the end of the First World War British leaders, particularly the Prime Minister, David Lloyd George, hoped for the continuation of a co-operative spirit in the peace, and were prepared to modify their policy towards the prospective League of Nations, particularly on matters such as territorial and political guarantees and sanctions as a way of resolving disputes, to mollify Wilson as a way of achieving this. But domestic opposition to the Covenant in the United States, the Senate's refusal to endorse American membership of the League of Nations, and the Republican victory in November 1920 with the election of President Warren Harding together with control of the Congress, largely on the basis of a platform of isolationism, left British leaders with a feeling of betrayal.[2]

Faced with Washington's determination to remain isolated from world affairs, London, unable to return to any form of splendid isolationism, had to negotiate with a former ally that not only had a markedly different outlook on foreign policy, but also domestically pursued a very different ideological goal with the Republican emphasis on big business, at a time when Britain was undergoing a social revolution with the ousting of the Liberals by the Labour Party and a commitment to trade unionism and Socialism.[3]

Economic and Financial Issues in the 1920s

Historians discussing the Anglo-American relationship during the 1920s have inclined to a concentration on the economic and financial issues.

This has perhaps resulted in tendency to equate American pre-eminence as the leading economic and industrial power with pre-eminence as the world political power, taking over Britain's mantle.

At the start of the First World War, Britain had been the pre-eminent financial power. Britain had supported its allies with loans, often raised on the American market. This meant that London borrowed in Washington and then lent the money to the Allies in Europe; by 1920 Britain owed the Americans $4,000 million (£850 million) and was due around $8,000 million (£1,825 million). After Congress passed the Debt Funding Act in February 1922, Washington invited its debtors to suggest ways of settling their debts. Britain, in the Balfour note of 1 August 1922, suggested the cancellation of all the inter-Allied debts, and reparations as well. The Americans would not accept the link between war debts and reparations, and Britain had to agree to repay over 62 years with an annual interest of 3.3 per cent.

The other debtors were able to negotiate less severe terms. Britain's payments came from the reparations it received: by 1931 Britain had paid $1,911 million, around $200 million more than it had received from reparations payments. Britain never paid all the debt and the issue was a source of friction and bitterness on both sides of the Atlantic. The United States, by the end of the 1920s producing almost half of the world's manufactured goods, imposed high import tariffs with the Fordney–MacCumber Tariff of 1922, and so made it difficult for its debtors to pay.[4]

There has been considerable recent debate as to the extent to which there was co-operation between British and American financiers. One school argues that bankers in both countries continued to work well together after the end of the First World War, but that there was still a struggle for economic superiority between London and Washington, and that the Americans increasingly dominated the financial relationship.[5]

Roberta Dayer, however, while acknowledging that there was co-operation between British and American bankers early in the 1920s, concludes that they did see themselves as rivals, and that the American bankers were particularly adept at pursuing their own ends. Dayer further argues that the financial leaders in Britain wanted to co-operate with their American counterparts over monetary policy. They thought that given certain concessions, the Americans would co-operate. With this in view, Dayer claims that London agreed to abrogate the Anglo-Japanese alliance, accept parity in capital ships in 1922, settle the terms of the British war debt to the United States in 1923 before agreeing on the level of German reparations in 1924, and to return to the gold standard in 1925. These concessions, however, were met by an American refusal to co-operate in currency regulation, a hoarding of American gold, and a refusal to reduce Britain's war debt. Britain, initially prepared to make concessions in the Far East to secure a European settlement, felt betrayed, and during the second half of the 1920s pursued its own interest and resisted American inroads.[6]

Naval Rivalry

The naval rivalry evidenced between London and Washington in the 1920s has been seen as a reflection of a competition for Great Power status. The settlement, first demonstrated in the outcome of the Washington Conference of 1921–2, is still described in a recent work as being evidence of 'British realism in adjusting to the rise of US naval power while maintaining friendly relations with her'.[7] John Ferris offers an interesting variation of the familiar theme in his diagnosis of the American naval challenge in the Anglo-American struggle for supremacy. J. R. Ferris argues that the British leaders were concerned with other powers' perception of British naval strength as a means of Britain achieving its objectives by diplomacy as well as war. The British felt that the United States had the resources to build an unrivalled navy, but doubted that country's will to do so. Lloyd George and those around him decided that the American will would not be there unless Britain appeared as a threat to the United States. This, Ferris shows, resulted in a 'naval diplomacy', a bargaining to lessen American naval ambitions which would not weaken Britain's real position in the world, especially in regard to other potential enemies such as France. While prepared to accept equality with Washington in capital ships – those over 10,000 tons, like battleships – Britain would not agree to equality in vessels below 10,000 tons, such as cruisers. Britain, Ferris argues, surrendered little at the Washington Conference, even against Japan: London only compromised on the symbol. Britain 'remained by far the greatest seapower, one well able to defend its maritime interests': 'Rather than being a defeat, the Washington naval treaty was Britain's last victory of the First World War.'[8]

In December 1921 the Four Power Treaty replaced the Anglo-

Japanese alliance: the powers would respect each other's Pacific possessions and negotiate if difficulties arose. The Nine Power Treaty of 1922, which also included Italy, Portugal, Belgium, the Netherlands and China, was an endorsement of the 'Open Door' for China's administrative and territorial integrity, and both Washington and London put pressure on Japan to give up its 1919 gains from China: Britain surrendered the lease of its naval base at Weihaiwei, and Japan gave up Kiaochow. This was the diplomatic background to the Five Power Naval Treaty of 6 February 1922 with the retention of capital ships in the approximate ratio of 5 : 5 : 3 : 1.7 : 1.7, which gave Britain and the United States ships of around 500,000 tons, Japan 300,000 tons, and France and Italy 175,000 tons each. There would be no more capital ships built for ten years, and Britain, the United States and Japan accepted limitations in the construction of new strategic bases. Britain and the United States had very different naval requirements: Britain with its imperial lines of communication to defend, needed a lot of lightly armed vessels; the United States's requirement, operating from home bases, was fewer ships but with heavy armour. These differences led to an abortive naval conference at Geneva in 1927. But the matter was settled by the London Naval Treaty of 1930: Britain gained an advantage in lighter cruisers within a total of 339,000 tons, and the Americans had an advantage in heavier ships.[9]

European Security

With its position in relation to the European continent Britain remained concerned with problems of European security. Central to this was the dilemma of France. The Anglo-American guarantee of French security lapsed in 1919 with the rejection of the peace treaties by the American Senate. In 1924 Britain, Belgium, France, Germany and Italy signed the Locarno Agreements, a treaty of mutual guarantee reflecting the territorial status quo in Western Europe and requiring a flagrant breach to precipitate any aid. The Americans undermined the Treaty of Versailles with the Dawes Plan that same year: a scheme of annual payments adjusted to Germany's capacity to pay reparations, backed by a private, largely American loan to Germany to assist payment. The French, tempted by the prospect of Anglo-American financial assistance, accepted this at the London Conference of July 1924, and effectively emasculated their authority over Germany. There were illusions of a possible American move away from isolationism with the signing of the Kellogg–Briand Pact (the Pact of Paris of 1928): eventually sixty-two nations renounced war as an instrument of national policy, but there was no way of enforcing this. London, like Washington, was not prepared to pledge itself in advance to act to stop war. Indeed, at the time of the Geneva Disarmament Conference in 1932, Britain concluded that, in Europe, there could be no undertakings beyond the Locarno Agreements. This meant that Paris felt threatened by Berlin as it had no real guarantee of protection against German aggression.[10]

The Far Eastern Crisis of 1931–3

The Far Eastern crisis of 1931–3 exposed the myth of the Kellogg–Briand Pact. The Japanese invasion of Manchuria in September 1931 coincided with the economic crisis in Britain, and limited any prospect of imposing sanctions on one of Britain's main trading partners at a time of anxiety over the balance of payments. Washington, in contrast, had greater trading interests with Japan than with China. In January 1932, Henry L. Stimson, the Secretary of State, proclaimed the Stimson Doctrine: the United States would not recognise territorial changes brought about by force. Britain was consulted, but did not associate itself with any move to sustain the policy of the Open Door in China. A mythology developed that Britain failed to follow Washington's lead, and indeed refused an offer of co-operation in the international sphere, the implication being that Stimson was actually prepared to do something against Japan. But the only action that Stimson had contemplated was a joint representation to Japan. When Stimson asked Sir John Simon, the Foreign Secretary, to join him in invoking the Nine Power Treaty against Japan, the British response was to work through the League of Nations. By 1933 there was little prospect of any common Anglo-American front in the Far East.[11]

The Great Depression

This deteriorating political relationship was mirrored in the economic realm. Washington had hoped for the re-generation of the gold standard as the basis of a stable world economy in which it could import raw materials and export industrial products with a home base protected by tariffs. As Alan Dobson has pointed out in a recent study: to achieve this the United States needed the German economy to revive, and Britain to return to the gold standard. In 1925, partly through American persuasion, Winston Churchill, as Chancellor of the Exchequer, returned Britain to the gold standard. Frank Costigliola has observed that this was a British policy goal, an attempt by Britain to strengthen its imperial links, to 'regain its position as centre of the world economy, and meet the American challenge'. But Britain had to cope with a world market in which the United States was rapidly increasing its share, and displaying a sensitivity to any British dominance. For instance, Washington accused Britain of trying to assume control of the oil reserves of Mesopotamia. This dispute was resolved in 1929 with a private agreement between the British owners of the Turkish Petroleum Company, the French Compagnie des Pétroles, and two American companies, Standard Oil of New Jersey and Socony-Vacuum, to form the Iraq Petroleum Company.[12]

Against the background of disputes over the naval programme in 1927 there were even official British calculations as to the possibility of war with the United States, but the situation was eased with the visit of the newly-elected Labour Prime Minister, Ramsay MacDonald, to the United States at the invitation of President Herbert Hoover who had just been inaugurated.

This political healing was damaged by the Wall Street crash of 1929 and the subsequent raising by the United States of its tariff with the Hawley-Smoot Act in 1930. Faced by economic crisis, Britain, on 21 September 1931, abandoned the gold standard. A general election returned a National Government in October 1931, with MacDonald, now expelled from the Labour Party, remaining as Prime Minister, but with Conservatives dominating the Cabinet including Neville Chamberlain as Chancellor of the Exchequer and John Simon as Foreign Secretary. The Conservatives advocated imperial preference and tariff protection, and at the Imperial Conference held at Ottawa in 1932, a system of Empire preference was accepted – members would collect lower tariffs from each other than from outsiders. This was seen as protectionist and offended Cordell Hull, President F. D. Roosevelt's Secretary of State.

To try to sustain the free-market policies in the world economy, Hoover, in 1931, had declared a one-year moratorium on debt and reparation payments. The suspension of reparation payments annoyed the French, who avenged themselves on the Americans at the Lausanne Conference of June 1932 by making the reduction of reparations contingent on the reduction of war debts. The World Economic Conference, planned by Hoover and MacDonald, met in London in 1933 with the intention of stabilising international currencies. It was undermined by the newly-elected President Roosevelt who insisted on maintaining the advantage American exports had achieved through the devaluation of the dollar and the departure from the gold standard. In 1934 Britain stopped paying war debts to the United States; Finland was the only country that continued to do so. Hitler's rise to power in Germany ended the reparations issue.[13]

Rearmament

The Far Eastern crisis of 1931–3, and Hitler's accession in Germany, confronted both Britain and the United States with the question of rearmament. Stimson realised that the American navy was inadequate and not even of the size allowed under the various naval treaties. Washington had no practical plan for a war against Japan, and, in any case, increased defence expenditure was unrealistic.

London, faced with obvious German rearmament, as well as the deteriorating situation in the Far East, examined its defence priorities. Germany was seen as the serious long-term threat; a committee which started examining the situation in November 1933 recommended achieving an understanding with Japan. When, on 22 March 1934, the British Cabinet discussed the direction of foreign affairs, it was thought that a policy designed to keep Britain out of all war in Europe and the Far East would mean adopting too narrow a view. Britain could not restore international peace and confidence by 'backing out of Europe and leaving others to take the consequences'.[14]

London realised that any understanding with Japan would have to overcome American suspicion of anything that resembled an Anglo-Japanese alliance; and any Anglo-American association could result in a modification of Japanese naval policy. Britain delayed decisions on increasing the size of the navy and the army, pending a naval conference envisaged for 1935. Washington refused a British compromise designed to get Japan to accept a programme based on minimum security needs, and on 30 December 1934 Japan gave notice that it would terminate the Washington Treaty. Roosevelt threatened that if Britain appeared to prefer Japan to the United States, he would appeal to opinion in the Dominions and there could be a repetition of the experience of 1920-1 when Dominion pressure had helped to break the Anglo-Japanese alliance.[15] On 18 June 1935, however, London revealed the Anglo-German naval agreement which allowed Germany to expand its fleet in excess of the Versailles limitations, provided that it did not go beyond 35 per cent of the total tonnage of the combined fleets of the British Commonwealth. Negotiated behind the backs of the French, this agreement torpedoed the Stresa declaration of April 1935, under which Britain, France and Italy had damned German rearmament and affirmed the status quo in Europe. Italy broke from the anti-German front when Mussolini invaded Abyssinia. In 1936 Hitler remilitarised the Rhineland.

The Neutrality Acts

With the deteriorating situation in Europe and the Far East, the American Congress tried to ensure that the United States would not be ensnared into another war in the same way as it was perceived it had been trapped into fighting the First World War. Against the background of the Manchurian crisis, in 1931, Henry Stimson had suggested a discretionary arms embargo which the President could apply in time of war against the side which had broken the peace. This resulted in debates about armaments manufacturers in the United States, and the extent to which they had benefited from the First World War. A Senate investigation, headed by Gerald P. Nye, sat between 1934 and 1936, and with the assistance of a willing press sensationalised findings about the lobbying activities and profits of the munitions industry. The conclusion was reached that the United States had been drawn into the First World War by financial interests. This growing isolationist lobby was also strengthened by the debates over the Allies' refusal to repay war debts.

Against the background of Mussolini's invasion of Abyssinia, Hitler's occupation of the Rhineland, and the Spanish Civil War, Congress passed successive neutrality acts. The 1935 act made it mandatory for the President to proclaim the outbreak of war between foreign states and to embargo the export of arms to such states. The 1937 legislation, however, while handicapping any belligerent country's obtaining war material or other supplies, aided Britain as it had command of the sea and the largest purse. The reason for this was the 'cash and carry' clause, which was introduced for a trial period of two years. This provision meant that any belligerent could purchase goods in the United States provided that it could pay for them in cash, and had the shipping to transport them.[16]

Chamberlain and Appeasement

Neville Chamberlain became Prime Minister on 28 May 1937 against the background of the patriotic fervour of King George VI's coronation and the meeting of the British Commonwealth leaders at the Imperial Conference in London. Damned for a generation by a school of British historians and politicians who had made their reputations denigrating his policy of the appeasement of Europe, condemned for rejecting Roosevelt's peace overture in 1938, and so, according to politicians like Winston Churchill, turning down the last possible chance to avoid a world war, Chamberlain was commonly seen as a Prime Minister who thought that it was impossible to count on nothing from the Americans but words, and one who effectively harmed Anglo-American relations at a time when Washington was considered as the most obvious and valuable ally.[17] The opening, from 1968 onwards, of the British documents for years immediately before the outbreak of the Second World War revealed a very different picture. But the popular mythology perpetrated by successive generations of anti-appeasers has, in the end, perhaps been little shaken by the results of academic scholarship. And, indeed, some of that scholarship has persisted in seeing Chamberlain as having a distressingly limited perception of the United States's potential at the time of the European descent into the Second World War, and indeed as a positive hindrance to Anglo-American relations.[18]

On a diplomatic level, before the outbreak of the Second World War, a 'special relationship' did exist between Britain and the United States: this was reflected in the full and frank exchange of information between the two governments. Roosevelt greatly admired Chamberlain and had a plan for aiding Britain; but he was hampered by domestic crises, and an isolationist Congress and public opinion. The President said that he could only go as far as the public would allow him, though he tried to go further. Chamberlain, conscious of Roosevelt's domestic predicament, was careful not to push the American President to the front, a caution that Anthony Eden, while Foreign Secretary, ignored. Even before he became Prime Minister, Chamberlain, as Chancellor of the Exchequer, pursued an Anglo-American trade treaty: at the Imperial Conference he appealed, in June 1937, for Dominion co-operation over something that cut across the Ottawa agreements and imperial preference. The Americans also initiated the suggestion that Chamberlain, as Prime Minister, visit the United States. Given the international situation Chamberlain thought that such a visit would achieve little, but he was careful to give the impression that he attached considerable importance to improved Anglo-American relations and let Roosevelt know on 29 September 1937:

> Perhaps the community of sentiment between our two countries as to the events in the Far East and the developments in the European situation may be doing something to create a favourable atmosphere and the conclusion of an Anglo-American commercial agreement when we have found ways of overcoming its obvious difficulties will undoubtedly be an important step in the right direction.[19]

Even before becoming Prime Minister Chamberlain had decided on the need to reduce international tension and to pursue talks with Germany and Italy. The attitude of Dominion delegates at the Imperial Conference convinced Chamberlain that his policy of preserving peace in Europe was the right one.[20]

Anthony Eden, as Foreign Secretary, regarded Anglo-American co-operation and American involvement in Europe as his primary goals. On this he and Chamberlain diverged. Chamberlain believed that some settlement with the dictators was feasible, and a vague chance of the United States moving out of isolation should not be allowed to jeopardise this end.

The Far Eastern Crisis of 1937

When, in July 1937, following the Marco Polo Bridge incident, it was evident that there was going to be a major clash between Japan and China in the Far East, Eden hoped to involve the United States alongside Britain in that area. He believed, together with some Foreign Office officials, that if this happened, the United States would automatically be involved with Britain in any war in Europe. But the United States refused joint action and would only take parallel action. Norman Davis, a presidential adviser, explained that his government was reluctant to 'get mixed up with all Europe in the Far East'. Cordell Hull, the Secretary of State, complained of embarrassing British pressure for American co-operation. In a minute of 27 August 1937 N. B. Ronald of the Foreign Office examined the British dilemma:

> Mr [Stanley] Hornbeck [a State Department official] is no doubt right when he says that if we want U. S. co-operation, we must consult the State Depart. before taking action: I would go further and say that we must always frame our approach to the State Depart. in such a way that any action which may ultimately be taken may be represented as an American idea acted on through American initiative. And we must never complain if the State Depart. act without consulting us. . . . In other words we must be prepared to take all the knocks and get none of the credit. But Anglo-American co-operation being so important, I venture to think that we should be wise to submit to this, humiliating though it may be.[21]

Any hope of closer Anglo-American co-operation in the Far East was nearly dashed by the response of isolationist sentiment in the United States to Roosevelt's 'quarantine speech' at Chicago on 5 October 1937. Roosevelt, aware of the international situation and of the need to educate public opinion, inserted the controversial paragraph himself:

> It seems to be unfortunately true that the epidemic of world lawlessness is spreading. When an epidemic of physical disease starts to spread, the community approves and joins in the quarantine of the patients tin order to protect the health of the community against the spread of the disease.

Reaction in the United States was immediate and vociferous: a telegraphic poll of Congress revealed a majority of two to one against common action in the Far East. Although British observers saw press comment as favourable, the State Department viewed the response as hostile and determined United States foreign policy accordingly. On 12 October Roosevelt let the British government know:

(1) It should not speak or think or act as though it were possible for me to be in any way an exponent of British Foreign Office policy.

(2) It should never forget I cannot march ahead of our very difficult and restive American public opinion; and

(3) It must not try to push me in any way to the front or to thrust leadership upon me. . . . I cannot and shall not try to impose anything upon our people or the world. I will seek most earnestly to co-operate with all nations that are working for freedom and for peace.[22]

Following an Australian initiative a conference of the Pacific powers including the United States met at Brussels to discuss the situation in the Far East. Eden and the American delegate, Norman Davis, established a rapport: Eden hoped to follow one of Davis's suggestions that Britain and the United States should refuse to take Japanese products. The Foreign Secretary went behind the backs of the Prime Minister and the Cabinet in pursuing this with the ambassador in Washington. Eden's hope was that joint Anglo-American action along the lines suggested by Davis might be the foundation for later co-operation in Europe. Because of the situation in Europe, Britain would be unable to deploy a vast naval force in the Far East, and would have to insist on a guarantee being forthcoming for the possessions of those applying sanctions. The United States would be implicated neatly.[23] The State Department dampened Eden's hopes.

Indeed, isolationist sentiment in the United States was considered to be so strong that even when the Japanese attacked the USS *Panay* and HMS *Ladybird* in the Yangtse in December, the United States would not take joint action with Britain and was eager to accept the Japanese apology.[24]

Naval Conversations

Against the background of this crisis, however, Roosevelt did raise the matter of naval staff conversations similar to the arrangement in 1916–17 when an exchange of secret information had been established between the Admiralty and the Navy Department. Captain R. E. Ingersoll of the United States Navy had talks in London in January 1938, and these conversations together with those of Commander T. C. Hampton of the Royal Navy in the United States in June 1939 helped to lay the foundation of the Anglo-American military alliance.[25]

Roosevelt's Peace Plan

While Eden was attempting to achieve Anglo-American co-operation in the Far East, Chamberlain concentrated on pursuing the appeasement of Europe in the hope that what Hitler had indicated was the outstanding obstacle to good relations with Britain, the question of colonies, would be settled, and that an agreement could be reached with Mussolini over the recognition of his conquest of Abyssinia. This difference of emphasis led to Eden's resignation. Eden increasingly felt it futile to try to reach agreement with the dictators. The best way of averting war, or possibly even preparing for it, was to involve the United States alongside Britain in the Far East, in the hope that if there were a European conflagration, the United States would automatically be committed as Britain's ally. The Foreign Secretary did not enlighten Chamberlain fully as to his aims.

It was against this background, with Eden on holiday in France, that Chamberlain, on 12 January 1938, received an overture from Roosevelt: the President 'proposed to issue a sort of world appeal to end international tension by a general agreement to abide by international law and order'. Chamberlain, in a considered and polite reply sent on 13 January, asked whether Roosevelt could not hold his hand for a short time to see what progress the British could make piecemeal in talks with Germany and Italy. Chamberlain realised that Roosevelt's message made it clear that the United States would maintain its traditional policy of 'freedom from political involvements'.[26]

Roosevelt 'readily' agreed to defer his peace plan for a short while.'[27] Eden's scheming had not changed from the time of the Brussels conference. The Foreign Secretary drafted a memorandum for his conversation with Chamberlain on 18 January. Eden deleted the key aspects of his thinking:

> The decision we have to take seems to me to depend upon the significance which we attach to Anglo-American co-operation. ~~What we have to choose between is Anglo-American co-operation in an attempt to insure world peace and a piecemeal settlement approached by way of problematical agreement with Mussolini~~. If as is clear to me we must choose the former alternative, then it seems that we should reconsider our attitude and strongly support President Roosevelt's initiative. As you know, I do not take the view that this initiative need injure the prospects of our negotiations with Germany, which I regard

as the most important of the two sets of negotiations ~~we were considering. In fact the closer the sympathy and co-operation between the United States and ourselves, the stronger will be our position in dealing with Germany.~~[28]

On 20 February 1938 Eden resigned. The apparent reason was disagreement over the timing of the Italian conversations. Eden insisted at the Cabinet meeting that the difficulties did not refer to Italy only, and mentioned Roosevelt's peace plan: 'He had not thought that the original answer was correct, and his view was that a mistake had been made. He himself would have recommended a different course.'[29] In the end the choice was 'either Europe or the United States'.

Chamberlain had good reason for assuming that little of immediate practical importance could have resulted from Roosevelt's initiative. Langer and Gleason, the official American historians, conclude: 'Conceivably, a really strong stand by the United States Government might have changed the course of events, but . . . nothing of that kind was ever remotely envisaged in Washington.'[30] During February it still seemed as if Roosevelt's plan could be launched, but on 12 March 1938 London was informed that the opportunity for presenting Roosevelt's plan was unlikely to occur. The *Anschluss* in Austria effectively ended the scheme.

The Irish Treaty

Although it seems that, conscious of American isolationist opinion, Chamberlain was doubtful about any American support over Europe and the Far East, he cannot be accused of not cultivating Anglo-American co-operation. This is shown by his handling of the Irish question and the settlement of the issue of the treaty ports. Informed by the ambassador at Washington of the influence of the Irish element in the United States on Anglo-American relations, Chamberlain saw that the settlement of April 1938 was constructive.[31]

The Anglo-American Trade Treaty

The awareness of the importance of cultivating Anglo-American co-operation was shared by many Foreign Office officials. Mr F. Ashton-

Gwatkin, head of economic relations at the Foreign Office, commented on his return from a six-weeks visit to the United States:

> In a play which I saw in London some years ago, a young Foreign Office secretary finds himself by accident, at a full meeting of the Cabinet . . . He is asked by the philosophical Prime Minister what he thinks is the most important thing in the world, and he replies without hesitation: – 'Love and Anglo-American relations'.
>
> I am glad to think that my department is popularly considered to have its fundamental policy so firmly based.[32]

This was reflected in the negotiations for an Anglo-American trade treaty. On 17 November trade treaties were signed between the United States and Britain and the United States and Canada.[33]

Roosevelt's Plans for Aiding Britain

During Hitler's moves against Czechoslovakia – reasoned in terms of allowing the Sudeten Germans to rejoin their homeland – at the height of the Munich crisis, on 19 September 1938, Roosevelt warned the British ambassador, Sir Ronald Lindsay, that in indefinable circumstances the United States might find itself involved in a European war, but so strong was isolationist opinion that even in such a case he thought it 'almost inconceivable' that he would be able to send American troops across the Atlantic. If Britain were invaded, however, it was possible that a wave of emotion would send the United States Army overseas. Roosevelt was anxious to help Britain fight a war by blockade. He suggested this again in August 1939. War by blockade would meet with approval in the United States if the humanitarian purpose were emphasised. He could not take the initiative but it was the constitutional prerogative of the President to declare a blockade effective, and he could then, under the neutrality act, forbid American vessels to enter a danger zone except at their own risk. Roosevelt was hesitant about the possibility of the American government turning a blind eye to any evasion of the prohibition of exports of arms and ammunition in Britain's favour. He did, however, suggest that the Western powers could overcome this difficulty by not declaring war on Germany. They could call their action defensive measures or something plausible. Even if Germany declared war on Britain, provided Britain did not reciprocate, he might then be able to find that Britain was not at war, and so avoid applying the arms prohibition.[34]

Roosevelt, after Munich, through his friend Colonel Arthur Murray, was able to let Chamberlain know that he hoped to provide Britain, if it were at war with the dictators, with basic materials – such as aluminium plates, steel casings for engines, and cylinder blocks – not covered by the neutrality acts, to enable the building of an extra 20,000 to 30,000 planes, to give superiority over Germany and Italy in the air. On the eve of war, on 30 August 1939, Roosevelt in an interview with the newly appointed British ambassador, Lord Lothian, in which he 'could not have been more friendly', said that he hoped and expected that if war broke out Congress would revoke the neutrality act. If hostilities were represented as police action, or some equivalent interpretation, he might be able to avoid applying the act altogether. In any event he would not declare aluminium sheets or engine blocks as aeroplane parts. Roosevelt developed ideas about arranging for the American republics to combine to patrol half the distance to the African and European coasts to prevent entry by 'belligerent vessels or acts of war'. This could relieve the strain on the British and French navies, as well as making possible the transport of food and war materials from the Pan-American coast to Halifax, Nova Scotia, from where they could be taken to Europe on Allied ships.[35]

Roosevelt also urged that King George VI and Queen Elizabeth extend their planned tour of Canada in May 1939 to include the United States. He hoped to be able to present them with the repeal of the neutrality acts. But isolationist opinion in the United States was strengthened early in 1939 when a top secret American aircraft crashed killing a French official on board. Congress refused to repeal the acts. Roosevelt was unable to bolster the deterrent policy Chamberlain embarked upon following Hitler's seizure of Prague in March 1939 with the guarantee to Poland. Public opinion in the United States, according to contemporary analysts, was inclined to blame Britain for not taking a strong enough stand against the dictators, rather than blaming Hitler. On the refugee issue it felt that Britain should do everything: few Jewish refugees were admitted to the United States.

The Tientsin Crisis of 1939

With the Russian negotiations in progress attention shifted to the Far East in June. Japanese intransigence and maltreatment of British subjects in the Tientsin concession meant that for a time it seemed as if war would start in the Far East and not in Europe. This meant a serious rethinking of British contingency planning. If war did start in the East, it was unlikely that Germany and Italy would be able to resist the temptation to move in Europe. Britain might have to fight on three fronts simultaneously. The despatch of a fleet to the Far East had to be questioned seriously, with obvious ramifications for Australia and New Zealand. It seemed that there was little that Britain could do in the Far East without United States assistance, or at least co-operation. Japanese motivations in choosing Tientsin for a showdown were probably partially influenced by a desire to drive a wedge between the American and British governments. The United States had no direct interest in Tientsin. The British ambassador in Tokyo warned of this late in May 1939.

On 15 June London asked Washington for assistance in the form of mediation, and on 19 June Cordell Hull made a statement which from the British point of view did not amount to much. After this, because of the seriousness of the situation in the Far East, and the independent action that Britain was taking, a Cabinet committee on 20 June 1939 paid particular attention to the strategic situation. If a fleet of sufficient size, namely seven capital ships, were sent to the Far East, there was the danger that the naval position in home waters and in the Mediterranean would be insecure. Chamberlain felt that this was a decisive argument for reaching an early settlement of the Tientsin dispute, provided that the Japanese did not make the British position intolerable. Lord Halifax, the Foreign Secretary, agreed, but pointed out that if the United States co-operated this choice would not have to be faced.[36]

On 21 June, Chamberlain explained to the Cabinet that measures against the Japanese could be effective only with the co-operation of the United States: any mention of American assistance could seriously jeopardise any amendment to the neutrality legislation, and Britain needed such a modification if war were to be carried on for long. The situation was so serious that contingency plans had to be changed to meet the eventuality of war in the Far East rather than in Europe. When the Committee of Imperial Defence considered this on 26 June, Chamberlain pointed to the need to establish priorities: Britain could not be as strong as it would like in all three parts of the world where its interests were threatened. The Prime Minister mentioned the disadvantage of withdrawal from the Mediterranean. He felt that unless Japan forced war upon Britain, Britain should not take retaliatory action which could lead to war against Japan and the Axis powers. He later said that 'experience showed the best way of obtaining anything from America was not to ask for it'. With these factors in mind the committee agreed that nothing should be done to jeopardise the success of the impending negotiations in Tokyo.[37]

Then on 26 July, without warning, the United States gave the required six months notice for the abrogation of its commercial treaty with Japan. American expectations were that Britain should take a firm stand against Japan. Halifax was aware of the difficult position Britain was in because of the consideration that had to be given to American opinion:

> It is cardinal to our general policy to promote in any way possible co-operation with the United States, or at least to do nothing that would make that co-operation more difficult, we have not really got much choice, and from this point of view . . . it is better to face the situation now.

A gradual surrender would alienate American opinion.[38]

By the end of August Craigie did manage to reach an agreement with the Japanese, and Roosevelt told Lothian that the conclusion of the Nazi-Soviet Pact would probably lead to Japan coming to terms with China, with the assistance of Britain and the United States. Roosevelt said further that if Japan became hostile again he had two more methods of pressure 'in the locker': first, to send aircraft carriers and bombers to the Aleutian islands, about 700 miles from the Japanese northern island; the second was to move the American fleet to Hawaii.[39]

In the Far East, after Hitler's occupation of Prague, Britain was in an impossible situation. War on three fronts was a real possibility and the likelihood of American support was slight. Yet the United States favoured Britain's taking a firm stand against Japan which would probably lead to war, and any American support was likely to be in proportion to the firmness of the stand. Britain, however, did not have to face war on three fronts: Chamberlain's cautious policy in the Far East, hampered by the attitude of the United States, succeeded. And, on the eve of war, Roosevelt did indicate his willingness to apply pressure on Japan if that country became hostile.[40]

The Special Relationship

Chamberlain explained his approach to the United States in a letter to

Lord Tweedsmuir (John Buchan), the Governor-General of Canada, on 19 November 1937:

> I have gone out of my way to encourage those sections of American opinion that seem to have welcomed the President's Chicago [quarantine] speech. I have done so because I wish to give the utmost possible support to any tendency towards a closer understanding and a more complete community of purpose between our two nations. Nevertheless I am very conscious of the difficulties that have still to be overcome by the President before it can be said that he has his people behind him. His Chicago speech can be regarded, I think, as evidence that he recognises the need for the education of public opinion; but I should doubt whether such education can yet be said to have pro-ceeded very far and it would seem likely that its development must take time. . . . These considerations, however, should not deter us from pressing forward and I shall continue to do everything that lies in my powers to ensure improvement in our future relations.[41]

To an extent estranged by economic and naval rivalry during the 1920s, refusing to co-operate in the face of Japanese aggression in the early 1930s, by the end of that decade the governments of Britain and the United States, faced with the deteriorating international situation in Europe and the Far East, had moved closer together. Indeed the full and frank exchange of information between London and Washington would suggest that a special relationship existed between Britain and the United States before the outbreak of the Second World War: on the whole the British sent the Americans the same material as was circulated to the Cabinet and the Dominions; the Americans reciprocated accordingly and even let London know of the ensuing Nazi-Soviet Pact, though the information did not get through to London in time because of a spy in the decoding department of the Foreign Office.[42]

By October 1937 Roosevelt was aware of the dangers of the inter-national situation and of the need to educate public opinion. The secret staff conversations between Britain and the United States in January 1938 and May 1939 were indicative of the President's intentions. He was anxious to help Britain fight a war by blockade, as he suggested in September 1938 and again in August 1939. But Roosevelt was hampered by domestic crises, Congress, and public opinion. He said that he could go only as far as the pubic would allow him. He tried to go further. Roosevelt's plans for aiding Britain were consistent from 1937 to 1939. Chamberlain always had United States opinion in mind. He secured Hitler's signature to the paper saying that the Munich agreement was a pledge that Britain and Germany would not fight, in the hope that if Hitler broke his word the Americans would realise what kind of a man he was.[43] British policy throughout these years was dictated by a concern for American opinion. When Britain went to war in September 1939 over the Polish guarantee, it had behind it a sympathetic United States, and Roosevelt's assurance that the industrial resources of his country would be at Britain's disposal. Given the state of the Anglo-American relationship when he assumed office, this could be said to be a considerable achievement of the Prime Minister, Neville Chamberlain, and his American admirer President Franklin D. Roosevelt.

3

THE SECOND WORLD WAR:
THE ANGLO-AMERICAN ALLIANCE

The wartime alliance between Britain and the United States was for many years viewed through the vision Winston Churchill presented of it in his memoirs of the Second World War, published between 1948 and 1954 at the time of the joining of the Cold War and the revival of the Anglo-American special relationship in what many statesmen considered its close and effective partnership, apparently evidenced during the Second World War. Churchill's memoirs reflect perhaps more the desired state of the Anglo-American relationship during the Cold War than what it was actually like between 1940 and 1945. In public, in the postwar era, Churchill spoke of the relationship in terms of a cultural unity shown by the English Speaking peoples, of this being the natural force for the peace and order of the world. Often he included the old 'White' Dominions in this grouping. It was this alliance which was seen as being the only one able to stand up to the Soviet menace.

Churchill's history, for a generation, coloured both the public perception and the academic history of the Anglo-American relationship during the Second World War. Indeed, as D. Cameron Watt has observed, the view Churchill gave, in his memoirs, of the relationship he enjoyed with Roosevelt was given with such authority that even the publication of three volumes of the actual correspondence between the two statesmen has had little impact outside a narrow circle of historians.[1] Churchill has even been accused of withholding intelligence information from Roosevelt about the forthcoming Japanese attack on Pearl Harbor to ensure American participation in the Second World War. But, above all, this impression of Roosevelt and Churchill collaborating intimately together led to a certain distortion in the academic literature on the origins of the Cold War, a literature initially mainly American, or East-European-American, in origin which inclined to the view of American-Soviet confrontation as being started by the Americans during the Second World War.[2]

In 1972 John Wheeler-Bennett and A. Nicholls published *The Semblance of Peace*, a work which showed Roosevelt and Joseph Stalin, the Soviet leader, working together and leaving Churchill in the cold throughout the wartime conferences, as well as the United States and the Soviet Union collaborating on plans for the postwar world to the exclusion of Britain. This work dismissed the writings and the case made by the so-called 'revisionist' writers who saw the events of these years as mainly American imperialism threatening a peaceful non-expansionist Soviet Union.[3] What was known as the revisionist-orthodox debate was largely an American debate, fought out against the background of the Vietnam War and a generation of American students anxious to find an intellectual justification for refusing to fight in Vietnam, a mood outstandingly conveyed by John Irving in his masterpiece, *A Prayer for Owen Meany*.[4] At a time of new-left faddism there were angry protests from reviewers about the 'frozen postures' taken by Wheeler-Bennett and Nicholls.[5]

To an extent American historians have persisted in writing about the Cold War as if, on the Western side, only the United States had a role to play.[6] As the British documents became available in the Public Record Office in London a group of historians has increasingly challenged this 'Americocentric' view of the origins of the Cold War, and has seen Britain as the original Cold War warrior, one determined to educate the United States to the realities of what it perceived as the Soviet threat.[7]

Roosevelt and Assistance for Britain

The enigmatic figure of President Franklin D. Roosevelt is central to any consideration of the nature of the Anglo-American relationship during the Second World War. The question has been posed as to whether the President deliberately exposed his country to being involved in a war without the support, or even the knowledge, of Congress and the American public: did he try to assist Britain 'through the backdoor'. Or were his actions more conspiratorial: hoping to repeat the experience of the First World War, did Roosevelt try to involve the United States in the war through first instituting patrolling in the Atlantic, and then convoying British ships, and even assisting these ships in the hunting of German submarines, by provoking a German attack? When this was evidently failing, did he then provoke Germany through sanctions and belligerent negotiations into firing the first shot, and so overcome an isolationist Congress which, the indications suggest, even after the Japanese attack on Pearl Harbor would not have declared war on Germany?

In his fireside chat on the outbreak of war, Roosevelt said that he could not ask the United States to be neutral in thought. This was in contrast to Wilson's demands from the American public on the outbreak of the First World War. Roosevelt implemented the plan he had outlined to Lothian on 30 August 1939. By the end of 1939 he had managed to force 'cash and carry' through Congress, arguing that it was a nonpartisan issue and wearing down reluctant isolationist senators through all-night sittings. This enabled Britain and France to collect weapons from the United States in their own ships, once they had paid for them. In October, the Declaration of Panama established a neutrality zone around North and South America, excluding Canada and 'the undisputed colonies and possessions of European countries'. Opinion polls at the end of the year reflected stronger isolationist attitudes in the United States than at the outbreak of the war. The isolationist lobby found focus with the American First Committee, led by the aviator Charles Lindberg; the administration worked through the Committee to Defend America by aiding the Allies. The Nazi invasion of Denmark and Norway in April 1940, with the obvious implications for Greenland and Iceland, showed that a policy based on continental America was not enough: Roosevelt proclaimed that 'obviously a defence policy based on [the continental America] is merely to invite future attack'.

David Reynolds asserts that throughout the period of the Phoney War Anglo-American relations were 'cool and distant': the British, with the experience of American isolationism, did not expect much practical help from Washington. Chamberlain and some of his colleagues, Reynolds argues, were also worried that dependence on Washington would expose Britain to American economic pressure and pressure to make peace in accordance with the principles outlined at the end of the First World War by Woodrow Wilson.[8]

This changed. From London, on 15 May 1940, Churchill, now Prime

Minister, asked the Americans for old destroyers and new aircraft, and an attitude of 'non-belligerency', one which openly took sides without actually fighting. The American ambassador in London, Joseph Kennedy, of Irish extraction and the father of a future President, effectively recommended that Britain be left to sink beneath the seas. But Hull and Roosevelt argued that the way to keep the fighting away from the United States's own backyard, was to keep Britain and France on their feet; Roosevelt asked Congress not to hamper the delivery of planes to the Allies. Hitler's invasion of Belgium on 10 May had aroused even the traditionally isolationist Middle West. At this stage public opinion appeared to be ahead of that of the administration on the matter of assisting the Allies.

On 10 June, on the eve of Italy's entry into the war, in a speech at the University of Virginia, Charlottesville, Roosevelt extended 'to the opponents of force the material resources' of the United States. This marked the change in the American attitude from neutrality to non-belligerency. As France was falling, Roosevelt felt unable to respond to Prime Minister Paul Reynaud's appeal for destroyers: Congressional consent was necessary and the isolationists showed no sign of weakening.

Roosevelt, as Joseph Lash has observed, felt that the critical situation enabled him to take the lead in influencing events.[9] On 20 June it was announced that Henry Stimson, the former Secretary of State, would return to the War Department, and that Frank Knox, who had stood as the Republican Vice-Presidential candidate in 1936, would become Secretary of the Navy. This meant that a majority of the Cabinet favoured aiding Britain and France. Their influence was soon evident in the Destroyers for Bases deal. Churchill reiterated his appeal for fifty old destroyers for use in the Atlantic against the German U-boats. Knox and Stimson found ways of bypassing Congress by using a statute of 1917. Negotiated at the height of the Battle of Britain, the Destroyer for Bases deal gave Washington ninety-nine-year leases on eight air and naval bases in Newfoundland and the British West Indies. The ships were of little use, and only nine were in service before 1941, but the act showed that the United States was no longer neutral, and Churchill was able to tell the House of Commons: 'This process means that . . . the British Empire and the United States will have to be somewhat mixed up together.'

Faced with an election in November 1940 and the power of isolationist opinion, Roosevelt told an audience that: 'Your boys are not going to be sent into any foreign wars.' This was the appearance of

Roosevelt's policy. In any case 'foreign' was open to interpretation. The reality was perhaps different. Britain was running out of dollars to pay for war material from the United States. Some Congressmen misguidedly thought that Britain had control of the dollar resources of the Dominions and Empire and could pay anyway.

It was Lord Lothian, the British ambassador in Washington, who convinced Roosevelt in the middle of December of the need to dispense with the dollar sign. In August 1938 Lothian had agreed to go as British ambassador to the United States. Earlier he had complained to Lord Halifax, the Foreign Secretary, of the aloof and arrogant atmosphere of the British embassy in Washington, which offended both American journalists and Congressmen. The embassy was known as 'the British compound'. The Senate Foreign Relations Committee characterised British *précis* as 'the British commands'. Lothian explained that the embassy staff usually consisted of old public school boys 'many of whom manifest a constitutional inhibition when dealing with the average politician either in the Senate or the House of Representatives'.[10] Lothian did a great deal to mobilise American opinion in support of Britain and won the trust of American leaders.[11]

At the beginning of January 1941 Roosevelt outlined what became known as Lend-Lease, and forced the bill through Congress between then and March. The legacy of war debts was side-stepped: Britain would be supplied with what it needed and settlement would be postponed until after the end of the war and then would be in kind or otherwise.[12] Kathleen Burk has argued that with Lend-Lease Washington had the objective of bringing about the collapse of Britain's external economic policy: Washington's plan culminated in 1945–6 with the negotiation of the American loan.

> Lend-lease was neither sordid nor unsordid. It was proposed by an Administration which saw it as a means by which the US could defend itself by proxy – perfectly in the British tradition – and agreed to by a Congress which in no way intended to give Britain and other recipients something for nothing. Lend-lease aid was always to be paid for in some sort of coin.[13]

Harry Hopkins went as Roosevelt's emissary to London to assess the British requirements, and convinced Churchill that Roosevelt was Britain's best friend. After that Churchill tried to smooth out any differences between London and Washington in an effort, at all costs, to secure American entry into the war. It could be asserted that in passing

Lend-Lease, Congress authorised Roosevelt to go to war: the debates showed an awareness that only American protection of British shipping could ensure that the goods crossed the Atlantic safely. Indeed Churchill hoped that the Americans would be drawn into the war by attacks on American shipping by German U-boats, repeating the experience of the First World War.

Initially Roosevelt increased the American Navy's patrolling operations, and it also had orders to inform the Royal Navy of the position of German vessels. In April 1941 the Americans occupied Greenland, and in June took over the garrisoning of Iceland, which had been occupied in 1940 by Britain. Iceland and Greenland were territories of German-occupied Denmark. American ships were moved from the Pacific fleet to escort American merchant ships carrying goods across the Atlantic to Britain. After a German submarine had torpedoed an American freighter, the *Robin Moor*, on 21 May 1941, Roosevelt proclaimed a national emergency and told the American public that American patrols were helping to ensure the delivery of supplies to Britain. The USS *Greer* was attacked off Iceland on 4 September 1941. This act led to American protection being extended to all merchant ships in the American patrol zone, and to a warning that all German and Italian ships would be fired on when sighted.

Two more destroyers, the *Kearney* and the *Reuben James*, were sunk in the second half of October. There is debate as to whether the Germans were provoked into this action by active participation by American aircraft and ships in attacks on German vessels. The President accused the Germans of firing on the *Greer* without warning. Information leaked to a Congressional committee led to the United States Navy admitting that the American ship had pursued a German U-boat after being told its position by a British aircraft.[14] Indeed Roosevelt explained to Churchill the extent to which he was restricted by isolationist sentiment in Congress, and encouraged the Prime Minister's belief that he was trying to provoke a shipping incident in the Atlantic that would lead to war. In November 1941 key sections of the neutrality act were repealed: Washington reclaimed the right to send its ships anywhere, and to arm and protect them. Arguably, by November 1941 the United States was involved in a shooting war in the Atlantic.

When Churchill and Roosevelt met off the coast of Newfoundland between 9 and 12 August 1941 and signed the Atlantic Charter – a set of principles on the peace settlement of a war which the Americans had not then joined – there were British hopes of further American commitments to go to war, but even if these were not made there was a public image of a common bond of interest between Britain and the United States. In effect, the Atlantic Charter, with its anti-colonial stance and multilateralist economic thinking, could be seen as pointing to potential divisions between London and Washington in the postwar settlement. Its principles included equal access to raw materials; the renunciation of territorial aggrandisement; and the restoration of self-government.[15]

The Intelligence Relationship

Between 1940 and 1941 the Anglo-American military alliance initiated before the outbreak of the Second World War was furthered. The basis for an intelligence relationship was laid, particularly during the secret staff talks that took place between 29 January and 27 March 1941 in Washington: military missions in London and Washington were to include intelligence officers from all the services. These staff talks considered what the strategy should be if the United States were compelled to resort to war. The agreement was reached that even if Japan were in the war, priority would be given to the defeat of Germany. The principles established in these ABC-1 war plans were followed by Washington and London throughout the war. Scientific and technical collaboration were also furthered, particularly by a mission led by Sir Henry Tizard in August 1940 who took information about radar, jet engines, chemical weapons, anti-submarine devices and uranium which was essential for the development of atomic weapons. The exchange of scientific information between the two countries was formalised during Hopkins's mission to London, in January–February 1941.[16]

The War in the Far East

Against this background of the evolving Anglo-American relationship, Roosevelt perhaps, unable to precipitate a war in the Atlantic, concentrated on the situation in the Far East. Or perhaps the President left it to his subordinates.

In 1940 Japan had forced Britain to close the Burma Road, the route for Western supplies to Chiang Kai-Shek in China, for three months, and this had led to American criticism. Churchill and the Foreign Office became convinced that Japan could not be appeased. Britain attempted to contain Japan, particularly in South-East Asia, and tried to set up a barrier to Japanese expansion, with the Netherlands, the United States, and to an extent China. The Japanese referred to this as the ABCD encirclement. As well as military planning it included the co-ordination of economic sanctions against Japan. The United States had two main weapons against Japan: the American fleet stationed since April 1940 at Pearl Harbor, over 2,000 miles from its American West Coast bases; and Japan's reliance on raw materials, the supply of which the United States controlled. Washington embargoed the sale of aviation fuel to Japan in July 1940, scrap iron needed for the manufacture of aircraft in September, and iron ore in December 1940.

In 1941 the key decisions were taken in Washington and Tokyo, and Britain was on the sidelines. Churchill, his Foreign Secretary, Anthony Eden, the defence chiefs and the Foreign Office probably all under-estimated Japanese intentions. After the German invasion of the Soviet Union in the middle of 1941, the Soviet Union was no longer seen as a threat by Japan. Japan occupied Indo-China. Faced by this new situation Washington sent heavy bombers to the Philippines, imposed a complete oil embargo against Japan, and froze Japanese assets. Eden felt that it was not in Britain's interest to take such harsh action against Japan, but that London had to take action parallel to that of Washington, and looked to Washington for assurance. Japan abandoned diplomacy and planned for war: its army needed fuel and without this Tokyo would have had to evacuate China and Indo-China. On 7 December 1941 the Japanese attacked Pearl Harbor; 2403 Americans were killed.[17]

Pearl Harbor and the Conspiracy Theory

Extreme conspiracy theorists have claimed that Roosevelt sacrificed the fleet at Pearl Harbor, and that the loss was deliberate rather than being the result of a series of blunders. A number of works published to mark the fortieth anniversary of Pearl Harbor did not resolve the issue.[18] Probably Roosevelt, understanding the seriousness of American sanctions instituted in July 1941, assisted by the diplomacy pursued by his Secretary of State, Cordell Hull, in his conversations with the

Japanese, which in the end amounted to giving a virtual ultimatum on 26 November with the Ten Point Programme, had anticipated a war. But the American military machine and the public experienced a psychological paralysis: a Japanese attack of the sort mounted had been thought impossible.

Some historians have claimed that Churchill withheld intelligence of the Japanese attack from the Americans to ensure Washington's entry into the war. Initially banned in Britain under a D-notice, a book based on the testimony of an Australian code-breaker, Eric Nave, and written by James Rushbridger, an author who later committed suicide in sensational circumstances, claimed that Britain had intelligence information of the Japanese naval commander Admiral Yamamoto's message to his task force on 21 November ordering the fleet to carry out the second phase of the operations: on 25 November to move out to sea, and on 2 December to 'Climb Niitakayama 1208', the time in Tokyo of the attack on Pearl Harbor. Nave and Rushbridger claimed that Niitakayama, the highest mountain on Taiwan, could only have been a coded and easily identifiable reference to Pearl Harbor. Desmond Morton, Churchill's Whitehall confidant, received intercepts of the Japanese coded messages.

The case was immediately challenged. Documents released in the Public Record Office in November 1993 on Britain's intelligence operations showed that Churchill's intelligence briefings started on 27 September 1940. The one relevant to the Nave and Rushbridger case, the report from the Japanese ambassador in Berlin to the Japanese foreign ministry, which outlined a conversation with Joachim von Ribbentrop, the German Foreign Minister, made no reference to the attack on Pearl Harbor.[19]

Economic 'Integration' and Rivalry

On the economic and military level Washington's participation in the Second World War was notable for the intimacy of its relationship with London. The two countries' economies were not completely integrated, but there was a pooling of their industrial and raw material resources. The foundation for this had been laid between 1937 and 1941 as co-operation had developed on the military and scientific level, and the application of Lend-Lease had helped to establish procedures on the economic front. The Combined Boards achieved co-operation over production. Grosvenor Square in London became the centre of a huge American administrative complex; in Washington, at the height of the war, around nine thousand British officials centred around the British embassy.[20]

Despite this inter-Allied partnership there was economic rivalry, particularly in Latin America over the policy of blockade as Britain had economic interests in Argentina. There was also mutual suspicion over access to Middle Eastern oil. The interwar years had seen a considerable increase in the American oil interests in Kuwait, Bahrain, Saudi Arabia and even Iraq. A Presidential committee on international petroleum policy under Senator Harry S. Truman reported in March 1943 that future American demand for oil was likely to be in excess of domestic production. There were accusations that the United States was providing a disproportionate share of the Allies' oil, and that Britain was engineering this to further its own imperial interests. James F. Byrnes, the Director of the Office of War Mobilisation, pointed out on 5 October that the facts did not support this impression. Senators were told that although the British and American contributions might have been 'unequal' they had not been 'inequitable'. Byrnes warned Roosevelt on 17 February 1944 that further public discussion on the economic rivalry between Britain and the United States in the Middle East could give rise to 'strong and dangerous anti-British feeling'. A mutually satisfactory settlement should be reached at a high level as this could be difficult at the peace table. The British denied following a selfish policy and Anglo-American diplomacy led in August 1944 to the two governments confirming their 'mutual respect for valid concessions and lawfully acquired oilrights'. But American oil interests regarded the agreement as an unnecessary interference, and the proposals were withdrawn by Roosevelt in January 1945.[21]

Divisions were also evident in the discussions on the postwar economic order. The British wanted multilateralism on particular terms, and wanted the Americans to encourage international liquidity both through making loans and by lowering the American tariff barriers. The Americans dominated the discussions, and scored a success with the Bretton Woods agreements of 1944, which established the International Monetary Fund on terms more rigid than those wanted by London. Although Washington appeared committed to a policy of economic internationalism, which could be considered a long-term British victory, Randall Bennett Woods has argued that London failed in its effort to

educate Washington away from isolationism and economic nationalism: 'British multilateralists made no headway against the forces of
economic nationalism'; American conservatives insisted that business
principles be applied to national and international affairs and that
'the principles of American capitalism when applied to foreign affairs
were incompatible with economic internationalism'.[22]

Strategic Co-operation and Disagreement

On the military side the Combined Chiefs of Staff, which evolved early
in 1942, had a general jurisdiction over strategic policy. Its headquarters
was in Washington, and the British Chiefs of Staff were usually
represented by deputies, headed by Sir John Dill. Dill worked intimately
with General George C. Marshall, the American Army Chief of Staff,
and this relationship oiled the Anglo-American military alliance. Anglo-
American strategy continued to be based on the 'Germany first'
principle: the concentration was to be on defeating Hitler while con-
taining Japan. Initially the Anglo-American plan was to build up forces
in Britain, an operation code-named 'BOLERO', with a view to an
invasion of the European Continent in either 1942 or 1943. This was
modified to the invasion of North Africa, TORCH, which started in
November 1942, and was followed by the invasion of Sicily, and then
mainland Italy in September 1943. The Japanese were held by the
American-led Allied forces in the Pacific. But there was major Anglo-
American disagreement over how the European operation should be
continued. The debates over what became OVERLORD, the invasion
of North West Europe in the spring of 1944, revealed not only a
differences in approach to the conduct of the war, but also markedly
divergent visions of how the postwar world was to be managed.[23]

Britain fought the Second World War as an imperial power with
worldwide commitments. Looking back on this experience, at a time
when the Labour government was considering once again the need for
Britain to undertake responsibilities for European defence, Sir John
Cunningham warned the Chiefs of Staff on 2 February 1948 that it had
been Britain's traditional policy in the past to avoid continental
commitments: 'Twice in the past we had given a guarantee to assist a
continental nation to the limit of our power by the provision of land
forces. On both occasions we had suffered severely, first on Mons and

more recently at Dunkirk.'[24] As the Second World War progressed, however, Britain's geographical position meant that its preoccupation with the envisaged alignments of power on the European continent grew. Churchill became increasingly worried that he could not persuade the United States to take a sufficiently long-term view of postwar problems. During 1943 Anglo-American military co-operation was close, both in the Mediterranean theatre and in preparation for the Second Front. But Roosevelt wanted Marshal Stalin as the close ally, and the President was worried that the Soviet leader might suspect that Britain and the United States were 'ganging up' on him.[25]

Roosevelt and Stalin versus Churchill

On his way to the Teheran Conference at the end of 1943 Churchill told Harold Macmillan: 'Germany is finished, though it may take some time to clean up the mess. The real problem now is Russia. I can't get the Americans to see it.' By that time statesmen in Britain and the United States had significantly different perceptions of Soviet intentions for the postwar world. Roosevelt probably envisaged the Soviet Union and the United States working for peace together. When these two countries were fighting side by side this vision was enlarged: the Soviet Union and the United States would manage world affairs under the aegis of the United Nations. Roosevelt, unlike Churchill, feared Nazi aggression more than Russian expansionism. Even after the Yalta Conference Roosevelt, in April 1945, appeared not to share Churchill's fears of a Communist take-over in Europe: he urged the Prime Minister to minimise the Russian problem and things would straighten out.[26]

    The United States had started planning for the postwar world before Pearl Harbor. This was shown by Sumner Welles's mission to Europe in 1940, and the Atlantic Charter of 1941, which embodied those freedoms the Americans considered basic to the continuance of international society. The United Nations Declaration was signed as early as January 1942. The general American attitude was that there was a need to move away from the old system of the balance of power, and allied blocs, and into a new era of efficient world organisation. The prospective United Nations appeared to be more important than alliances. Colonialism had to go, and this meant conflict with Britain. By 1942 Britain suspected that the United States was trying to overthrow British rule in India.[27]

Britain was, perhaps, more pragmatic, and more concerned with the realities of power on the European continent. This meant an increasing suspicion of Soviet intentions, and an anxiety over seeming American blindness to them. Differences in attitude between Britain and the United States towards the Soviet Union were evident at the Cairo meeting in November 1943 which preceded that at Teheran. Churchill had to face suspicions that British military planning in the Mediterranean and the Far East was a scheme to defend or recapture Britain's imperial possessions. The United States also feared that Britain was trapping its allies into activities in the Balkans. Lord Moran, Churchill's doctor, recorded in his diary that 'to the Americans the PM is the villain of the piece; they are far more sceptical of him than they are of Stalin'.

Because of the attitude of the United States, the two countries went to face the Soviet Union at Teheran without a common policy. Evidently the President played the role that he had envisaged: a sort of arbiter between Churchill and Stalin. On Eastern Europe Churchill had a proposal to create a Danubian confederation. Stalin did not like this, as it seemed to imply that Britain would re-establish the balance of power in Europe. Roosevelt supported Stalin, who insisted that Romania, Austria and Hungary should become independent powers again. Churchill resisted, as he felt that Stalin was aiming at the Balkanisation of Eastern Europe. Roosevelt and Stalin agreed on the need to keep Germany weak. Churchill was probably more concerned that the Soviet Union would become too strong. In his private conversations with Stalin Roosevelt discovered common ground that separated the two men from the British: they were both concerned to liquidate Western colonial empires, and agreed that Indo-China should not be returned to France. Churchill was appalled by his impotence at Teheran: he realised that he could not rely on Roosevelt's support and that the Russians knew this.[28]

But there was little that Churchill could do. By the time of the next meeting of the Big Three a year later, Britain and the United States had still not co-ordinated their policies. There were even military differences between the two countries: on the issue of the Second Front, it was the United States and the Soviet Union that were in step. Roosevelt suspected British efforts to carve a sphere of influence in Eastern Europe. Because of Anglo-American closeness the differences between the two countries were accentuated. It was general American policy that no decisions on frontiers should be made until the end of the war, when divisions would be settled by a world organisation. The Soviet Union was free to pursue its special interests in Eastern Europe. Britain's lack of faith in the prospective world organisation focused American resentment on Britain rather than on the Soviet Union. Churchill, anxious to stop the Soviets and to bring the United States around to his view of the postwar problems, could do neither.[29]

The Italian campaign revealed real differences between Britain and the United States. But for British statesmen what mattered more was their influence on affairs in Central Europe. Churchill and Eden wanted to exploit the victory in Italy to play a more influential part in Central Europe. The United States opposed this, using strategic arguments. Churchill and Eden felt that political inhibitions about becoming involved in the Balkans were the real reason. In 1944 Eden advised that the only way of checking Soviet influence in the Balkans was to consolidate Britain's position in Greece and Turkey.[30]

The British Cabinet had no doubts over Moscow's intentions in Eastern Europe. On 25 January 1944 Eden told it that what Russia had in mind for Poland was probably 'a puppet Government under Russian control and a Soviet Republic'. In May, Churchill, referring to disagreements over Romania, admitted that Foreign Minister Vyacheslav Molotov's attitude 'led him to despair of the possibility of maintaining good relations with Russia'. On 9 October 1944 Churchill met Stalin in the hope of securing British control in Greece, and some influence in Bulgaria, Hungary and Yugoslavia. The Prime Minister suggested an informal division of influence in Eastern Europe. Stalin agreed. For Churchill this was, apparently, only a guide, and did not set up a rigid sphere of interest. This 'percentage split' agreement did not commit the United States.[31]

By early 1945, however, despite earlier differences, Britain and the United States did achieve agreement on the Polish question: it was decided at Malta that the Soviets should be asked to agree to an interim government in Poland with a council including Stanislaw Mikolajczyk, the leader of the London Poles. Britain had also secured American acquiescence in its policy in Greece; Roosevelt had been furious over British action there as he felt that it involved shooting those Greek Communists who had been allies in the fight against Nazism. This, however, was achieved by consummate diplomacy rather than through a similar assessment of the Soviet Union's intentions. When the Big Three met at Yalta in February 1945 Anglo-American policies were not co-ordinated, and this lack was largely through American engineering. Churchill found the President unreceptive to the idea that 'only a solid understanding between the United States and Britain could keep Stalin's appetite under control'. At Yalta, Churchill and Roosevelt did not work easily together, and the Prime Minister saw that 'the map of Europe will be redrawn in red ink'. There was nothing that Churchill could do about it.

Roosevelt was preoccupied with the idea of the United Nations. With his worldwide view, he was determined to maintain co-operation with the Soviet Union as the key to world peace. Churchill appeared uninterested and showed his lack of faith in the world body. Roosevelt was under the influence of Admiral William D. Leahy, who thought Europe unimportant, and the Far East more an American concern. The President negotiated in secret with Stalin, without consulting his Chinese or British allies, and reached an agreement to cover the Far East. Eden was opposed to signing this agreement, but Churchill thought it necessary to try to safeguard British authority in the Far East. Britain and the United States fell out over the issue of a world charter to deal with territorial trusteeships and dependent areas. Churchill would tolerate no interference with the British Empire and won his point: the allies would not interfere with one another's sphere of influence. But this victory was double-edged. It left the Soviet Union virtually free to do what it liked in the occupied territories of Eastern Europe.[32]

The weeks following the Yalta communiqué showed the markedly different assessments of Soviet intentions on the two sides of the Atlantic. Roosevelt maintained his anti-colonial stance – possibly weakening only on his deathbed – and his insistence on independence for such territories as French Indo-China. This stand, however, was personal, and in making it Roosevelt was not supported by his bureaucracy or by his national security advisers, who were concerned that such a stand would threaten American rights to its Pacific possessions.[33] Indeed on 2 April the research and analysis branch of the Office of Strategic Services argued that if the United States stood aside after the war, the Soviet Union would be able to dominate Europe and establish its hegemony over Asia. The United States should safeguard its own position and encourage Britain and other powers to do the same. It was in the American interest that the British, French and Dutch colonial empires be maintained. Furthermore, the United States should encourage the development in West European states of independent, economically prosperous democratic regimes which could, in alliance with Britain and the United States, serve as 'a counterweight to Russian power and a bulwark against further Russian expansion'.[34]

There was also a division in Britain between the leadership and some of the bureaucracy. The Foreign Office, like Roosevelt, viewed the Soviet objectives as limited. Churchill did not. He hoped for Western democratic institutions in south-eastern Europe, and was unwilling to believe that Soviet control could not be stopped. American support was essential to halt Soviet advances in Europe. This action had to be taken quickly at a time when Anglo-American military strength in Europe was at a maximum. Churchill wanted a meeting of the Big Three, at which the United States and Britain would face the Soviet Union with the threat that if they did not honour their agreements at Yalta, the Anglo-American armies would stay their ground.

The Prime Minister's wish for a stronger bargaining position against the Russians was thwarted by the United States, and especially General D. D. Eisenhower. In Churchill's estimation what was needed was a rapid military advance on Berlin. Eisenhower had other plans, of which he informed the Russians, without authorisation from the combined Chiefs of Staff, on 28 March 1945. To the United States, Berlin was not a particularly important objective. The American Chiefs of Staff also supported Eisenhower's plan not to advance his troops across the Elbe in mid-April. The new President, Harry S. Truman, would not consider Churchill's view of the political consequences of the military objectives. The pattern was repeated in Czechoslovakia. On 13 April Eden sent a message to the American ambassador in London urging the United States to liberate Prague before the Russians did. In the British view, the liberation of Prague and as much as possible of western Czechoslovakia might influence not only the postwar situation in Czechoslovakia but also that in nearby countries. Marshall and the American Chiefs of Staff were opposed to operations conducted with a political rather than a military purpose. Eisenhower, after a protest from the Soviet high command, halted his troops when they could easily have entered Prague and at a time when there were no Russian troops in Bohemia. Washington anticipated that Czechoslovakia would develop as an independent state not subject to pressures from either East or West.

Truman's Attitude towards Britain and the Soviet Union

Truman, even more than Roosevelt, was determined that there should be no Anglo-American collaboration against the Soviet Union. Instead of accepting Churchill's plan to negotiate a real settlement with the

Soviets, he delayed the next meeting of the Big Three and tried a unilateral approach to Stalin with the mission of Harry Hopkins to Moscow. The Hopkins mission did secure a paper agreement on Poland. But it appeared to the British, and especially to Churchill, that the Americans were not alive to the dangers of a Russian advance in Europe. Churchill seemed to be concerned that Truman, like Roosevelt, would not want to commit American forces to a long stay in Europe. On 12 May 1945 Churchill sent a telegram to Truman about his fears for Europe when there might be only a few French divisions against two or three hundred Russian. The Prime Minister saw an 'iron curtain' being drawn down upon the Russian front. He felt that it would soon be open to the Soviets to advance to the North Sea and the Atlantic. It was necessary to achieve a settlement with the Soviet Union before British and American strength was dissipated.[35]

It could be argued that Truman's cancellation of Lend-Lease to the Soviet Union on 11 May 1945 showed a hardening of attitude on the part of the new President towards the Soviet Union. Perhaps he considered economic pressure as an option to use against the Soviet Union. It is more likely Truman thought that he was giving in to anticipated Congressional pressure: Lend-Lease was intended only to help fight the war and not for reconstruction. Though the Soviet Union was affected, Lend-Lease to Britain was cancelled as well. Perhaps as Gabriel Kolko has argued, though his particular case has been devastatingly exposed, this was part of a carefully calculated American plan to force Britain to conform to the United State's postwar economic schemes. But if it was a carefully calculated scheme, Truman does not seem to have been a part of it. He carelessly did not even read the document cancelling Lend-Lease. Britain, if it were to continue as an economically viable country, needed a vast loan after the war. In the autumn of 1945 Lord Keynes tried to negotiate such a loan in Washington. Indeed the British expected an outright gift. But Keynes soon discovered that there was a gulf separating Washington from London. The American administration and 'its immeasurably remote public opinion' was not interested in British 'wounds though incurred in the common cause', but in British 'convalescence'. Bolstering Britain as a bulwark against the Soviet Union did not seem to be in the American scheme of things.[36]

Truman, initially, had made some sort of stand against the Soviet Union on the Polish issue before the meeting at San Francisco to prepare for the Charter of the United Nations. This was probably because of his inexperience and his consequent reliance on certain sources of advice. In late April, Truman told Molotov that the United States wanted friendship with the Soviet Union, but not 'on the basis of a one-way street'. Molotov protested that he had never been talked to like that in his life. Although Eden would have preferred the weighting of American policy to be towards a strong stand against the Soviet Union, the success of plans for the United Nations still had top priority. There were differences at the conference on the issue of the veto and the seating of Argentina, but the American policy of giving priority to the idea of the United Nations and ameliorating relations with the Soviet Union lest it walked out, was successful in that the Charter was finally drawn up on 26 June.[37]

The Big Three finally met at Potsdam in July. Britain did not succeed in securing a preliminary Anglo-American meeting, but, because of Stalin's late arrival, there was an exchange of views between Foreign Office and State Department delegates on 14 July. At Potsdam, the United States, for the first time, found itself closer to the British position than to that of the Soviet Union. Truman, accompanied by a new Secretary of State, James F. Byrnes, had something to do with this. From the outset the President avoided giving the Soviets the impression that their two countries had interests in common that Britain did not share.

There were still important differences of emphasis between British and American policy. When the news came of the explosion of the atomic bomb, Churchill hoped that this might dampen American enthusiasm for Soviet participation in the war against Japan. Washington had no alternative plans for ending the war in the Far East other than with Soviet help. Churchill was anxious that the Soviet Union should not acquire so much German territory. But Truman would not listen. On Eastern Europe the United States, supported by Britain, demanded the fulfilment of the Declaration of Liberated Europe: Stalin refused supervised elections and the proposals for political freedom were worthless. American idealism about the pattern of postwar relations began to crumble as the United States began to realise how powerful the Soviet Union's armies of occupation made its position, and to comprehend what Britain had understood by the 'sphere of influence'. The United States, however, though ready to resist Russian pressure in Iran and Turkey, showed less interest in Soviet claims to be a trustee of an Italian colony in North Africa, a prospect which alarmed Churchill, as it seemed to threaten British interests in the Mediterranean.

At Potsdam the news came through of the election of a Labour government in Britain. Churchill was replaced by Clement Attlee. The new Prime Minister of a Socialist government chose, admittedly for reasons of internal party politics, Ernest Bevin as his Foreign Secretary. Bevin proved to be a man well suited by temperament to deal with what he increasingly regarded as an aggressive and unco-operative Soviet Union. Bevin consulted Eden on problems of foreign policy. Though it pursued ideals of socialism at home, the British Labour government did not extend these to foreign policy. Perhaps the British position was weakened at Potsdam with the new delegation as it was less able to stand up to the American concessions than Churchill and Eden had been. But, as Churchill had realised, it was too late: 'the time to settle frontiers had gone. The Red Army is spreading over Europe. It will remain.'[38]

Potsdam also saw the finalisation of plans for ending the war against Japan. One writer has argued, though he has subsequently modified his case, that the dropping of the atomic bombs was seen by key American officials as being relevant to the political outcome in Europe. There is little evidence for this. The United States wanted to end the war quickly: it had no alternative plan for the defeat of Japanese forces in China other than with Soviet aid. What the United States did insist on and secure was mastery of the fate of postwar Japan. On 11 August Truman signed a memorandum stating that whatever the Allied contingents in Japan were, the United States alone would designate a centralised commander of a unified occupation government. British and Soviet opposition to the arrangement had no effect. This was in line with American wartime policy of keeping the Pacific theatre to itself, and even excluding its ally, Britain, where it could.[39]

4

THE COLD WAR:
EDUCATING THE AMERICANS

The period of Attlee's Labour governments has been seen as the time of the revival of the 'special relationship' between Britain and the United States, a relationship revived to face the threat of the Soviet Union at the time of what Walter Lippmann, the American journalist, described in 1947 as the 'Cold War'. Like Neville Chamberlain's policy for the 'appeasement' of Europe in the late 1930s, myths and legends have proliferated about the origins of the Cold War. 'Inevitability' has been invoked; 'ineluctable forces' mentioned; 'accident' offered as an explanation. The Cold War was a name, given in hindsight, to what appeared as a Soviet threat, first to some British, and then afterwards to American statesmen. The phrase, in inverted commas, began to appear in British official minutes around 1948. By 1949 it was accepted, and written in small letters.

Most of the literature on the origins of the Cold War, particularly that of American origin, viewed the post-1945 world in terms of bipolar rivalry between the United States and the Soviet Union.[1] Interpretations of the Truman era, in terms of a Western response initiated and managed by the United States, persisted well into the 1980s: Bradford Perkins, in analysing Anglo-American relations, continued to insist that the 'Americans, like the Romans, never permitted challenge to their authority'.[2] As F. M. Carroll observed, this writing failed to 'keep abreast of the most recent scholarship on Britain and the origins of the cold war'.[3] That work showed that there was no indication, initially, that Truman intended to build up Britain as a bulwark against the Soviet Union, or even to be particularly helpful in restoring Britain's economy

58

and preserving its military forces. Truman continued the wartime accommodation of the Soviets. It was left to the British Foreign Secretary, Ernest Bevin, to be the architect of the Western alliance that was built up to contain the Soviets.[4] Furthermore, the strategy devised to deal with the new situation was global: in the years immediately after the end of the Second World War, the Cold War was almost global in scale, extending across Europe and Asia, penetrating the Middle East and Africa.[5] London had to educate Washington to what it saw as the reality of a Soviet and later general Communist threat, not only in Europe, but in the Middle East, Asia and even Africa.

American Economic Aid to Britain

This was at a time when it was only with American money that Britain could maintain the illusion of being a world power. In December 1945, London accepted a $3.75 billion loan at 2 per cent interest. At the same time British debts under Lend-Lease were effectively written off. Given the state of public and Congressional opinion in the United States the terms were generous: no other nation was treated in such a favourable way. But Parliament and the British public viewed the agreement in a sour mood. When the loan went to Congress the American administration endorsed the British cause at a time when Washington was beginning to stand against Moscow. Many Americans thought that London could use the money to sustain the British Empire, or implement the socialist programme of nationalisation, or fight the Zionists in Palestine, of all of which they disapproved. Increasing Soviet intransigence, however, helped the administration's case, and Truman was finally able to sign the agreement on 15 July 1946.

The freezing winter of 1946-7 in Britain brought that country more effectively to a standstill than had the Nazi bombs, and waiver clauses over the interest payments on the loan had to be operated. London effectively broke the agreement by suspending the convertibility of the pound sterling. Britain did not have the money to sustain its worldwide obligations. Britain's deficit in 1946 could be attributed to military payments. Increasingly, however, in American eyes, British weakness was a threat to American security: an economically strong Britain was seen as politically necessary for the United States. With this prevailing mood, Britain managed to preserve a system of imperial preference and the sterling area. Despite Marshall Aid, however, London was forced to devalue the pound sterling against the dollar in 1949. The Labour governments of 1945-51 implemented their Cold War foreign policy against a background of continuing economic crises. They were able to do this only with American backing.

Against the background of the overriding need to rebuild Britain economically, Attlee's government faced a new strategic situation. Jet engines, rockets, guided missiles and the atomic bomb practically eliminated the sea as a significant defence. If the Soviet Union were the most likely enemy, the British navy would be of limited use against a land-locked power. This meant that, despite the financial straits, the army would have to be maintained. In addition Britain had the victor's obligations to occupy Japan, Germany, Austria, Venezia Giulia and Greece. Troops were also needed to keep order against terrorism in Palestine. The Labour governments retained conscription in peacetime. This was seen as necessary. By December 1946 Britain needed 400,000 more troops than had been anticipated; the British military establishment totalled almost 1,500,000. During the fiscal year of 1946–7, 18.7 per cent of men were in military service; in comparison only 10 per cent of American men were under arms. That year Britain's defence expenditure accounted for 18.8 per cent of the national income; in the United States it was only 10.6 per cent. Attlee was forced to slow down demobilisation.

British Options for Postwar Planning

In August 1945 Britain, if it were to remain a significant force in the world, was faced, in effect, with three options: it could develop the Commonwealth as an alternative power bloc, a course often favoured by the Labour left; or it could revive the wartime Anglo-American alliance to stand against the Soviet Union. These alternatives were not mutually exclusive, and Churchill spoke of them as being interlocking.

The European option was not acceptable: indeed until 1948 the Middle East rather than Europe was considered to be Britain's first line of defence.[6] During the Second World War, Attlee had had hopes of the Commonwealth. But it was evident at the conference of Commonwealth leaders in London held during April and May 1946 that although there might be agreement as to the nature of the Soviet threat, the Dominions were reluctant to compromise their independence in any way. The 1948 Commonwealth Conference evidenced a similar hesitation. It was only really in 1949, following the election of the anti-communist Afrikaner Nationalist government in South Africa,[7] and with the joining of the Cold War in Asia, that Britain was able to enter into bilateral defence discussions with the old 'white' Dominions. Until then Bevin chose to stress the Anglo-American special relationship.[8] As the Cold War was joined in Europe he manoeuvred the United States, Canada, and the West European powers into a defence system with which to face the threat of the Soviet Union. As the Cold War spread to the Middle East, Asia and the African continent, Bevin broadened the emphasis on the Anglo-American special relationship to embrace, possibly in a looser form, and through bilateral discussions, the old 'white' Dominions.

Anglo-American Co-operation as the Basis of British Foreign Policy

In February 1949 Bevin agreed to the establishment of the Permanent Under-Secretary's Committee, under William Strang, to consider long-term questions of foreign policy, and how Britain could in the future maintain its status as a Great Power. That committee recommended that neither the Commonwealth alone, nor Western Europe alone, nor even the Commonwealth plus Western Europe would be strong enough, either economically or militarily, to stand on their own against the forces opposing them, and that the full participation of the United States was essential to sustain the free world, which the Soviet Union was trying to undermine. Effectively the British Government, at the end of 1949, endorsed the conclusions of Strang's committee that the prevailing policy of close Anglo-American co-operation in world affairs should continue, and that such co-operation would involve Britain's sustained political, military and economic effort. When, early in 1951, the principle of the Anglo-American special relationship as the corner-stone of British foreign policy was seriously challenged in Cabinet, against the back-ground of Western reverses in the Korean War, a dying Bevin, assisted by Strang, and Hugh Gaitskell, fought to sustain the recommendations of the Permanent Under-Secretary's Committee. What Britain had to do was to 'exert sufficient control over the policy of the well-intentioned but inexperienced colossus on whose cooperation our safety depends'.[9]

Atomic Weapons

The major shortcoming of the Anglo-American relationship during the years of the emergence of the Cold War, the American refusal to share the military and industrial secrets of atomic energy, to the development of which Britain had significantly contributed, was evident with the end of the Second World War. Initially the development of the atomic bomb had been regarded as an equal partnership, and Roosevelt and Churchill had agreed at Quebec in 1943 that the collaboration should continue after the end of the war. This was reaffirmed in 1944. Prompted by the Chiefs of Staff, Attlee raised the issue with Truman on 17 August 1945, urging that means should be sought to enable the frank collaboration and exchange of information to be continued.[10] The Americans refused. Bevin and the Chiefs of Staff discounted Truman's case that a plant in Britain would be vulnerable, presumably either from enemy attack or from sabotage. The American administration lent its support to the McMahon Bill in Congress which proposed restrictions on the disclosure and exchange of information on atomic energy. The Bill became law on 1 August 1946. It was not until attempts were made to reconsolidate the Anglo-American relationship in the aftermath of the Suez crisis of 1956 that the McMahon Acts were finally repealed.[11]

Accommodation of the Soviets

It has been claimed that possession of atomic weapons enabled the United States to threaten the Soviet Union.[12] But Britain and the United States could not challenge the Soviet Union's position in Eastern Europe: they wanted some influence to try to secure a democratic framework. Soviet occupation forces enabled the communists to prevail in all these areas except Czechoslovakia, and by the end of 1946 the resistance of independent political forces was broken. Despite rhetoric, it appears that Britain and the United States accepted the Soviet Union's apparent need for a rim of friendly states on its borders. In a memorandum of 18 October 1945 Charles E. Bohlen, who was special assistant to the Secretary of State, James F. Byrnes, drew obvious parallels with the Monroe Doctrine. He observed that while the United States had not tried to deny the Soviet Union 'the legitimate pre-rogatives of a great power in relation to smaller countries resulting from geographic proximity', it seemed that Stalin was seeking 'complete Soviet domination and control over all phases of the external and internal life' of neighbouring states.

On 9 November 1945, the Turkish ambassador warned Bevin that the Soviet 'war of nerves' over Turkey was aimed at forcing Turkey out of the British and into the Soviet orbit. In November autonomists in the region of Iran, with the support of the Russian army, staged an open revolt. In reacting to this the United States would not co-operate with Britain. It ordered the evacuation of American troops, and Byrnes urged Britain and the Soviet Union to do likewise. Britain favoured rapid evacuation as well, but not at the risk of the Soviets overrunning Iran.

Against this background Byrnes, without consulting Bevin, suggested to Molotov that the Big Three should meet again. Bevin did not want this meeting to take place as he felt that the Soviet Union would be the only gainer. The meeting took place in Moscow, where on 17 December 1945 Bevin warned Byrnes that it looked as if the Soviets were trying to undermine the British position in the Middle East, particularly in Greece, Turkey and Iran. Byrnes's response was that he did not intend to raise the question of the Straits: the Soviet Union was challenging Turkey's right to close them. After reading the communiqué of the Moscow Conference Truman recorded: 'There was not a word about Iran or any other place where the Soviets were on the march. We had gained only an empty promise of further talks.' He noted down to inform Byrnes on 5 January 1946: 'I do not think we should play compromise any longer. . . . I'm sick of babying the Soviets.'

The Origins of Containment

In Moscow, George F. Kennan, the American counsellor, and Frank Roberts, Minister in the British embassy, friends from the Second World War, discussed Soviet policy together. At the beginning of 1946 Roberts advised the Foreign Office that the Soviet Union would be active in countries on its borders and not yet under communist control. Britain had to be resolute in its determination to keep the Soviet Union out of Turkey and Iran. American support would make that more effective.[13] That support came in the form of a telegram from Kennan to the State Department on 22 February 1946 explaining the Soviet Union's behaviour: in the Soviet Union there was a 'political force committed fanatically to the belief that with U.S.A. there can be no permanent modus vivendi'; the United States should be prepared to guide the peoples of Europe, because if it did not, the Soviet Union would.

If the American administration were to have a new policy towards the Soviet Union it first had to educate public opinion to the realities of the Soviet threat. American opinion at this time can be gauged from the reaction to Churchill's speech of 5 March 1946. Speaking at Fulton, Missouri, in the company of the President, he stated: 'From Stettin in the Baltic to Trieste in the Adriatic, an iron curtain has descended across the Continent.' Churchill called for the unity of the English-speaking peoples, 'a special relationship between the British Commonwealth and the United States', to meet the menace. But such was the reaction of isolationist sentiment in the United States that Truman had publicly to dissociate himself from the speech.

In Britain, however, the Prime Minister wanted a policy of considerable disengagement from areas where there was a risk of Britain clashing with the Soviet Union: the situation would only be different if the United States became interested, and that country was withdrawing into isolation. Attlee's proviso, however, was met when the new American policy of standing up to the Soviets was first evident in Iran. The Soviets broke their undertaking to withdraw troops, and when the Americans finally associated themselves with the British stand in the United Nations, the Soviets withdrew from Iran.

The pattern was repeated in Turkey. Late in 1945, Turkey, backed by Britain and the United States, refused the Soviet Union special rights to garrison the Straits area. In March 1946 Washington considered sending a powerful fleet into the Straits. On 7 August 1946 the Soviet Union requested joint Turkish-Russian defence of the Dardanelles. Truman's advisers concurred: if the Soviet Union dominated Turkey it would be difficult to stop Moscow from gaining control of the Near and Middle East. The Soviet Union could only be deterred by a threat of force. The United States used a show of gunboat diplomacy. Britain was not involved in this American response.[14]

Britain, however, remained uncertain as to how long the Americans would stay in Europe. The Foreign Office hinted that if there were war against the Soviet Union, there should be as many Germans as possible on the side of the West. Bevin, on 23 July, was still worried that the Americans would 'leave him in the lurch' over the proposed unification of the British and American zones in Germany. Then, on 6 September, in a speech at Stuttgart, Byrnes mentioned a provisional government for an economically self-supporting Germany and stated that American forces would remain in occupation. This was the first indication that American troops were going to stay in Europe. The single economic and political unit, the Bizone, was formed on 1 January 1947. The United States was preparing to block Soviet expansion in Europe. Byrnes's Stuttgart speech signified that Roosevelt's grand design of co-operation with the Soviet Union had failed.[15]

While in New York for the signing of the peace treaties at the end of 1946 Bevin met Molotov privately. Molotov asked why Britain kept in such close touch with the United States and not with the Soviet Union. Bevin explained that this was so because it was possible to exchange views and ideas between British and American statesmen and officials. Bevin commented that it was ridiculous to think that the British Empire wanted to attack the Soviet Union: 'We wanted to be friends. It was the Soviet Government which was making things difficult.'

Bevin Chooses the Anglo-American Alliance

Bevin chose the Anglo-American alliance. As early as 13 February 1946 he had written to Attlee:

I believe that an entirely new approach is required, and that can only be based upon a very close understanding between ourselves and the Americans. My idea is that we should start with an integration of British and American armaments and an agreement restricting undesirable competition between our respective armament industries.[16]

Talks towards this end took place in the United States in September 1946 between B. L. Montgomery, by then Chief of the Imperial General Staff, and the American Chiefs of Staff. In December 1946 it was accepted that the wartime practice of American and British naval vessels using each other's ports should be continued indefinitely. By the end of 1946 the British and American air forces were exchanging officers to study tactics and equipment. In Washington, American, British and Canadian military experts discussed arms standardisation, weapons research and common tactical doctrines. Britain had offices in the Pentagon, close to the Joint Chiefs of Staff: the British Joint Staff Mission handled matters of common interest. The Combined Chiefs of Staff, in some ways the only Anglo-American organisation that survived the end of the Second World War, continued until 1949 when the North Atlantic Treaty Organisation was formed. Britain and the United States had an informal military alliance by December 1946. Bevin, in shaping this alliance, was challenged by Attlee. The Prime Minister was disturbed by signs that the United States was trying to make a safety zone around itself, while leaving Britain and Europe in no-man's-land. Greece, in particular, troubled Attlee. He reiterated his conviction that British military advisers overrated the strategic importance of the Mediterranean. If Britain left Greece, only the United States could take its place. During the second week of December Bevin told the Secretary of State that Britain would continue to help with military equipment, but that he hoped that the United States would provide economic assistance. Early in the new year an American economic mission arrived in Greece headed by Paul A. Porter, assisted by Mark F. Etheridge. On 17 February 1947 Etheridge warned that the Soviets thought of Greece as a 'ripe plum ready to fall into their hands'. Two days later Porter told the State Department that economic and political stability would only be possible if there were an all-out effort on the part of the United States. On 21 February, before the arrival of Britain's message that it would have to leave by 31 March, George C. Marshall, the new Secretary of State, instructed Dean Acheson to prepare the 'necessary steps for sending economic and military aid' to Greece.[17]

Against the background of the freezing winter of 1947, economic chaos and disruption, Bevin, despite the opposition of his Prime Minister, chose to emphasise the Anglo-American special relationship as the foundation-stone of British foreign policy. Convinced of the Soviet Union's expansionist intentions, the Foreign Secretary was determined that nothing should endanger the development of an alliance which he saw as being essential for Britain's security. He realised Britain's dependence on the United States, but felt that Britain had to maintain its independence and its seat at the table of Great Powers. He was conscious of the difficulties of American public opinion. George Kennan, in March 1947, thought that Britain was trying to lessen the stigma of being an imperial power with this in mind. On 28 January of that year Britain announced the future constitution of an independent Burma; on 14 February it was known that Britain would refer the Palestine question to the United Nations, an issue on which there had been major Anglo-American disagreement; on 20 February Attlee said that India would be independent no later than June 1948; negotiations with Egypt were in progress.[18]

By 11 February Bevin had concluded that policy towards Greece had to be reviewed. On 21 February Washington received two messages from London. The first noted the strategic importance of keeping Greece out of the hands of the Soviet Union and suggested that the British and American Chiefs of Staff urgently consider the situation in the Eastern Mediterranean. British aid would have to end on 31 March. The second note said much the same about Turkey. Earlier that day Marshall had given instructions for the necessary preparations to be made for sending aid to Greece and Turkey.[19]

The State Department immediately started preparing specific plans for aid to Greece and Turkey. On 12 March 1947 Truman outlined what was to become known as the 'Truman doctrine' and 'containment' to both houses of Congress. Congress bickered, but on 15 May it appropriated $400 million for Greece and Turkey. This, though not an open-ended commitment to containment, was the first step. Zionists in the United States tried unsuccessfully to link American relief of Britain's financial position in Greece with forcing Britain to accept the displaced persons in the American zone in Germany into Palestine. Senator Robert Wagner of the American Christian Palestine Committee raised the matter with a fellow member, Arthur Vandenberg, in the middle of March.[20] But by then Greece was an issue within the framework of the emerging Anglo-American alliance, and Washington was reluctant to endanger that. Marshall persuaded Bevin in March to allow the British mission to stay in Greece; the Secretary of State also wanted to leave military affairs in Turkey to the British. British troops remained in Greece until 1954.

Bevin and the Preparation of Europe for Marshall Aid

In March 1947 Bevin had no assurances that the United States would go further than supporting Greece and Turkey. He knew, as he told the Cabinet on 3 February, that Britain would be placed in an impossible position if the United States withdrew from Europe. Britain, however, was not prepared just to rely on the United States. Truman's abrupt cancellation of Lend-Lease, and American Palestine policy dictated by domestic pressures, together with the revocation of the Quebec and Hyde Park agreements, convinced a group of British ministers that Britain should build its own atomic bomb. The decision was taken on

10 January 1947. With an eye on the situation in Europe, and with the hope of reducing the influence of the Communist Party in France and of balancing the attraction of the Soviet Union, Bevin at the beginning of 1947 negotiated the Dunkirk Treaty with France. At the time it was not seen as the beginnings of a military alliance with which to face the Soviet Union. The idea that the Anglo-French alliance could be extended to include Belgium and the Netherlands was dismissed: 'more harm than good may be caused by trying to go too quickly'.

Within the American administration warnings about Britain's economic plight, France's instability, and a growing awareness that other countries could face the same problems as Greece and Turkey, led to suggestions for better planning and more co-ordination in the use of American resources to meet the threat. In the early stages planning for a European recovery programme was focused on the newly formed Policy Planning Staff under George Kennan, and on a special agency of the State-War-Navy Co-ordinating Committee.[21] At Harvard University on 5 June 1947 Marshall spoke of the need for recovery in 'Europe as a whole'. The United States would give financial support and provide 'friendly aid' in drafting a recovery programme. It was up to the Europeans to show initiative and responsibility.

Bevin acted on his own initiative. He assured the Americans that there would be a response, and on 9 June suggested joint action with the French. He argued, unsuccessfully, that Britain should be treated as a partner in the Marshall programme, rather than being lumped together with the other European countries. Bevin contacted the French, saw that the governments of Belgium, the Netherlands and Luxembourg drew up proposals, and even approached Italy. The Foreign Secretary succeeded in convincing the French that they should go ahead with the plan even if the Soviet Union attempted obstructionist tactics. For Bevin it was important that 'there should be no delay' and that the proposals should embrace 'as large an area of Europe as possible'.

In Paris, at the end of June, Molotov suggested that each nation should establish its own recovery programme. France and Britain refused, and stood by the American idea of the programme being Europe-wide. Molotov walked out, and in a week the Molotov plan was announced for the Soviet Union's satellites. Sixteen West European nations met in Paris between July and September, drew up a pro-gramme, and gave the United States a shopping list. The Americans and some of the French argued for an economic integration of Europe, but this was resisted by Britain. The Labour government did not want to become part of Europe. The British view prevailed: economic co-operation was to be multilateral and functional. Truman presented the European Bill to Congress on 19 December 1947. But there it met with intense opposition. The Republicans disliked steps towards socialism in Europe.

On 4 December Britain learnt that Truman had approved the conclusions that had arisen out of the informal political and strategic talks on the Middle East held in Washington from 18 October to 7 November between British and American officials. The conclusions reached by the participants on both sides were that the security of the Middle East and the Eastern Mediterranean was vital to both Britain and the United States. The two countries would co-operate in the area and abjure any desire for one country to replace the other. The United States would support and strengthen the British strategic, political and economic position throughout the Middle East, and assist Britain to obtain strategic facilities in the area.

Anglo-American Divisions over the Middle East

The Middle East had been an area of major Anglo-American dispute between 1942 and 1947. At the end of the Second World War the Middle East, to the British military mind, had an importance second only to that of the United Kingdom. The experiences of Mons and Dunkirk lingered, British land armies should not again fight on the European continent. That was a job for Europeans. The security of the British Commonwealth depended on protecting the United Kingdom, maintaining vital sea communications and securing the Middle East as a defensive and striking base against the Soviet Union.[22]

This strategic policy meant that the British Empire in the Middle East, acquired almost accidentally earlier in the century, had to be maintained and consolidated. In effect British strategic policy for the Middle East was dependent on a British military presence in Palestine. In August 1945 the Chiefs of Staff opposed the partition of Palestine into separate Zionist and Arab states: it would be drastic and irrevocable.

At this point Truman intervened. He had sent Earl G. Harrison to investigate the condition of displaced persons in Europe. Harrison recommended that Washington should, under existing laws, allow reasonable numbers of Jewish refugees into the United States. Truman, realising that Congress would not relax the immigration quotas, chose instead to assign the responsibility to Britain. In doing this he overrode the advice of the State and War Departments. There was an election in New York, and the Jewish vote seemed crucial. Truman wrote to Attlee on 31 August suggesting that the main solution lay in the quick evacuation of Jews to Palestine. Harrison had recommended that 100,000 be admitted.

Bevin, who could not accept that Jews could not live in Europe, suggested to the Cabinet an Anglo-American commission to investigate the refugee problem. The American response was hesitant, at a time when British soldiers were being killed by terrorists in Palestine, because of Zionist agitation in the New York election campaign. Bevin wanted to involve the United States. Increasingly worried about Soviet advances in the Middle East, Bevin saw the area as essential to Western security at a time of the emergence of the Cold War. To maintain its position, Britain had to negotiate treaties with the new Arab states. This would hardly be possible if Britain were seen as the sponsor of a Zionist state in Palestine, to be achieved through Jewish immigration.

An Anglo-American commission was appointed, heard evidence in Washington, London, Europe and the Middle East and reported in April 1946. On 30 April, without consulting London, Truman endorsed the recommendation of this commission that 100,000 certificates be issued for Jewish immigrants to go to Palestine, and also two other aspects favourable to Zionism. Those favourable to the Arabs were dismissed as long-range considerations. The British public was outraged: British soldiers had just been murdered by Zionist terrorists. Truman had succumbed again to Zionist pressure, and to threats of electoral punishment in the forthcoming November Congressional elections.

Anglo-American differences over Palestine were temporarily resolved when delegates from both countries met in London in July 1946 and suggested a scheme of provincial autonomy. In Palestine, Menachem Begin and the Irgun, with the co-operation of the Haganah, blew up the King David Hotel, one wing of which was used as British Army headquarters; 91 were killed. Zionist propaganda throughout the world publicised what was construed as an anti-Semitic statement by the British Army commander, and as a result, turned a terrorist outrage into a Zionist victory. Under the threat of Zionist electoral punishment, Truman withdrew his support from the provincial autonomy scheme. But by the beginning of October, Bevin anticipated that Jewish delegates could be brought into the Palestine conference even before the return of the Arab delegates. Truman ruined this hopeful prospect. The Zionists, working with Robert E. Hannegan, the Chairman of the Democratic National Committee, with an eye on a forthcoming election in New York and the Presidential election of 1948, urged Truman to make an immediate statement in favour of partition. The State Department advised against this, as did the Joint Chiefs of Staff: partition might alienate the Arabs form the West. Attlee asked Truman to delay. But on 4 October, the eve of the Jewish Day of Atonement, Truman said that a solution along the lines of partition originally proposed by the Jewish Agency on 5 August 1947 would 'command the support of public opinion in the United States'.

In December 1946, Attlee suggested that Britain should withdraw from the Middle East. The Prime Minister wanted to hand over the mandate for Palestine. The Chief of the Air Staff, Lord Tedder, warned that a solution to the Palestine problem which alienated Arab goodwill would be unacceptable. Britain would be denied freedom of movement through an essential area, and its wider interests in the Middle East would be endangered. The Chiefs of Staff reiterated their insistence that Britain had to be able to station forces in Palestine. Airbases were needed for imperial communications. With Egypt being evacuated, apart from the Canal Zone, Palestine was the only area able to accommodate Britain's Middle East reserve. Tedder told the Cabinet on 15 January that there were three cardinal requirements for the future defence of the British Commonwealth: the defence of the United Kingdom and its development as a base for air offensive; the maintenance of sea communications; and the retention of Britain's existing position and influence in the Middle East. These were the three 'vital props' of Britain's defensive position. They were all interdependent and if any one were lost, 'the whole structure would be imperilled'. Palestine had to be held, as a screen for the defence of Egypt. As Britain had undertaken to withdraw from Egypt, it had to be able to use Palestine as a base for the mobile reserve of troops which had to be kept ready to meet any emergency throughout the Middle East.

Despite warnings from the Chiefs of Staff, on 14 February 1947, the Cabinet decided to submit the Palestine problem to the United Nations without any recommendations for a solution. On 15 May the United Nations Special Committee on Palestine (UNSCOP) was established, with broad powers of investigation. During the UNSCOP inquiry British morale in Palestine was eroded. The *President Warfield*, renamed *Exodus*, arrived off Palestine with 4,493 illegal immigrants. These were returned to their French port of embarkation. In retaliation for the execution of Zionist terrorists, the Irgun hanged two British sergeants and booby-trapped their bodies. These were found on 31 July. There were outbreaks of anti-Semitism in Britain. As Bevin explained, Britain had no alternative but to ship the refugees on the *President Warfield* back to Germany. This gave the Zionists the most notable propaganda success of the time.

UNSCOP, in a majority report, recommended in effect the creation of a separate Zionist state. Bevin told the Cabinet on 20 September that the UNSCOP proposals were unacceptable. Attlee did not think it reasonable to ask the British administration to continue in the prevailing circumstances. The Cabinet accepted the policy of withdrawal.

On 26 September Arthur Creech Jones, the Colonial Secretary, told the United Nations that if the General Assembly recommended a policy not acceptable to the Arabs and Jews, Britain would not be able to implement it. The Soviet Union, on 13 October, 'mystified' Britain and the United States by announcing its support for the partition of Palestine. Bevin thought that the Soviet Union hoped to pour enough indoctrinated Communist Jews into Palestine to turn it into a Communist state in a short time. He observed: 'The New York Jews have been doing their work for them.' The Chiefs of Staff became worried that a Communist regime could be set up in Palestine after the British withdrawal on 15 May 1948, but Bevin insisted on a British attitude of neutrality in the United Nations. The calculation probably was that partition would not secure the necessary two-thirds majority. On 24 November Bevin dined with Marshall, and told him that Britain would abstain in the United Nations vote. 'This great issue' had been handled by the United States more with 'the electoral situation in New York City in mind than the large issues of foreign policy which were involved'. Before the murder of the two British sergeants Bevin had felt that the situation in Palestine could be held. He told Marshall that Britain could not be committed to a position which might involve military action against the Arabs.

On 29 November the General Assembly voted for partition. Before the vote the American Zionists exerted unprecedented pressure on the American administration, and delegations to both the United Nations and their governments, to secure the necessary majority. The situation in Palestine deteriorated. The Arab reaction was worse than Bevin had expected. On 17 December he warned Marshall that the Middle East could 'blow up'. There would be serious consequences, even for the

United States. The Soviet Union might profit when the Zionists and Arabs started fighting.[23] In the end, however, as Zionists in the United States realised, Bevin managed to isolate the Palestine question from the overall development of the Anglo-American special relationship, and from the problems of the Middle East as a whole.

The English-Speaking Alliance

On the evening of 17 December 1947 Bevin outlined to Marshall the gist of a policy that he was formulating to deal with the Cold War. Bevin felt that it was important to take a wider view of the situation, and not just regard it as a dispute between the Soviet Union and the Western powers. A positive plan was essential for the association of the Western democratic countries – including the United States, Britain, France, Italy and others – and the Dominions. This was not to be a formal alliance, but 'an understanding backed by power, money and resolute action', 'a sort of spiritual federation of the West'. A powerful con-solidation of the West would show the Soviet Union that it could not advance any further. Marshall commented that it was necessary to distinguish between themselves as soon possible on immediate objectives: 'They must take events at the flood stream and produce a co-ordinated effect.'[24]

On 8 January 1948 Bevin outlined to the Cabinet a suggestion that Britain should try to form, with the backing of the United States and the Dominions, a Western democratic system. The memorandum was sent to Marshall. Bevin approached France, and on 22 January told the House of Commons that talks had been proposed to the Benelux countries. He referred to a 'Western Union' to meet the threat of the Soviet Union. Marshall asked London at what point he could suggest the participation of the United States in Bevin's plan. For a while the Americans hesitated: there was opposition to the Americans under-taking a direct commitment. Bevin had problems with the Chiefs of Staff. Sir John Cunningham, Admiral of the Fleet, on 2 February 1948, reminded the Committee that it had been the traditional British policy in the past to avoid European continental commitments: 'Twice in the past we had given a guarantee to assist a continental nation to the limit of our power by the provision of land forces. On both occasions we had suffered severely, first at Mons and more recently at Dunkirk.'[25]

While the Chiefs of Staff were evolving a strategic policy to implement the new British foreign policy, little progress was being made in Washington. Further advances by the Soviet Union changed that. On 25 February there was a coup in Czechoslovakia, the country which in 1945 the United States had anticipated would develop free from interference from East or West. Apparent Soviet moves against Norway seemingly led Bevin to conclude that the time was right for a specific approach to the United States: on 11 March Marshall received a message from the Foreign Secretary asking for immediate consultations on the setting up of an Atlantic security system. Marshall consulted Truman, ignored his obstructionist State Department officials, and replied on 12 March that Washington was 'prepared to proceed at once in the joint discussion on the establishment of an Atlantic security system'. He wanted British representatives in Washington early the following week. On 17 March the Treaty of Brussels, initiated by Bevin, was signed: it set up the Western European Union, which was to last for fifty years. The five signatories, Britain, France, Belgium, the Netherlands and Luxembourg, were to come to the aid of any one of their number which was attacked. It was understood that other powers could join. Bevin told the French that he wanted the Americans to underwrite the Brussels Treaty.

Opinion was changing in the United States. The day the Brussels Treaty was signed Truman asked Congress for selective service to maintain the strength of the American armed forces. The coup in Czechoslovakia so shook Congressmen that the bill for Marshall Aid had a relatively easy passage. It was against this background that delegates from Britain, Canada and the United States met in the Pentagon between 22 March and 1 April.[26] The Americans blocked French participation on the grounds of security. One of the British delegates, however, was Donald Maclean, the Soviet spy, and it seems evident from an article in the Polish press that Moscow knew what went on. In the end the issue focused on whether the Americans should propose a collective defence agreement for the North Atlantic area as a whole, or whether a presidential declaration of support for the Western European democracies would be enough. Bevin thought that the Soviets would not be deterred by a presidential declaration, and in any case Britain would be lucky if Truman and the leaders of the Senate pronounced in favour of 'a treaty binding the United States for the first time in her history to accept positive obligations in the way of the defence of her natural associates and friends'.

Like the British, the Canadian delegates wanted a treaty rather than a presidential declaration. It was hoped that the Americans would summon a conference to discuss the new 'Security Pact for the North Atlantic Area' in May, after the Italian elections. Later in April Robert A. Lovett, the Under-Secretary of State, saw Senator Arthur Vandenberg. As a result of this meeting, helped by a declaration by Louis St Laurent, the Canadian Foreign Minister, the Senate adopted Resolution 239 on 11 June: it recommended the 'association of the United States, by constitutional process, with such regional and other collective arrangements as are based on continuous and effective self-help and mutual aid, and as affect its national security'. In the end the negotiations with all the states concerned did not start until 6 July 1948.

But the British embassy in Washington warned that the Americans were in no hurry: they did not regard themselves as equal partners in the enterprise. 'They still feel that they are in the position of a kind of fairy godmother handing over favours to the less fortunate European countries – provided always that the latter can justify their claims for such favours.'[27] Bevin, however, was confident. He was not shaken by the Soviet 'peace offensive', which took the form of exchanges between the American ambassador in Moscow, Walter Bedell Smith, and Molotov during April and May 1948. Without meaning any offence, the Foreign Secretary explained that 'he realised that America had not so much experience in foreign affairs as we had and that while she was developing a sense of responsibility remarkably well, there must occasionally be setbacks to which he did not attach excessive importance'.[28]

The Zionist Lobby and Truman's Recognition of Israel

The British were succeeding in educating the American administration and public to what they saw as the reality of a Soviet threat to Europe. This was at a time of British disenchantment over Truman's shifting policy in the Middle East, and his recognition of the State of Israel in the interests of helping to secure his re-election as President.

Early in 1948 the American Joint Chiefs of Staff had warned that partition would lead to Arab hatred, the loss of oil, Soviet penetration in the area in the guise of enforcing the United Nations plan, and a call for American troops for Palestine. On 29 January George Kennan, then a senior State Department official, explained that British relations with the

Arabs and the remaining British strategic positions in the Middle East were among the few 'real assets' the United States still had in the area. James V. Forrestal, the Secretary for Defense, said that without Middle Eastern oil the Marshall Plan could not succeed. The United States began to move away from partition. In Britain the Chiefs of Staff were instructed to investigate accelerating the British withdrawal.

Zionists working through Clark Clifford, Truman's electoral adviser, George M. Elsey, Clifford's assistant, and Max Lowenthal, a White House consultant with Jewish Agency connections, secured a reversal of American policy. Truman, concerned about the significance of the Zionist vote in the forthcoming presidential election, recognised Israel on 14 May 1948. At midnight HMS *Euryalus* left Palestinian waters with Sir Alan Gordon Cunningham, the High Commissioner, on board. Britain was no longer the paramount power over the Zionists. David Ben-Gurion proclaimed the State of Israel at 4 p.m. the same day. On 15 May carious Arab armies entered Palestine. On 21 May Kennan's Policy Planning Staff advised Marshall that American policy threatened 'not only to place in jeopardy some of our most vital national interests in the Middle East and the Mediterranean but also to disrupt the unity of the western world and to undermine our entire policy toward the Soviet Union'. From London the ambassador, Lewis Douglas, warned that the widening crevasse between Britain and the United States over Palestine 'cannot be confined to Palestine or even the Middle East: it is already seriously jeopardising foundation-stone of US policy in Europe – partnership with a friendly and well-disposed Britain'.[29]

The Berlin Blockade and American Bases in Britain

On 28 July Attlee approved a Foreign Office paper, endorsed by Bevin, to be used in preliminary discussions with the Americans. It stated that the Soviets had established themselves solidly in eastern Europe, and from that secure entrenchment they were trying to infiltrate into western and southern Europe. Special attention was given to Germany. Britain wanted a Western Germany forming part of the Western defence system. That would be the most effective barrier against the spread of Communism across Europe. By then the Soviet Union had blockaded Berlin. The West had to remain in Berlin.

The Berlin blockade[30] marked the joining of the Cold War. The

Soviet Union imposed a partial blockade on the city on 1 April 1948. On 12 May A. V. Alexander, the Minister of Defence, finally agreed with Montgomery that British forces stationed on the European continent would stay and fight in an emergency. By the end of May the Americans had agreed that their forces would stay in Germany. On 24 June the Soviet Union severed the rail, road and water routes between the Western zones and Berlin. Britain and the United States supplied Berlin by air. Bevin urged the Americans to take military measures by increasing the airlift, and sending the B-29 bomber to Britain. The National Security Council on 15 July agreed to despatch these 'atomic bombers' to Britain from where they could reach Moscow. Sixty bombers were sent to East Anglia, and the first American Air Strategic Air Command base was established on British soil. At the time it was not known whether these B-29s did carry atomic bombs. But it was a psychological move.

The modified B-29s capable of carrying atomic bombs did not arrive in Britain until the summer of 1949. American bombers on British soil might have made Britain an obvious target for the Soviet Union, but it also probably ensured that the United States would fight at Britain's side. Britain would not have to wait for a Pearl Harbor. The Cabinet did not accept the principle that there should be a permanent American base in Britain, and the matter was not reported to Parliament. At the end of 1949, in any case, Britain was prepared to formalise the American presence in 'an adequate, proper and agreed arrangement'. The psychological threat of the B-29s, Western resolution and the technical success of the airlift forced the Soviets to give way. At the end of May 1949 they lifted the blockade. On a military level, in mounting the Berlin airlift the Anglo-American alliance had been revived almost on its Second World War footing. With the arrival of the B-29 bombers Bevin had the practical assurance of the American commitment to Europe.[31] The Anglo-American special relationship was working.

The Formation of NATO

The Berlin blockade encouraged Western unity, and was a favourable background for the negotiations leading to the establishment of the North Atlantic Treaty Organisation. During these, Bevin was irked by unofficial hints, spurred on by speeches from Churchill, that Britain should become part of a united Europe. He told Marshall that Britain was not 'a small country of no account'.[32] On 19 October 1948 Bevin explained to the Commonwealth Prime Ministers meeting in London that he did not favour an immediate attempt to establish a united states of Europe. Within the foreseeable future it was not practicable: 'It was alien to the British inclination to create grandiose paper constitutions.'[33] At this gathering Bevin also tried to complement the Washington discussions with his earlier scheme to involve the Dominions. Following the Commonwealth Prime Ministers' Conference, bilateral defence discussions and strategic planning were started between Britain, Australia and New Zealand.[34] Talks with South Africa began in 1949.[35]

By the end of 1948 the caution of the American delegates negotiating the Atlantic Pact evaporated. In the summer they had been worried about committing Congress, and the likelihood of Truman losing the presidential election. But Truman was returned against all the odds, and opinion in the United States moved strongly in favour of a pact. The North Atlantic Treaty was signed in Washington on 4 April 1949 by twelve governments. Bevin felt that the pact had 'steadied the world'.

The Global Cold War

It was, at one time, easy and fashionable to dismiss the events of these years as British and American imperialism threatening a peaceful non-expansionist Soviet Union. To do this neglects the real sense of threat felt in Britain and the United States. At one time it appeared that the agitation of the Communist Parties in France and Italy might easily lead to those countries falling under Soviet influence, and after that there would not be much of Europe left. British and, by 1946, American statesmen were inclined to think of Europe in terms of what later became known as the domino theory when it was applied to Asia. After its rejection by the Soviet Union the Marshall Plan was used to stop the dominoes from falling. It can be said that the emergence of the Cold War marked a transitional period in relations between Britain and the United States, and the Western world and the Soviet Union. The United States took over Britain's mantle of world leadership – which British statesmen, in view of the supposed Soviet threat, saw as necessary. Even during the Second World War, Churchill had been obsessed with the need to secure a firm American commitment to Europe. Bevin, the

Foreign Secretary of a socialist government, continued in the Churchillian tradition and achieved the objective. Although British and American statesmen had, at various times, markedly different views of the Soviet Union's intentions, by the beginning of 1946 these were beginning to coincide. Only then was unified action possible, though there were earlier indications of the United States and Britain acting on parallel lines. But in the United States public opinion lagged behind the perceptions of the statesmen. Though it is possible to make too much of 'left-wing' criticism of Truman, he nevertheless had to move carefully to secure Congressional support for his programme. Bevin did not have to educate the British public to the same extent. On 17 December 1947 he envisaged an association of the Western democratic countries – including the United States, Britain, Italy and others – and the Dominions. By the middle of 1949 the North Atlantic Treaty had been signed, and defence discussions had been initiated with Australia, New Zealand and South Africa. Bevin saw the Cold War not just in European but in global terms. It was spreading to the Middle East, Asia and Africa.[36]

5

THE COLD WAR:
GLOBAL STRATEGY

By early 1946 Bevin had the long-term aim of reviving the old wartime Anglo-American alliance. Initially, it seemed only possible to do this on the level of military co-operation. By the end of 1946 that was well under way. Co-operation was close, except in the atomic field. And there was the suspicion that Britain could not always rely on the United States. The Foreign Office was accused by some State Department officials of spreading propaganda that the United States was a 'conglomerate of ill-assorted groups'.

The Anglo-American Relationship as the Basis of Britain's Cold War Foreign Policy

William Strang's Permanent Under-Secretary's Committee, which in 1949 outlined the basis of British foreign policy, pointed out that Britain had no other option than to rely on the United States. The Commonwealth and the nations of Western Europe between them were not strong enough to deter the Soviet Union.

A detailed paper surveying Anglo-American relations, present and future, was revised at various stages during 1949, particularly in the light of conversations in Washington. It was considered so sensitive that initially it had only a very limited circulation. In October 1949 certain ministers were allowed to see it, but at the end of November Bevin decided that it was not to be circulated to the Cabinet as a whole. Strang sent Bevin the first 'final draft' on 24 August 1949 with the warning that it was more controversial than the others. Bevin minuted: 'I will not circulate this.' This version suggested that there need be no fundamental conflict of interest between Britain and the United States in any part of the world provided that Britain could achieve a position closely related to that of the United States, and yet sufficiently independent of it to be able to influence American policy in the desired direction. If Britain ceased to exist as a leading world power there would be a risk of major divergence, and the United States could withdraw from commitments in the Middle East, the Mediterranean and Africa. The United States could also decline to accept any responsibility in South and South-East Asia and might limit its responsibility in the Far East and the Pacific.

The committee offered an analysis of the difficulties resulting from American traditions, and in particular the extent to which local minority groups often used their electoral importance to exert a disproportionate influence on national and international policies. The anti-colonial tradition also inspired a prejudice against 'imperialist' rule. This and a deep-seated isolationism made Americans reluctant to intervene in the affairs of other countries. Washington always hesitated to take responsibility for other nations or territories, and when it did assume this responsibility it demanded absolute control and imposed its own solutions. The problem of Israel occupied a special place in Anglo-American relations. Of the 10 million Jews in the world, about 5 million lived in the United States and many were concentrated in the politically key state of New York. The committee observed:

> The sympathy of the strong Zionist element of American Jewry for the establishment of Israel and the political pressure which this element has been able to exert on the White House have imposed a considerable strain on relations with the United Kingdom, whose position in the Middle East would be fatally compromised if she were to lose entirely the friendship of the Moslem world.

It was hoped that this problem would diminish now that Israel existed, and since then British and American policy towards the Middle East had been virtually identical.

Other possible sources of political friction between Britain and the United States were the Irish problem and the anti-British feeling amongst the Roman Catholics, who largely because of the influence of the Irish Americans, viewed Britain as the largest Protestant power.

There were difficulties in the field of economic relations. Though the two countries were seen as having similar international objectives, progress towards these appeared to many Americans to have been impeded by 'restrictionist policies and methods which have robbed the British economy of its competitive strength and sapped the will to work of the British people'. American suspicion of 'colonialism' also inspired a fear that Britain, through the Sterling Area, was exploiting the resources of the Commonwealth and the Colonial Empire for its own benefit. Strang's committee warned that if friction were allowed to increase or even continue in the economic field, it would threaten the basis on which strategic and political collaboration with the United States rested.

The second revision of this version, at the end of 1949, argued that following the victorious wartime alliance, collaboration between Britain and the United States had been closer than ever before; the United States maintained closer relations with Britain than with any other country. In the military field the partnership had been maintained by the combined Chiefs of Staff organisation. For the United States, Britain remained the principal military partner and ally, and the United States wanted that partnership to endure. British interests were likely to be best served by the maintenance and consolidation of the existing relations between the two countries. Any British attempt at self-sufficiency, even with the support of some Commonwealth countries, would entail 'a sharp contraction of political influence and material prosperity'. If it failed, Britain would be forced to beg once more for the benefits of association with the United States, not as an independent partner, but instead as 'a client existing on permanent doles from the American tax payer'. Strang's committee advised that Britain had to continue to shoulder the political, economic and military burden of playing a leading role in world affairs, in close association with the United States, but not necessarily dominated by its policies.

The Anglo-American partnership would for some time be an unequal one, and might eventually need a more formal expression. The inherent inequality could be ameliorated by Britain and the United States working closely in conjunction with other friendly states, such as the members of the Commonwealth, particularly in Asia and the Far East. Indeed it was in this region that Britain thought the alliance would be least effective. Here American naivety and selfishness seemed particularly evident. Inexperience could account for the narrowly conceived American policy towards China. The treatment of Japan, however, was an instance of the 'somewhat unimaginative tendency of the Americans to graft their own way of life on to rather improbable stock', and the insistence on restoring the low-cost Japanese economy on multilateral principles took little account of British economic interests. But an American 'stake' in the area was of great importance for the consolidation of Western influence. Although the United States was likely to maintain a line of strategic defence in the Pacific, the degree to which it would extend this westwards was dependent on the extent to which Britain and the other members of the Commonwealth could contribute. American resources were not unlimited, and the United States appeared unwilling to contemplate any major effort in South Asia. Therefore, Western resistance to the spread of Soviet influence in the region depended largely on Britain.

Strang's committee concluded, despite all the reservations – and this conclusion was acknowledged to be the corner-stone of British foreign policy: 'The interests of the United Kingdom therefore demand that her present policy of close Anglo-American cooperation in world affairs should continue. Such cooperation will involve our sustained political, military and economic effort.'[1]

Bevin's Global Strategy

The British Cabinet at the end of 1949 collectively endorsed Bevin's pursuit of the Anglo-American relationship. By then, in Europe, Bevin had initiated the Western Union and the North Atlantic Treaty Organisation. But Bevin's vision extended far beyond Europe. As he told the Commonwealth Prime Ministers at Colombo in 1950, Britain was a world power. The Foreign Secretary had outlined his global strategy to Marshall in December 1947. The democratic nations had to get together to meet the Soviet threat. Britain, the European democracies, the United States and the Dominions should co-operate. Bevin had a low opinion of Europe. By May 1950 he had refined his ideas: Britain and Western Europe had to be able to rely on the full support of the English-speaking democracies of the Western hemisphere. Seemingly Bevin did not think that the West Europeans could provide much. In August 1950 he said that people in Britain were pinning their faith 'on a policy of defence on a Commonwealth-U.S.A. basis – an English-speaking basis'. Britons who had been bombed by Germans during the war could not rely on them for defence: if the Germans wanted to help that was all right. The French were defeatist.

'Reliance must be placed on America and the Commonwealth.'

In practice Bevin started to implement this vision at the Commonwealth Prime Ministers' Conference of 1948. There was general agreement amongst the 'old' Dominions about the nature of the Soviet threat. South Africa, under a new Afrikaner Nationalist government, was particularly co-operative. The Nationalists, though nurtured on a hatred of English-speaking South Africa, feared Communism and were prepared to work closely with Britain as an ally to meet the apparent threat in Africa, and the shield of Africa, the Middle East. The Labour government decided that for economic, strategic and other reasons a close relationship between Britain and South Africa was in Britain's direct interests. Though the South African leaders did not speak English as their first language, South Africa too became part of Bevin's scheme for the English-speaking alliance. The Nationalist Prime Minister, D. F. Malan, had a particularly high opinion of Bevin. After Bevin's death, Patrick Gordon Walker, the Secretary of State for Commonwealth Relations, outlined the specific terms of Britain's mutually interdependent relationship with South Africa cemented with the Cold War.[2]

British Responsibility for the Middle East

The Commonwealth was of particular significance for the defence of the Middle East. Washington had interests in the area, particularly in ensuring that Iran was strong enough to prevent it from collapsing from Soviet penetration, and Saudi Arabia where oil interests were at stake. The Petroleum Division of the State Department, in December 1949, pointed to the unrestricted increase of British-controlled production in Iran, Iraq, Kuwait and Qatar. This increase could stalemate Saudi progress and jeopardise the unique friendship that existed between Washington and Jedda. If the American-controlled oil company in that country, the Arabian-American Oil Company (ARAMCO), were economically healthy it could fight the advance of Communism by providing the local populations with a livelihood.

Anglo-American talks on the Middle East in 1949 showed an American interest in the area, but a reluctance to assume any new responsibilities. Washington did not want to compete with, or hinder, London in the Middle East. London, as Sir Michael Wright, the Foreign Office's Middle East expert, told the Americans in November 1949, felt that the United States should increasingly concern itself with the Middle East.[3] But Washington saw this area as being a British and Commonwealth responsibility.

During the First Arab-Israeli War the United States did honour its agreement with Britain of November 1947 over the Middle East. When at the end of 1948 the Israelis were pushing into Egypt, London warned Washington that under the terms of the 1936 Anglo-Egyptian Treaty Britain was obliged to assist Egypt in case of attack, and that unless the Israelis withdrew, Britain would fulfil its treaty obligations. There could arise out of this situation 'the gravest possible consequences, not only to Anglo-American strategic interests in the Near East, but also to American relations with Britain and Western Europe'. London hoped that Washington would place pressure on the Israelis so as to make this step unnecessary. Washington obliged. But the Israelis did occupy the heights above the border town of Rafa, and on 7 January 1949, under Ezer Weizmann, a former Royal Air Force officer, the Israelis shot down five Royal Air Force planes, which they claimed had strafed Israeli troops. London argued that the planes were over Egyptian territory and the attack was unprovoked. Britain sent troops to Aqaba and alerted its Mediterranean ships. Egypt demanded evacuation of the Rafa heights before starting negotiations. London reminded Washington of the Middle Eastern talks of November 1947 and of the support offered by the United States to maintain Britain's position in the Middle East. The Under-Secretary of State, Robert A. Lovett, warned that the position might arise where Britain would be arming one side in the dispute and the United States the other, with the Soviet Union as the permanent beneficiary. The Israelis withdrew their offending troops.[4]

Early in 1950 Anglo-American relations in the Middle East once again became the tool of the Zionist lobby in Congress. Just as in 1946, when the Zionist lobby in the form of the American (Christian) Palestine Committee had demanded that Congress make the American loan to Britain subject to allowing Jewish refugees into Palestine, and again in 1947, when it had tried to insist that Washington should make Britain stay in Greece and pay for British troops there by an enforced withdrawal of British troops from Palestine, so on 28 March 1950, Democratic representatives mainly from New York, Illinois and Pennsylvania, along with two Republican representatives from New York, told Acheson of a growing sentiment in the House that there would be an amendment to cut the recovery aid to Britain if Britain continued to arm the Arabs. Acheson explained that when the arms embargo had been lifted at the end of the First Arab–Israeli War in 1949, the American ambassador at the United Nations, Warren Austin, had stated that Washington did not want to see an arms race in the Middle East and would only permit the exportation to the Middle East of such arms as it thought necessary for internal security and legitimate self-defence.

The Secretary pointed the congressmen to the two problems involved: the Arab–Israeli relationship; and the defence of the Eastern Mediterranean, which was a matter of vital importance to both Britain and the United States and because of which Britain had a modest programme of providing the Near Eastern countries with arms to repel an attack. Early in April the Department of State drafted a plan to obtain British and French agreement to minimise the damage that shipments of arms to the Middle East could bring about. This idea was developed into the Tripartite Declaration of 25 May 1950, under which Britain, the United States, and France acknowledged that the Arab states and Israel needed to maintain a certain level of armed force for the purposes of legitimate self-defence of the area as a whole. The three powers agreed to consider all applications for arms or war materials by the countries of the Middle East in the light of these principles.[5]

On 7 June the British Chiefs of Staff submitted a paper entitled 'Defence Policy and Global Strategy', which though slightly revised in 1951, laid down the principles of British policy until 1952 when they were changed by the new Conservative administration. Full collaboration with the United States in policy and method was vital. After stabilisation of the European front, the next most important objective should be to secure an agreed Allied military strategy in the Middle East and East Asian theatres. It was also necessary to obtain the fullest possible political, economic and military collaboration in the British Commonwealth as a whole.

The British Chiefs of Staff pointed out that Britain, itself, could not afford all the forces required for the Middle East, in addition to those required to defend itself and Western Europe. Additional forces had, therefore, to be found from other parts of the Commonwealth and the United States. Anglo-American military talks, however, revealed that although Washington was prepared to cultivate a new interest in the Middle East and even to play a role there, this did not mean that it was willing to relieve Britain and the Commonwealth of what had already been agreed was a British and Commonwealth responsibility to defend for the West.

London and Washington diverged on policy towards Saudi Arabia and ARAMCO's attempts to limit British oil interests in Iran and in the Gulf, and there was open conflict over Iran. Dr Muhammad Mossadeq nationalised British oil interests there at the beginning of May 1950. Washington objected to any British use of force. Roger Makins, a Deputy Under-Secretary of State at the Foreign Office, advised on 11 August 1951 that the maintenance of the Anglo-American partnership was difficult because the power and resources of the United States were increasing at a rate much faster than those of Britain. But the Americans continued to regard Britain in a special way and this could be sustained provided that Britain kept itself independent of economic aid and that it did not always expect the Americans to do things the way Britain wanted them done. The hard fact was that Britain needed American support to keep up its end in the Middle East. Makins recorded that the dispute had dealt a heavy blow to British prestige, and that Britain had brought this on itself by allowing the oil company too much freedom of action when vital national interests were at stake.[6] Attlee advised the Cabinet that Britain could not afford to break with the United States, and that although the loss of the oil facilities at Abadan would be humiliating, Britain would have to leave. The evacuation of Abadan was completed on 4 October 1951.[7]

The British position in Egypt where there was resentment at a continued British presence in the Canal Zone, and in the Middle East generally, increasingly exercised the Americans. George McGhee, an Assistant Secretary of State, after a tour of the Middle East and talks in London, discussed these issues with the Joint Chiefs of Staff on 2 May 1951. He warned that the Americans had to consider carefully whether they could support British policy in the Middle East. Britain was opposed to the rising tide of nationalism throughout the area, was increasingly unpopular, and a liability to the United States. Indeed the liability was such that it could exceed the military value of co-operating with the British in the Middle East. McGhee pointed to the Egyptian rejection of the British proposals on withdrawal. The Egyptians were prepared to force the British out. There was a difficulty in that there was not a meeting of minds between the Joint Chiefs of Staff and the British Chiefs of Staff about division of responsibility in the area.

In response to the accelerated American aid to the Middle East, Britain expanded its British Middle East Office. Sir William Strang, at a Foreign Office meeting on 29 July 1951, emphasised the need for Britain to encourage economic development in the Middle East as a means of influencing the course of events there. Strang warned that it was important to understand what the Americans meant by partnership with the Middle East states: the Americans were prepared to take executive action under the cover of political arrangements in which local government would participate as equals. This did not seem to the Americans to be colonialism.[8]

Britain pursued the idea of the Middle East Command. If Egypt were invited to join, that could solve the problem of an Allied presence on Egyptian soil, which was considered essential by the Chiefs of Staff to hold the Middle East and Africa against the Soviets in the event of war. Australia, New Zealand, and South Africa were prepared to join the discussions. The Pentagon agreed to the plan, but on 9 October Egypt denounced the Anglo-Egyptian treaty although it knew that the Middle East Command proposals were about to be presented. Cairo formally rejected the proposals on 16 October 1951.

At the time of the fall of the second Labour government in October 1951 Britain could still be regarded as the paramount power in the Middle East. But its position was being steadily eroded. This was something of which British officials were acutely aware. The British Minister at Beirut, E. A. Chapman-Andrews, attributed this British decline to the British eagerness not to offend the United States, who 'in turn, so far as Israel is concerned, is completely in the hands of American Jewry'. Chapman-Andrews complained that in the case of Syria, Britain had been supine in the face of French activity. Britain's leadership of the Arab world, secure since 1918, had from 1945 been successfully challenged by the United States and France. Chapman-Andrews concluded: 'neither one nor the other is capable of taking our former place and both are largely for their own hand'. In the Foreign Office, G. W. Furlonge did not like this analysis: it was 'jejune', and did not merit a reasoned reply.

This reaction reflects what at the time was a common dichotomy in the perception of British policy in the Middle East at the joining of the Cold War. Many of the officials in the field, along with some of those in London, did not get on with their American counterparts, and were suspicious of what they perceived as an American intention to replace Britain in a traditional British sphere of influence. But British official policy had moved away from the idea enunciated in September 1945 that other powers were, if possible, to be excluded from the area, and that American penetration, even commercial, was to be resisted. As the Americans started to show an interest in the Middle East in the late

1940s, so the British, in response, welcomed what they increasingly saw as a necessary support for their position.

Britain was left with responsibility for the area in war. This was something Britain tried to resist. In the military conversations with the Americans the British representatives tried initially to shy away from this obligation, which, given Britain's financial state and military preparedness, it was impossible to meet. Australia, New Zealand and South Africa were reluctant to enter into definite commitments in the area as well. Britain was in a position where it had to do everything it could to encourage the American interest, and play down divergences of policy over Iran and Saudi Arabia. And Washington did support the British position in Egypt.

In the United States the new interest in the Middle East revealed divisions between the State and Defence departments, and rivalries between the armed services. These slowed down the evolving policy. There was a political perception that British influence in the Middle East was declining, and that many countries in the area were looking more and more towards the United States. But the United States remained reluctant to commit forces there in time of war. It was willing to increase its economic stake, and London was aware that if it did not do the same the Americans might lose interest and Britain would be left in an impossible situation. After all, the Middle East, in 1951, remained one of the three cardinal pillars of Britain's defence.[9]

Securing the American Commitment in South-East Asia

With an American commitment to come to the defence of Europe,[10] and an increasing interest in the Middle East, when the Cold War was joined, with the Berlin blockade, there was an obvious weakness in the line drawn to stop the advance of Communism: Asia. South-East Asia was an area of British, French and Dutch influence; the Americans had few interests in the region. During the years immediately following the end of the Second World War, London had persuaded Washington to see the dangers in parts of the globe through British spectacles. Or at least that was how it appeared to some officials in the Foreign Office. At the beginning of 1949 the immediate problem seemed to be how could the same vision be achieved over South-East Asia? That area, in the view of the British Chiefs of Staff, on 7 June 1950, was 'critically important' even if, as had been proved between 1939 and 1945, it was not 'vital to our survival in war'.

Malcolm MacDonald, the British Commissioner-General in South-East Asia, enunciated the domino theory long before President D. D. Eisenhower. At the beginning of 1949 the Foreign Office decided that something had to be done about the Communist threat to South-East Asia. London had been conscious of this at the end of the Second World War: in 1946 Lord Killearn was asked to make an assessment of Moscow's influence in the area. The Communist insurgency in Malaya and the deteriorating situation in Indo-China made the situation more pressing. Britain could not do anything on its own. The Foreign Office thought that only the United States would stop the Communist advance in Asia. After the experience of supporting Nationalist China – where it had given everything possible in terms of money and weapons and support short of fighting a land war in Asia – the United States refused, initially, to become involved in Asia. British policy for Asia was developed in the Foreign Office and by Strang's Permanent Under-Secretary's Committee. It was put across to the Americans by Bevin. In mounting this policy Britain had to take American sensibilities over the recognition of Communist China carefully into account: in the United States important foreign-policy issues could be decided by domestic considerations. In November 1949 George Kennan's Policy Planning Staff was shown an edited version of the Strang committee's policy for South-East Asia. At the end of December, Truman endorsed NSC 48/2, a document outlining an American policy set to stop Communist expansion in Asia, which reflected a remarkable congruence of views with Strang's policy paper. After that the United States started support-ing the French position in Indo-China. In effect, in an area of traditional British and French interest, the United States was once again 'pulling British and French chestnuts' out of the fire. In many ways Britain had been the instigator, if not the initiator, of this policy.[11]

The Recognition of Communist China

The Permanent Under-Secretary's Committee observed in 1949 that the Anglo-American alliance would be least effective in Asia and the Far East. In that area American naivety and selfishness were particularly evident. The spread of Mao Tse-Tung's Communists across the Chinese mainland emphasised Britain's predicament, especially as Britain, initially, relying on the analysis of the Soviet spy Guy Burgess, regarded the Chinese as orthodox Communists. By 1949 the British Joint Intelligence Committee, though it did not have proof, felt that the Soviet Union had delegated to the Chinese Communist Party at least some responsibility for building what Mao Tse-Tung called 'a bulwark of world Communism in Asia'. The difficulty for the Soviets was to ensure that they retained the ultimate control of the movement in Asia. The Chinese, on the other hand, had to overcome the suspicions of many Asian races about Chinese motives. Six months later the Joint Intelligence Committee was more certain: 'Russia had made clear to Communists throughout the world that she has confidence in the loyalty of the CCP. and is prepared to back it to the hilt.'[12]

Although the United States spent over $3.5 billion to sustain the Chinese nationalists, it was Britain that had the major Western economic interest in China. This economic interest, together with the position of Hong Kong and the attitude of some Commonwealth countries, led to the British recognition of Communist China. Officials anticipated that friction could develop between the Soviets and the Chinese, and that Britain should keep 'a foot in the door'. Some State Department experts agreed with this diagnosis, but, in the end, American policy was determined by domestic political factors. For Britain, the importance of the Anglo-American special relationship was such that policy towards the Chinese Communists had to take into account American sensibility. The Cold War had been joined. The United States was the only country that could hold the communist advance in Asia. The Anglo-American alliance in Europe could not be endangered by serious disagreement in the Far East.

Bevin, in Washington, explained to Dean Acheson, the Secretary of State, in August 1949 that Britain was in no hurry to recognise Communist China, but it had commercial and trading interests in China that the United States did not share. Bevin felt that if the West were too obdurate China could be driven to the Soviet Union; alternatively, with care, the Soviet Union's grip could be weakened. Acheson replied that the Americans doubted 'if recognition is a strong card in keeping China out of Russian hands and they will be there anyway'. There was agreement on the need for continued close consultation. Guy Burgess minuted that the emerging American policy of severing trade links and non-recognition had been irresponsibly adopted by the State Department 'for reasons of internal self defence and muddled thinking'.[13]

Despite the agreement on close consultation, early in October, Britain in effect gave de facto recognition to the Chinese Communists. Truman told Acheson that he thought that the British had not 'played very squarely' with the Americans over this. M. Esler Dening of the Foreign Office had to plead with Arthur R. Ringwalt, the First Secretary of the American embassy in London, that no 'skulduggery' had been intended, but that his overworked and undermanned staff had committed two stupid errors: the Far Eastern department had 'blundered outrageously' in not checking with its legal adviser whether the note sent to the Chinese Communists about establishing 'informal relations' amounted to *de facto* recognition; and the text of this note to be conveyed to the Americans had been sent by airmail instead of being telegraphed. American anger over apparent 'deliberate' failures on the part of the Foreign Office was misplaced: this was a genuine mistake. The French pointed out to the British that a note they had sent to the Chinese Communists amounted to *de facto* recognition. W. E. Beckett of the legal branch of the Foreign Office confirmed the French view: Britain had acknowledged that there was a Central People's Government, and that it had territory under its control. This was the same as saying that it was recognised as the *de facto* government of that territory.[14]

On 6 January 1950 Britain recognised the Central People's Government as the *de jure* government of China, and said that it was willing to enter into diplomatic relations. Immediately after the recognition, the American administration went out of its way to be helpful. Indeed Sir Oliver Franks, the British ambassador in Washington, thought that, judging from the press, American recognition would follow in around three months. Then the Communists seized American property in the Peking barracks incident. The reaction in the United States meant that domestic political considerations determined an important foreign-policy decision. It seemed unlikely that the United States would return representatives to China until American public opinion had settled down, and that would not happen quickly.

With the outbreak of the Korean War the Chinese Communists reacted violently over the American declaration on Formosa that Communist occupation of the island would be a direct threat to the security of the Pacific and the United States forces. Acheson thought it unlikely that British and American policy over the seating of China at the United Nations could be harmonised. At a meeting of British and American representatives in Washington between 20 and 24 July a difference of emphasis emerged in policy towards Communist China.

Britain wanted to avoid any further involvement of Western forces on the Asiatic mainland. Bevin was particularly anxious that a 'possible gradual drift of the Communist regime away from Moscow might not be interrupted', and thought Chinese Communist intervention in Korea unlikely as Peking would not act at Soviet direction without material advantage. The Americans argued that Peking was under strong Kremlin influence, and the Kremlin might wish Peking to fight the West. Chinese Communist intervention in Korea was not unlikely. Britain underestimated the closeness of the Moscow–Peking axis.[15]

The Korean War: The Americans Should Not Feel Lonely in their Great New Task

The test of American commitment to a global strategy designed to stop the Communist advance came on 27 June when troops from North Korea invaded South Korea. Washington, working through the United Nations, stood firm and troops were despatched. From Washington the British ambassador, Sir Oliver Franks, pointed to the 'steady and unquestioning assumption' that Britain was 'the only dependable ally and partner'. In Korea the American government and people had 'instinctively followed their high destiny in the world'. That was 'a very great thing for all of us'. But Americans felt lonely: Britain should offer to send land forces to reassure them. The Chiefs of Staff did not want to do this, and the Defence Committee was worried lest the Korean conflict diverted attention from other danger-spots in Asia, and blinded Britain to the risks to which it was exposed in Europe. But by the end of July the need for Anglo-American solidarity outweighed the military dis-advantages, and the Cabinet agreed to the formulation of a brigade group to operate in Korea under American command. Attlee explained to the Cabinet on 1 August that Britain had to accept positive sacrifices to align its policy with that of the United States: British oil and strategic exports were being denied to Communist China, and it might be unrealistic to alienate the Americans over the issue of the seating of Peking at the United Nations.

The measures Britain took during the first six weeks of the Korean crisis, in the view of Franks, prevented a crisis in the Anglo-American relationship. The ambassador pointed to the dichotomy between the American view of the Britain it had helped during the previous five years and the Britain it had known in the world wars. With the aggression in Korea, American opinion swung back from its postwar views about the economic weakness of Britain and the efforts that Britain was making to recover, to the older view of a Britain from which more should be expected and demanded. British troops in Korea prevented this split mind from fomenting trouble. On the administrative level, however, the Americans were showing that they thought that 'the effectiveness of the Anglo-American partnership' was reviving.[16]

Britain Initiates the Objective of a Unified Korea

For London, from the beginning of September 1950, the original intention of the Korean operation began to change from merely repelling the 'aggressor' north of the 38th parallel, to the original United Nations objective of establishing a unified and democratic Korea. On 6 September, Air Vice-Marshal C. A. Bouchier reported the 'feeling' that with the defeat of the North Korean army the United Nations' forces would cross the 38th parallel; this was necessary to stop Communist China and Soviet troops advancing from Manchuria unopposed to the 38th parallel and restoring the stalemate. With all Korea occupied, Bouchier anticipated a general election, and a government representative of Korea as a whole. Following MacArthur's victories, Attlee, on 21 September, informed Bevin, then in New York, that he favoured a declaration from the United Nations that it would take responsibility for the rehabilitation of the whole country. The Prime Minister felt the Chinese would not be sorry if Soviet influence were eliminated from Korea. The Chiefs of Staff, however, warned against any lasting British military responsibility in Korea, and suggested that forces sent north of the 38th parallel should be kept to a minimum. Bevin agreed with Attlee about the need to forestall the Soviets, and took the initiative in drafting a resolution for the General Assembly authorising the crossing of the 38th parallel with a view to establishing a unified, independent and democratic government of all Korea. The Americans revealed in conversation with the British that they appreciated that a certain amount of risk was unavoidable in crossing the 38th parallel, but the dangers had to be accepted, and there was no evidence of any move by Chinese or Soviet forces. Attlee told the Cabinet on 26 September about these developments and secured approval for the policy of a united Korea, though it was emphasised that British commitments in Malaya and elsewhere should prevent it from playing a substantial part in a prolonged pacification. As it was evident that the Americans had given little thought to its specific terms, the drafting was left to the British who incorporated amendments suggested by the Americans, and then sent the document to nine allies.

When it seemed evident that the United States did not have a policy, Britain was quick to find one for it. The change of intention of the Korean operation from being merely to repel the aggressor north of the 38th parallel, to one of bringing about a unified Korea, was Britain's initiative. Britain organised the United Nations resolution endorsing the crossing of the 38th parallel. When the Communist Chinese entered and there were reverses, the British Cabinet was told that whatever might be said in the House of Commons, Britain was just as responsible as the United States.[17]

Bevin Ensures that the United States becomes Part of Europe's Defence

The Americans did not go over to an 'Asia first' policy. During the early stages of the Korean crisis Bevin secured a change in the nature of the American commitment to Europe: the United States became more than just committed to go to Europe's defence, it became part of Europe's defence. In December 1950 Attlee and Truman agreed on what was, in effect, a 'Europe first' policy. The British Prime Minister also understood that Truman had said that, except in the case of an attack on the United States, Truman regarded the atomic bomb as the possession of Britain, Canada and the United States and would consult the Allies before using it. The American public had a slightly different version, but not much was made of that at the time. Bevin was worried that the deterrent threat of the bomb, so successfully used during the Berlin crisis, would be lost.

It was Bevin, ill and dying, with the able assistance of Strang and other Foreign Office officials, who managed to quell the anti-American revolt led by John Strachey, the Secretary of State for War, and seemingly even supported by Lord Mountbatten early in January 1951. It was decided that Britain, the countries of the Western Union and the Commonwealth – even if such an alliance were possible – could not stand up to the Communist threat on their own. The full participation of the United States was 'essential to sustain the free world which Soviet Russia is trying to undermine'. What Britain had to do was to 'exert sufficient control over the policy of the well-intentioned but inexperienced colossus on whose co-operation our safety depends'. London felt that it did that.[18]

The American Sphere: Asia and the Pacific

Britain, in 1951, also felt that it was helped by the responsibilities undertaken by Australia and New Zealand working with the United States in the Pacific. The tripartite security pact, ANZUS, was regarded by Attlee and most of his colleagues as being in line with their idea of the evolution of the modern Commonwealth, in which member states would take the lead in areas of their particular interest.[19] The Labour government was also satisfied with the Japanese peace treaty: Herbert Morrison, the Foreign Secretary, found John Foster Dulles most co-operative and felt that Dulles had, as Truman's ambassador, allowed Britain to contribute a great deal to the treaty.[20] In planning for defence policy and global strategy with the Americans it was agreed that Asia and the Pacific were an American sphere.

Britain Not Part of Europe

Whatever ideas Bevin might have had about closer West European co-operation from 1945 onwards,[21] he made it clear to the Americans and the Commonwealth that he did not want Britain as part of Europe. In 1950 he angrily said that Britain was not just another Luxembourg, it had a very special position. When the issue of American aid for Europe was first raised, Bevin even hoped that this would be Anglo-American administered. But such a scheme was unacceptable to the Americans.

Bevin resented bitterly unofficial American pressure for Britain to become part of Europe, and told Marshall so, despite the assurances that this was not the policy of the American administration. When it seemed that this might be the policy of the American administration in 1950, Bevin fought it resolutely. The British people were pinning their faith on a defence alliance between the 'old' Dominions, Britain and the United

States. The West European countries were not reliable. In any case Bevin disliked the French approach to European unity: formal written constitutions were simply not British. The Foreign Secretary told this to the Commonwealth Prime Ministers. At the Colombo Conference in 1950 Bevin said that Britain would 'resist ill-considered plans for the integration of the UK economy with that of other European countries'. Britain refused to accept the French approach in the Schuman Plan of 1950, a plan for a supranational 'High Authority' to control the coal and steel industries, open to France, Germany and any other country which wished to join. A gulf opened up between France and Britain. It is not clear that the Europeans wanted Britain in anyway.[22] In March 1950, however, the Defence Committee finally agreed that, in the event of war, two British divisions would be sent to Europe. They would take three months to arrive, and would only go if the line were holding. The military inclined to the view that the next time, the Europeans should do their own fighting. The West Germans would have to be rearmed. On 4 September 1951 the Cabinet agreed, in principle, to the idea of a 'European army'.[23]

The Anglo-American Special Relationship

The foundation stone of British policy during this period was, as Strang's committee suggested, the Anglo-American special relationship. This was sustained and revived by men and women on both sides of the Atlantic who spoke the same language, and, in most cases, enjoyed a common heritage. Some of the Americans concerned had been educated at Oxford under a scheme established by the great imperialist Cecil John Rhodes for fostering co-operation in the English-speaking world. Some of the Britons had American family connections and felt at home in the United States anyway. Bevin, at the end of 1946, explained to Molotov that the two leading 'Anglo-Saxon' – perhaps a loose and inaccurate term – nations were just able to get on with one another in a natural sort of way. At the top, personal relations were not especially good. Bevin in particular, but Attlee as well, never forgave Truman for pursuing a policy in Palestine in the interests of his own re-election at a time when British soldiers were being murdered in the mandate with weapons bought with American subscriptions that were tax free. Later Bevin could not understand Truman's insensitivity over the question of the one million Arab refugees. But it was through the skilful diplomacy of officials, both British and American, that the Palestine issue was kept outside the deepening current of the Anglo-American special relationship. Bevin and Marshall were frank with each other, and there seems to have been a friendship based on trust and liking. The two men exchanged books: Marshall enjoyed George Orwell's *Animal Farm*. Those two men did a great deal to foster the Anglo-American special relationship at a time when Americans were discovering hyphenate identities that challenged a concept of 'Anglo-Saxondom'.[24] Bevin, the trade union official who had been born in poverty and left school at the age of eleven, also enjoyed the warm companionship of Marshall's successor, Dean Acheson. Although from radically different social backgrounds – Acheson's father had been born in England, become Bishop of Connecticut and sent his son to the equivalent of an English public school, Groton, and then to Yale and Harvard – the two men liked and respected each other.[25]

It was men like these who oversaw with great skill, and perhaps a little regret, the transformation from the *Pax Britannica* to the *Pax Americana*.

6

ONE AMONG A NUMBER OF ALLIES

The years of Winston Churchill's peacetime premiership, and that of his heir-apparent, Anthony Eden, were a period of adjustment in Britain's foreign responsibilities. A public tired of rationing, conscious of the booming standards of living of the vanquished West Germany and Japan, was more interested in being able to buy bananas than in Britain's status as a Great Power. In the West End John Osborne's play *Look Back in Anger* was seen to be symptomatic of what became known as the mood of the 'angry young man', Jimmy Porter. Critics perhaps failed to notice the sympathetic and heroic portrait of the colonel leaving India with the arrival of Independence. Osborne went on to write *West of Suez* (1971), in which he argued that the only people left with values in Britain were those who had returned with the narrowing of the reigns of Empire. Domestic circumstances, economic straits partly brought about by Mossadeq's nationalisation of Iranian oil, meant that the Conservative governments initiated foreign and defence policies that moved away from the global commitments of their Labour predecessors.

Central to the postwar Labour foreign and defence policies had been the Anglo-American special relationship as the corner-stone. Although those at the top had not got on, bureaucracies on both sides of the Atlantic had successfully and sympathetically managed the transition from the *Pax Britannica* to the *Pax Americana*. With the return of Churchill as Prime Minister and the election of his old wartime friend Dwight D. Eisenhower to the presidency, it might have been expected that the Anglo-American relationship would blossom. There was a Republican administration in Washington, one which did not regard itself as having been returned by the Zionist vote, and one which seemed less likely than its predecessor to dictate, under pressure from minority pressure groups, a policy to an ally, inimicable both to itself and to the ally. But under Eisenhower, Britain was no longer the special relation. It was merely one among a number of allies. The Republican administration felt that the United States could not function in the United Nations in the face of the emerging neutralist and anti-colonial bloc with Britain at its side. At times Britain used this to its advantage. In the talks at Geneva in 1954 Eden complained that the Americans seemed to have forgotten that Britain had allies, with the Commonwealth members at the head. But at Geneva Eden achieved his great diplomatic victory: his diplomacy enabled Britain and France to retreat from Indo-China (Vietnam) and left the Americans with the responsibility.

Much has been written about the Anglo-American relationship suffering because Eden and the Secretary of State, John Foster Dulles, disliked one another. Dulles has been described as controlling American foreign policy, with the latitude of his President who valued his experience. But over the last few decades a different picture has emerged: Eisenhower was firmly in charge.[1] The school which considered Dulles as bedevilling the Anglo-American relationship has increasingly been forced to look at Eisenhower and his personal obsession with being re-elected President, as the real culprit. Papers in the Public Record Office, London, and the Eisenhower Library, Abilene, confirm the pioneering work of Leonard Mosley in his depiction of Dulles's close co-operation with Eden during the Suez crisis. Indeed, at a time when Eisenhower had devalued the special relationship, Dulles virtually acted as the British spokesman in the negotiations with the Egyptians about the withdrawal from the Suez Canal base.[2]

Conservative Defence Policy

In the second half of 1950, particularly with the deteriorating situation in Malaya and Indo-China, British defence planners had placed increasing emphasis on South-East Asia. More forces were needed to stop the Communist threat. More money had to be spent on defence. On 25 January 1951 the Cabinet accepted a huge increase in Britain's defence budget: £4700 million was to be spent over the years 1951–4.[3] In May 1951 the Iranian Prime Minister, Muhammad Mossadeq, nationalised the Anglo-Iranian Oil Company, forcing Britain to buy oil for American dollars. The balance of payments crisis helped to precipitate a general election in October 1951, and a Conservative administration was returned with Winston Churchill as Prime Minister. The new Chancellor of the Exchequer, R. A. Butler, when examining the treasury accounts, decided not only that the British economy could not sustain the rearmament programme, but that the Sterling crisis was also likely to challenge the nature of Britain's foreign and defence commitments, and, in effect, the position of Britain as a Great Power.[4] Churchill gave his Minister of Defence, Field-Marshal Alexander, the task of economising on Britain's military commitments.

The Chiefs of Staff, in a paper dated 17 June 1952, revised Britain's global strategy. The Allies were, in 1952, in a position to launch a devastating attack on the Soviet Union at the very outset of war. In considering what preparations to make for a war, the Chiefs of Staff argued that it was necessary to take into account three major developments: the increased accuracy and power of atom bombing; the advent of the small bomb for tactical use; and the economic situation. The Chiefs of Staff decided that it was economically impossible to prepare and build up the necessary reserves for a prolonged war. Efforts had to be concentrated on producing forces and equipment for an intense, all-out conflict of short duration. In the view of the Chiefs of Staff in the Cold War period, the main effort had to be directed to the prevention of world war. In the Cold War, Europe had to be given top priority, with the Far East next, and after that the Middle East. In a hot war Europe should remain a top priority, but the Middle East should be given priority above the Far East owing to the importance of communications through the Middle East, its oil, and the 'necessity to prevent Communism from spreading throughout Africa'.

The 1952 Defence Policy and Global Strategy Paper outlined what the Chiefs of Staff regarded as 'reasonable' preparations for hot war. Their recommendations were undermined by the Treasury under R. A. Butler, who was concerned that the rearmament programme would reduce living standards in Britain. He was assisted by Duncan Sandys, the Minister of Supply, who attacked the navy's carrier and cruiser programme and argued for the strengthening of the strategic bomber and air defence fighter forces. But fears that the Royal Air Force's V bombers would be vulnerable to Soviet surface-to-air missiles, and NATO requirements for three carrier groups in the north-east Atlantic, helped to save the navy. Sir Rhoderick McGrigor, the First Sea Lord, looked to the destroyers and frigates equipped with missiles, and carriers with vertical take-off strike aircraft. The successful test of the American hydrogen bomb in November 1952 also contributed significantly to a new defence review which further undermined the 1952 Defence Policy and Global Strategy Paper. Churchill insisted that Britain needed a hydrogen bomb to remain a Great Power. Butler hoped that such a thermo-nuclear weapon would lessen expenditure on conventional forces. The Chiefs of Staff concluded that with thermo-nuclear weapons, provided the United States maintained its lead, another war was unlikely, but the Cold War would go on. The main British deterrent should be nuclear forces. This move towards a global strategy based upon the nuclear deterrent alongside conventional forces stationed in Europe, with a reduction of British forces in the Middle East, was outlined in the February 1955 Statement on Defence.[5]

Churchill's Foreign Policy

The foreign policy of Churchill's peacetime administration coincided with the new defence policy. The development of the hydrogen bomb and the revised British defence policy and global strategy meant that the Middle East was no longer cardinal for Britain's security. With the negotiation of the withdrawal from the Suez base in 1954, it was hoped that manpower from there could be diverted to colonial wars in Kenya, Malaya and Cyprus. Churchill, personally, wanted to get the Americans involved in the Middle East – in what had been agreed between Washington and London was an area of British responsibility. British integration into Western Europe seemed even less attractive than it had been to the previous Labour administration. But the Cold War meant that NATO, in British eyes, had to be strengthened, and there was the question of the rearmament of West Germany. It was the collapse of the idea of a European army and the proposed European Defence Community, on which the American Republican administration had based its European policy, that forced Anthony Eden, as Foreign Secretary, to announce in September 1954 that British troops would be committed to Europe: Britain would maintain for an indefinite period four divisions in Europe and the tactical air force. Eden did this to allay American threats of a withdrawal from Europe, and to calm French fears about German rearmament.[6]

In the Far East and South-East Asia British policy increasingly diverged from that of Washington. That was particularly evident in the two countries' approach to Communist China, and to the Geneva Conference of 1954 over Indo-China.[7] There was, however, a temporary resolution of the Anglo-American differences with the signing of the Manila Treaty on 8 September 1954: this Treaty established the South-East Asian Treaty Organisation (SEATO).

Churchill hoped to become the Prime Minister of peace as well as of war, and initiated peace overtures to Moscow: he personally was worried that the Americans might force a 'showdown' with the Soviet Union while Washington still enjoyed nuclear superiority.

Eisenhower's Revision of the Special Relationship

Throughout most of Churchill's premiership the corner-stone of British postwar foreign policy, the Anglo-American special relationship, did not exist. Eisenhower, when he assumed the presidency, demoted Britain from being the special ally to just being one among a number of allies. In January 1953, Eisenhower hinted at this revision of the special relationship when he told Churchill on the Prime Minister's visit to the United States that while Britain and the United States should work together in the Middle East, there should be 'no collusion'.[8] Churchill bitterly resented Eisenhower's demotion of Britain to the status of just another ally. The Prime Minister complained to Eden in April 1953 that he did not like Britain being treated by the United States as if it were one of an equal crowd.[9]

As Prime Minister, Churchill dominated foreign policy. Eden was often ill, and Churchill took official control. And when Eden was not ill, the two men fought. Churchill did not always win, as over Egypt. But it was his personality and possibly outdated imperial views which dominated the making of British foreign policy during most of his last premiership. Neville Chamberlain in the late 1930s, and Bevin in the late 1940s, had based British foreign policy on the English-speaking alliance, an association with the old 'white' Dominions and the United States.[10] Churchill, as he told the Cabinet in November 1951, saw the first objective of British policy as the unity and consolidation of the British Commonwealth and what was left of the former British Empire. The second objective was the 'fraternal association' of the English-speaking world. The third was a united Europe, to which Britain was 'a separate, closely and specially-related ally and friend'.[11]

Churchill and 'Getting' the Americans into the Middle East

Immediately on becoming Prime Minister, Churchill commented that it was 'of the utmost importance to get America in' to the Middle East.[12] Furthermore, Churchill did 'not understand how and when the anticipated Russian threat against the Middle East would eventuate'.[13] The Prime Minister did not regard the Middle East as a British prerogative. Indeed he consistently wanted to lessen Britain's role there, and preferably get the Americans involved. When, in January 1954, the Cabinet considered a suggestion of the American government that Washington's offer of military aid to Pakistan should be linked to the initiation of military collaboration between Pakistan and Turkey which could eventually be developed into a system of collective defence in the Middle East, Churchill favoured the building of a military association between Turkey and Pakistan as being to Britain's advantage.[14]

For Churchill, the United States was also central to any handling of the situation in Iran, where Dr Muhammad Mossadeq, the Prime Minister, had challenged British paramountcy in the Middle East by nationalising the Iranian oil industry, including the Anglo-Iranian Oil Company, on 2 May 1951. Just before handing over to Churchill, Attlee had told his colleagues that Britain could not afford to break with the United States on an issue like this. In the end the United States was convinced that Mossadeq was not the only alternative to Communism in Iran. British external intelligence, MI6, and the Central Intelligence Agency, arranged the overthrow of Mossadeq and the return of the Shah. The American ambassador, Loy Henderson, worked with his British counterpart, Sir Roger Stevens, to secure a satisfactory arrangement over oil. But it meant that the share of British capital invested in the oil industry of the Middle East dropped from 49 to 14 per cent, and the British share of oil production from 53 to 24 per cent. The American share increased from 44 to 58 per cent, and the American companies controlled 42 per cent of the capital. The image of British power faded in Arab eyes. Churchill, on 25 August 1953, warned the Cabinet about his fears of an American take-over in the area and supported the arguments of Lord Salisbury, the Lord President, that Britain needed to give financial aid to the new Iranian government along with the United States to find a solution to the oil dispute, or 'sacrifice all prospect of re-establishing British influence in Persia'. Churchill hoped that support of the new Iranian government would be undertaken on an Anglo-American basis.[15]

Saudi Arabia, furthermore, made moves towards the British-protected sheikhdoms in the Gulf, and in August 1952, a Saudi expedition seized the Buraimi oasis. Relations between Britain and Saudi Arabia were strained. The attempted annexation had been arranged by Kim Roosevelt of the Central Intelligence Agency: the Saudis had tempted the Americans with the offer of oil concessions. But the British-led Omani scouts drove the Saudis out. Roosevelt then attempted to bribe people in Abu Dhabi to concede the oasis to King Saud to open the way to the American firm ARAMCO, and to close it to the British-controlled Iraq Petroleum Company. But Britain was informed, and took the dispute to an international court where the Central Intelligence Agency tried to bribe the arbitrators.[16]

Churchill's Middle East policy was also driven by his overriding wish to help Israel, which he described as 'the great experiment', 'one of the most hopeful and encouraging adventures of the 20th Century'. The Chiefs of Staff also wanted Israeli co-operation in the Middle East. A British military mission went to Tel Aviv in October 1952, and had exploratory talks with the Israelis. Churchill complained that 'the late Mr Bevin, who had a strain of anti-Semitism in his thought, put the Foreign Office in on the wrong side when Israel was attacked by all the Arab States'. Churchill insisted that Israel was the most powerful fighting force in the Middle East and 'could come in very handy in dealing with Egypt if [Muhammad] Neguib [Egyptian Prime Minister] attacks us'.[17] But, despite Prime Ministerial interference, the Cabinet insisted that Jordan be informed, in July 1954, that if Israel attacked, Britain would honour its obligations under the Anglo-Jordanian treaty.[18]

It was, however, the Anglo-Egyptian agreement of December 1954 which marked both Britain's lessening of interest in the Middle East and a significant decline in British power in the area. Under the agreement British troops were to be withdrawn within twenty months, and the Suez base would be maintained by 1,200 civilian technicians. The British Empire lost an area the size of Wales: it was seen as the biggest retreat from Empire since the division of the Indian subcontinent. British forces moved to Cyprus and had to contend with mounting terrorism on the Mediterranean island. Opposed by Eden, the Foreign Office and the military, Churchill was reluctant to give up Egypt. Churchill wanted American involvement. The Cabinet debated the whole approach on 22 June 1954. It was emphasised that Britain's strategic needs had been radically changed by the development of thermo-nuclear weapons. It was no longer expedient to maintain so large a concentration of stores, equipment and men within the narrow confines of the Canal Zone. In the end, Churchill accepted the military argument for redeploying the British forces in the Middle East. Churchill wanted an agreement between Britain and the United States on one side, and Egypt on the other. But he acknowledged that the Americans would not participate unless invited to do so by the Egyptians. On 7 July 1954, Churchill confessed that he was satisfied that the withdrawal of British troops from Egypt could be justified fully on military grounds. Britain's requirements in the Canal Zone had been radically altered by Turkey's admission to NATO and the extension of a defensive Middle East front as far east as Pakistan. Thermo-nuclear weapons had increased the vulnerability of a concentrated base area and it would not be right to continue to keep in Egypt 80,000 troops who would be better placed elsewhere.[19]

It was Churchill's peacetime administration which oversaw the dramatic change in British foreign and defence policy, the move away from considering the Middle East as one of the three cardinal pillars of British strategy, towards the conclusion that it was an area of more limited significance in the age of thermo-nuclear weapons and at a time when Britain's financial strictures meant a limitation of its world role. Churchill felt in any case that the Americans should become involved in an area for which Britain had undertaken responsibility in the agreement made between their two countries at the end of 1947. In this respect Churchill's Middle East policy was radically different from that of Attlee's first Labour government, which had decided that the Middle East was a British preserve, and one from which the Americans should be excluded. John Foster Dulles, the American Secretary of State, on his visit to the Middle East in 1953, concluded that Britain could no longer meet its responsibility for the defence of the Middle East on behalf of the West. In July 1953 the National Security council advocated 'greater independence and greater responsibility in the area by the United States vis-à-vis Britain'.[20] Churchill's last government welcomed the beginnings of the transfer of power in the Middle East from Britain to the United States.

Divergences in South-East Asia and the Far East

Between 1951 and 1955 British policy in South-East Asia and the Far East diverged increasingly from that of its American ally. Following its demotion to being just one among a number of allies, a demotion reconfirmed at the Bermuda Conference of December 1953, London resented Eisenhower's letter to Churchill of 4 April 1954 urging a combined military operation as two special allies to assist the French in Indo-China. At the Geneva Conference of 1954 Eden secured a settlement which enabled France's withdrawal, and the presence of three buffer states which could contain Communist China. The Foreign Secretary often acted independently of Washington and it marked a major period of tension in Anglo-American relations. Throughout, Britain was concerned over what it considered an American policy which lacked understanding of the area and could have led to war, particularly with Communist China.[21]

Britain also diverged increasingly from the United States in its policy towards Communist China. In 1949 the British, under the inspiration of Guy Burgess, the Soviet spy, had viewed the Chinese as orthodox Marxist-Leninists. But Britain, as it had the major economic stake in China, and wanted to keep a foot in the door as the Communists took over the mainland, changed its emphasis, and through a mistake, initially gave *de facto* recognition to Communist China in October 1949, and followed this by *de jure* recognition on 6 January 1950. It was anticipated that Washington would follow. In the late 1940s Washington did not have a monolithic view of Communism. But attacks on American property in Peking in January 1950 meant that domestic pressure determined American policy towards Communist China. During the Korean War there were significant divisions between Washington and London: Washington departed from its wedge strategy – the idea that it was possible to separate Peking from Moscow – and from August 1950 American officials argued that in general foreign policy Peking would follow Moscow; London argued that the Chinese were xenophobic and would not follow Moscow's line. The British did not attach the same importance to Taiwan as did the Americans. The British were apt to dismiss the Chinese Nationalist leader, Chiang Kai-Shek, as a '*palooka*', and failed to understand his ability to manipulate American domestic politics to involve the American government in his struggle with the Communists. London objected to Washington's defence of the off-shore islands of Quemoy and Matsu during the 1954–5 crisis. Britain pursued a policy of Mao-Tse-Titoism, of trying to separate Peking from Moscow; in the 1950s Washington saw Communism as monolithic.[22]

The European Question

Keeping Washington committed to the defence of Europe was an overriding concern of the Churchill administration. Central to this was the rearming of West Germany and the proposed European Defence Community. It was the United States which, in December 1950, proposed the creation of a West German army. NATO divided on this: Britain was ready to accept the principle; France wanted to know what would happen.

On 24 October 1950 the French Prime Minister, René Pleven, proposed the rearmament of West German troops as part of a supranational European army, under a single European defence minister. Bevin preferred an Atlantic force, which would avoid the creation of a continental bloc under French leadership, and he condemned any idea of a 'third force'. Herbert Morrison, however, following the advice of the Permanent Under-Secretary's Committee, together with Dean Acheson, the American Secretary of State, and Robert Schuman, the French Foreign Minister, made a statement in September 1951 aiming at the inclusion of a democratic Germany in a continental European community which would form part of a constantly developing Atlantic community. But Churchill's Conservative administration showed no enthusiasm for joining supranational organisations in Europe. It felt 'goodwill' and wanted to be associated with the work of the supranational bodies, but not to be members of them. Britain's defence considerations, its connections with the Commonwealth and its leadership of the Sterling area, inhibited it from 'subordinating' itself to any supranational European authority.

It was the French who defeated the idea of a European Defence Community. Some French politicians opposed West German rearmament. Strong armed forces seemed unnecessary in the apparent era of détente which followed the death of Stalin in March 1953 and the end of the Korean War in July 1953. The commitment of French troops to Indo-China aroused fears that German forces would dominate the European Defence Community. Eden tried to overcome this fear by negotiating a treaty of British association with the European Defence Community which meant the inclusion of a British army division as well as institutional links. But in August 1954 the French Assembly rejected the European Defence Community. Britain, to allay American threats of a withdrawal from Europe, and to calm French fears about German rearmament, in September 1954 committed British troops to Europe. At the conference in London in September 1954 Eden also proposed the extension of the Brussels Pact of 1948, formed by Britain, France and the Benelux countries, to West Germany and Italy. The expanded pact became the West European Union in 1955. It was agreed that German rearmament should be carried out under NATO auspices, and that West Germany should join NATO as a sovereign state.[23]

Churchill himself, following the death of Stalin, wanted a summit meeting with the new Soviet leaders. He even suggested to Eisenhower that he, Churchill, should make the initial contacts with the new Soviet leaders. Eisenhower did not encourage this. Initiatives were further delayed when Churchill had a stroke, and with the need to delay any announcement until after the French vote on the European Defence Community. In June 1954 Churchill did win Eisenhower's approval for an Anglo-Soviet meeting. Churchill sent his own message to the Soviet leader, Vyacheslav Molotov. Some members of the Cabinet threatened to resign. London was saved by a Soviet proposal that there be a foreign ministers' conference to discuss European security and the future of Germany. Discussions over German rearmament delayed matters until May 1955 by which time Churchill was no longer Prime Minister.[24]

It was Eisenhower who assisted in arranging a Great Power summit meeting at Geneva in July 1955 to help Prime Minister Eden's general election prospects.[25] The month before, the issue of a full-scale common market had been raised by the six members of the European Coal and Steel Community at a meeting at Messina in Sicily. A committee under Paul Henri Spaak of Belgium was set up to study the matter. The British government, just returned to office in the general election, as an associate member, sent a representative. But the six wanted supranationalism. Britain, unsuccessfully, tried an alternative proposal of bolstering the Organisation of European Economic Co-operation, originally established to supervise Marshall Aid. At Venice in May 1956, however, the ministers from the European Coal and Steel Community decided to draw up two treaties: one for an atomic energy authority (EURATOM); the other for an economic community, the European Economic Community. The French, alienated by the British stand during the Suez crisis of 1956, hastened the talks, and the EURATOM and European Economic Community treaties were signed in Rome on 25 March 1957. By then Britain had opted for a revived Anglo-American special relationship of the sort that had existed before Eisenhower became President and demoted Britain to being just one among a number of allies. Proposals which Selwyn Lloyd, the Foreign Secretary, put to the Cabinet for closer links with France and Europe, were rejected.[26]

Eden and the 'Flexing of British Muscles': The Baghdad Pact

Early on in Eden's premiership Britain achieved a better working relationship with the United States in the Middle East. This was evident in plans, code-named 'Operation Alpha', initially secret, jointly drawn up for a settlement of the Arab-Israeli dispute which, at the start, it appeared would be at the expense of Israel.[27] Britain, in April 1955, joined the Turco-Iraqi Pact signed in February 1955, as a means of securing a satisfactory renegotiation of the Anglo-Iraqi treaty. This became known as the Baghdad Pact. Pakistan and Iran also joined. Washington, sensitive to Israeli demands and Arab nationalist reactions, did not. London hoped that if there were a settlement between the Arab states and Israel along the lines of 'Alpha' Washington would join the Baghdad Pact.[28]

When the Czechoslovak arms deal with Gamal Abdul Nasser was announced, London saw Moscow opening a third front of the Cold War in the Middle East. Eden felt that he had extended the hand of friendship to Nasser, but he now suspected Nasser of anti-Western sentiment. On 4 October 1955 Eden told the Cabinet:

> Our interests in the Middle East were greater than those of the United States because of our dependence on Middle Eastern oil, and our experience in the area was greater than theirs. We should not allow ourselves to be restricted overmuch by reluctance to act without full American concurrence and support. We should frame our policy in the light of our interests in the area and get the Americans to support it to the extent we could induce them to do so. Our policy should be based on the need to help our acknowledged friends and allies such as Iraq and the Trucial States on whom our oil depends.[29]

As relations between London and Cairo deteriorated, Eden had talks with Eisenhower and the Canadians in Ottawa at the beginning of February 1956. On Europe, Washington showed an enthusiasm for economic integration and the European atomic authority similar to that it had evidenced for the European Defence Community. Eden reported that on the Far East, differences between the two governments 'had not been fully bridged', particularly in relation to Chiang Kai-Shek, but there were signs that Eisenhower might relax some of the strategic controls over trade with Communist China. In the Middle East, however, the United States agreed to give its full moral support to the Baghdad Pact. Washington also wanted to avoid an arms race in the Middle East, and despite it being election year, was prepared to take a firm line over Israel. Eisenhower had also undertaken, once again, to increase American co-operation in the exchange of atomic intelligence, offers which were likely to save Britain money and time.[30]

Following the dismissal of the head of the Arab Legion in Jordan, Sir John Glubb, by King Hussein in March 1956, Eden warned the Cabinet that Britain's general policy in the Middle East had to be founded on the need to protect British oil interests in Iraq and the Persian Gulf. The main threat to those interests was the growing influence of Egypt. Britain had tried to counter this by strengthening the Baghdad Pact: 'there was no doubt that United States adherence to that Pact would be the greatest single contribution which could be made towards the easing of our present difficulties in the Middle East'.[31] The Foreign Secretary, Selwyn Lloyd, told the Cabinet on 15 March that his conversations with the Egyptian leader had convinced him that Nasser was aiming at the leadership of the Arab world and was willing to accept the help of the Soviet Union. Britain's first task needed to be to seek Anglo-American agreement on a general realignment of policy towards Egypt.[32] Britain also thought that the United States, which had transferred its principal base from Morocco to Libya, could be expected to bear a greater share of the cost of supporting Libya at a time when Britain was reappraising the value of its strategic connections with Libya.[33] This was at a time when London was reassessing its whole foreign and defence policy in the light of economic strictures and the new world situation.[34]

The Suez Crisis

The origins of the Suez crisis of 1956 lie partly in a mythology, current in the West in the 1950s, of Chamberlain's policy for the appeasement of Europe, and in the perhaps dangerous and inaccurate idea that history can repeat itself – that historical analogy can determine political policy. Eden, as he recorded in his memoirs, viewed the events of the 1950s through the spectacles of the 1930s. Nasser's nationalisation of the Suez

Canal not only threatened Britain's national economy, dependent on supplies of oil from the Middle East,[35] but the Egyptian leader was also viewed by the British Prime Minister as another Mussolini. This time Eden felt that the 'dictator' should not be appeased, and should be stopped before he went any further. In the end Britain worked with France and Israel to secure this. Britain rejected suggestions for a form of organic association with France: it preferred investigating a wider association between all the countries of Western Europe.[36]

Eisenhower wanted to play for time, and instructed Dulles accordingly: he could hardly run for re-election on the platform as the Prince of Peace if Washington's two main allies were fighting what the Americans might perceive as an old-style colonial war. Dulles went to London and saw Lloyd and Christian Pineau, the French Foreign Minister, on 1 August. Washington did not exclude the use of force, but it needed to be backed by world opinion. Lloyd explained that Britain might have to use force in the end. Dulles conceded that Nasser would have to be made to 'disgorge'. Dulles was obviously playing for time: he thought it would take three weeks to prepare for the envisaged conference, but 16 August was the compromise date agreed. Dulles was cheered by a crowd in Downing Street and was pleased. He also saw Macmillan and was told that the question for Britain was one of survival.

The Secretary of State met Eden privately the next day. In view of their clash at Geneva in 1954, the two men appear to have had a friendly talk. Dulles was particularly flattered by the Prime Minister's suggestion that he would go down in history as one of the great foreign ministers. It appears he gave Eden the assurance that he understood the Anglo-French position, and that Britain could count on the moral support and sympathy of the United States. Eden apparently offered the details of the Anglo-French military preparations, but Dulles interrupted to say that it would probably be better if Washington did not know. Presumably Dulles had possible domestic complications in mind; and the Central Intelligence Agency's activities were such that it would find out anyway; friendly exchanges between American and British military officials would also keep American officials apprised. After this warm talk both London and Washington were relieved and pleased. Later, the Egypt Committee was informed by Lloyd on 27 August that he had discussed the request from the American military attaché for information about the movements of British troops, and that Dulles had indicated that Washington would prefer that such information should not be passed to their military authorities. Lloyd informed Makins that Dulles had informed both him and Eden on at least two occasions that it would be an embarrassment for Washington if it were given this military information. But, if the State Department were complaining, it was possible that Dulles had not told Eisenhower or the State Department of this.

Eisenhower became increasingly involved in his election campaign. He wanted to delay the use of force until after its successful conclusion, and was probably disturbed by Eden's letter to him of 5 August. The Prime Minister did not think Nasser a Hitler, but the parallel with Mussolini was close. Thus Nasser's removal, and the installation of a regime less hostile to the West, was important. If the forthcoming conference ensured that Nasser disgorged his spoils, he would be unlikely to maintain his internal position. Eden concluded that London was determined that Nasser should not get away with it, because if he did the British people's existence would be at Nasser's mercy.[37]

Harold Macmillan, then Chancellor of the Exchequer, favoured the Users' Association, and London decided Dulles was acting in good faith with this suggestion. But the government's precarious position in the House was undermined when Dulles, during a debate on 12–13 September, said that the United States did not intend to shoot its way through the canal. Britain took the affair to the United Nations, and revised the military plans with France to allow for more time.[38]

Between 20 September and 1 October Macmillan was in the United States. He saw Eisenhower on 24 September, and found the President very keen to win his election. Eisenhower was sure that Nasser had to go. The question was how to achieve this. Macmillan made it clear that Britain could not play it long without aid on a large scale. Macmillan also saw Dulles, and told the Secretary of State that he devoutly hoped that there was no question of the president's re-election. Dulles hoped that Britain would do nothing drastic that would diminish the Republican chances. Macmillan recalled how helpful the Americans had been with Eden's general election in that they had arranged an appropriate summit conference to enable Eden to project an image of being a world statesman. Dulles said that he felt there was a basis for some reciprocity. Macmillan said that 'he quite agreed'. When he returned, the Chancellor assured Eden that Eisenhower was determined to stand up to Nasser. Dulles had given no indication that he did not recognise Britain's right to use force. Macmillan acknowledged later that he should have attached greater weight to the date of the presidential election. The Chancellor arrived back in Britain to Dulles's statement that he did not know of any teeth in the Users' Association.

Under criticism from sections of his party for not taking more resolute action and from others who opposed force, threatened by the French that the weather would preclude military action after the end of October, and believing that Pineau did not want a settlement at all, and faced with an opposition determined to undermine national unity, Eden's health deteriorated. The Prime Minister collapsed on 5 October, and had to resort to Benzedrine. Before that, on 1 October, he had reiterated his 'appeasement' thesis to Eisenhower: there was no doubt that Nasser was effectively in Soviet hands, 'just as Mussolini was in Hitler's'. Eden drew the parallel of showing weakness to placate Nasser with showing weakness to Mussolini. The result would be the same in that the two would be brought together: Cairo would join Moscow just as Rome had joined Berlin.[39]

On 25 October, Eden told the Cabinet that if Britain declined to join France in a military operation against Egypt, France would 'take military action alone or in conjunction with Israel'. Eden said: 'We must face the risk that we should be accused of collusion with Israel.' Lloyd supported Eden: 'unless prompt action were taken to check Colonel Nasser's ambitions, our position would be undermined throughout the Middle East'. Doubts were expressed in the Cabinet lest the envisaged British action 'would cause offence to the United States Government and might do lasting damage to Anglo-American relations'. It was thought that there was no prospect of securing the support or approval of Washington.[40]

On 2 November Lloyd warned the Cabinet about the strength of feeling the Anglo-French action in Egypt had aroused in the United States. The Foreign Secretary advised that if no concession to these feelings were made, it was possible that oil sanctions would be imposed against Britain. Britain could then be compelled to occupy Kuwait and Qatar, the only suppliers of oil which were not members of the United Nations. Britain would alienate, perhaps irretrievably, all the Arab states. Syria had already broken relations with Britain. It was possible that Iraq, Jordan and Libya would follow Syria's example. That could mean the fall of Nuri and the overthrow of the King. Britain 'could not hope to avoid serious difficulties with the Arab States for more than a very short time longer, certainly not for as long as it would take us to complete an opposed occupation of Egypt'. Dulles was effectively out of the way for the rest of the immediate crisis. In the middle of November he protested from his hospital bed to Eisenhower and Lloyd about Britain's not going through with the venture and dispensing with Nasser. The Secretary of State later attributed his hostile stand in the United Nations to his illness. After all, throughout the Suez crisis, Britain and the United States had the same objective: to dispose of Nasser. The only difference was in the timing.[41]

But that timing was crucial for Eisenhower. Few doubted that he would be re-elected, but Eisenhower felt that the least Eden owed him for arranging the summit conference in 1955 to help his general election was to hold off the Suez operation until after the presidential election. Shortly after the Anglo-French invasion, Eisenhower confessed to Air Chief Marshal William Elliott that he had known that Britain intended to strike at Nasser, but had thought that it would be after the American elections. London adhered to Dulles's wishes that no official information be passed about the military operation: both Eisenhower and Dulles were worried that Adlai Stevenson could use that against them in the election campaign if he found out. But Washington knew through un-official contacts. By 2 November, Eisenhower was aware of the Sèvres discussions; Dulles knew of the impending Israeli attack by 28 October.[42]

Before the election results came through in which the Republicans, Eisenhower's party, lost both Houses of Congress – though Eisenhower himself was returned as President – Eisenhower seemed open to Eden's reasoning. The President's secretary, Mrs Ann Whitman, recorded that on 30 October, at the time of the Israeli invasion of Sinai, Eisenhower while drafting a message to Eden was in 'remarkably good humor', and that the President that day spent all his free moments reading his own book on the Second World War, *Crusade in Europe*. Eisenhower, however, did write to Alfred M. Gruenther on 2 November about Eden's reaction in the Victorian manner, and the pointlessness of entering into a fight to which there could be no satisfactory outcome, and one in which the rest of the world viewed Britain as the bully, and that even the British population as a whole was not able to back. The following day Eisenhower confided to his friend Lew W. Douglas that he thought that the British had been stupid, that the leaders had allowed their hatred of Nasser to warp their judgement and that they were trying to deflate the Egyptian leader in the wrong way. The President wrote that it was clear that France and Israel had concocted the crisis, but the evidence of Britain's involvement in the hoax was less persuasive. Although Eisenhower felt that Britain must have known something of what had been going on, the President was not prepared to use the British government as a whipping boy.

On 5 November, the Prime Minister explained to the President that he had always felt that the Middle East was an issue on which, in the last resort, Britain would have to fight. He appreciated that Dulles thought that Britain should have played it longer. But Eden remained convinced that if the affair had been allowed to drift, everything would have gone from bad to worse: 'Nasser would have become a kind of Moslem Mussolini and our friends in Iraq, Jordan, Saudi Arabia and even Iran would gradually have been brought down.' Nasser's efforts would have then spread westwards and Libya and all North Africa would have been brought under his control. The French and British 'police action' had to be carried through: this was 'our opportunity to secure an effective and final settlement of the problems of the Middle East'. If Britain and France withdrew, the Middle East would go up in flames. They had to hold their positions until responsibility could be handed over to the United Nations: 'we shall have taken the first step towards re-establishing authority in this area for our generation'. Eden assured Eisenhower that he believed as firmly as ever 'that the future of all of us depends on the closest Anglo-American co-operation'. The temporary breach in this had been a sorrow for Eden. But Britain had acted with a genuine sense of responsibility not only to itself but to all the world.

On 6 November, London accepted a cease-fire. Eisenhower told Eden over the telephone that he did not care a damn how the election went. Eden wrote to Eisenhower the following day about the lack of understanding, since the end of the Second World War, between Britain and the United States on the Middle East. London and Washington needed to work towards common objectives there. Should the Soviet Union seize the opportunity of intervening by giving substantial support to Nasser, there could be major war. Eden had been going to Washington to see Eisenhower. The Republican losses in Congress changed that. Eisenhower would have to consult with the new Congressional leaders.[43]

Before the cease-fire, Eisenhower concerted action with the anti-British Secretary of the Treasury, George M. Humphrey, and Herbert Hoover, the Under-Secretary of State. Intelligence information was not passed to Britain, with the exception of the American assessment that the Soviet nuclear threat was a bluff. Eisenhower and Humphrey co-ordinated economic sanctions against Britain: the American Federal Reserve sold quantities of sterling: they held up emergency oil supplies to Europe; and in Macmillan's view almost illegally blocked Britain's drawing rights on the International Monetary Fund. No documentation on this had been found in the Department of State files. It has been argued that Macmillan's allegations of heavy selling of sterling in New York were unfounded, and that the figures he gave to the Cabinet about the drop in the reserves were also untrue. There is evidence, however, that Eisenhower did bloc Britain's drawing rights on the International Monetary Fund. That act forced Britain to stop a successful military operation before it had secured both ends of the canal. The parity of sterling was considered important.[44]

As Eisenhower took revenge – something he went on record later as regarding as the greatest mistake of his presidency[45] – the British Cabinet stressed more and more the need to re-establish close relations with the United States. On 30 November the Cabinet was informed that Washington had announced that it would view with the utmost gravity any threat to the territorial integrity or political independence of the Middle East members of the Baghdad Pact, and that it would maintain the oil supplies to Europe.[46]

The American administration considered a proposal for a new Middle East grouping which would merge the Baghdad Pact into a larger body. Britain also began to review Middle East policy. It was suggested to the Cabinet on 7 December 1956 that the military value of agreements such as the Anglo-Jordanian Treaty had been shown to be less than Britain had hoped, and could be expected to decline still further in the future. Britain's whole Middle East policy needed to be re-examined urgently. It might emerge from such a review that it would be preferable to rely on financial subventions to the Arab countries rather than on the maintenance of bases in their territories.[47]

Towards the end of 1956 relations between Washington and London were such that the two administrations hardly seemed to be speaking to one another. It seemed to the Americans that yet again, as had happened over the use of force to drive the Saudis out of the Buraimi oasis, and the despatch of the Templar mission to Jordan in November 1955, London had acted without informing Washington, this time about the invasion of the Suez Canal. London viewed the American policy as prevaricating, dictated by oil interests over Saudi Arabia and showing scant regard for British interests in the Gulf, on which the British economy was to a certain extent dependent, and, as had happened during the period of the end of the British mandate in Palestine, dictated by American domestic elections.

It was particularly over the aspect of the timing of the operation in relation to Eisenhower's presidential and the Congressional elections where the British miscalculated. And here it is not so much Eden who was responsible but Harold Macmillan. Macmillan had visited the United States, and had heard that Eisenhower expected the same consideration from Eden in relation to his election as Eden had had from the President over his general election in 1955, when Eisenhower had obliging arranged a summit conference so that Eden could project his traditional image of the suave foreign statesman. It has been argued too that Macmillan misled the Cabinet over the state of sterling, and it was that advice which forced the British withdrawal from the Suez Canal. Perhaps Macmillan saw his chance to become Prime Minister. He had resented Eden as the younger man and the heir apparent to Churchill, and when Eden had become Prime Minister probably saw his ambition for the premiership thwarted. The relationship between Eden and Macmillan was not easy. Macmillan resented Eden's interference when he was Foreign Secretary, but only agreed to move to the Exchequer on the understanding that he remained as the number two in government, that position traditionally having been reserved for the Foreign Secretary. It was Macmillan who was chosen by Queen Elizabeth II as her Prime Minister. His relationship with Eisenhower during the Second World War and his American connections – his mother was American – were a consideration. Macmillan was seen as the man best able to restore the relationship with the United States.

By early December, both British and American officials saw the need to re-establish the close relationship between London and Washington. During the years of the first Eisenhower presidency that relationship had not been 'special': Eisenhower from the outset had insisted that Britain was only one among a number of allies. His close advisers Hoover and Humphrey disliked the British, and often viewed them as colonialists who wanted the Americans to pay for the safeguarding of British interests in the Middle East while still leaving the British in command.

Eden, as Prime Minister, exerted a distinctly British policy in the Middle East. Churchill had wanted to involve the Americans in the area and to get Washington to assume more of the responsibility of defending the area in the interests of the West. Eden felt that the British dependence on Middle East oil, and the experience the British had had of the area, meant that London had to be prepared to mount a policy in the Middle East, if necessary, without the full agreement and support of Washington. Both Washington and London concluded that Moscow had opened up another front in the Cold War by agreeing to supply the

Egyptians with arms. Where they differed was in their diagnosis of how to deal with the Arabs over this. Britain felt that its Arab allies might react favourably to firmness. Washington thought shows of force would drive the Arabs to Moscow. Britain, as a means of securing a favourable renegotiation of the Anglo-Iraqi Treaty of 1930, initiated the Northern Tier concept that had initially been an American brain-child as early as 1950. The Americans, and particularly Dulles, had seen the Northern Tier primarily as a means of defence against the Soviet Union. Dulles felt that the British version, the Turco-Iraqi Pact which became known as the Baghdad Pact, was mainly about inter-Arab politics, and had little to do with defence against the Soviet Union.

After the Suez crisis, however, there was increasingly a common Anglo-American diagnosis of the danger of the Soviet Union moving into the vacuum in the Middle East, a vacuum that had been referred to for some time, as Britain increasingly withdrew from the area. During Eden's premiership the main objective of British policy in the Middle East was to ensure the flow of oil in Iraq and the Gulf. This brought London into head-on clashes with Washington. Washington, and Eisenhower as President, could not grasp the importance of the Gulf for Britain. Eisenhower chose King Saud as his man in the Middle East. He confessed that he knew little about Saud. But ARAMCO and American oil interests dictated that Saud should be humoured. Eisenhower could not understand why Britain was not prepared to allow Saud to take over Buraimi, and effectively Muscat and Oman as well. To Eisenhower this seemed a small sacrifice to pacify Saud. Of course it was a sacrifice that Britain would have to make. But Britain refused to co-operate. Eisenhower was aided in his assessment of British motives by Hoover.

Britain chose Nuri. Iraq saw Egypt as its rival for the leadership of the Arab world. Britain saw Nasser challenging its position not only in the Middle East, but in Africa and in the Muslim world. Nasser had to go. With this the Americans agreed. The Anglo-American difference hinged on the timing of this. The Suez crisis confirmed the need for the reappraisal of British foreign policy already initiated by the Eden government in June 1956.[48]

7

MUTUAL INTERDEPENDENCE

Harold Macmillan was chosen as Prime Minister by Queen Elizabeth II, acting on advice. Perhaps he was seen as the man best able to heal the breach with the United States. Eden had to go. The reason given was his health. In his message to Eden about this, Eisenhower omitted any mention of 'regret', and merely referred to past associations. Macmillan told the Cabinet on 9 January 1957 that when the history of the Suez crisis was written, it would be recognised that Eden had been inspired by motives of the highest patriotism.[1]

On 8 January 1957, just before Harold Macmillan assumed the premiership, Lloyd outlined to the Cabinet a suggestion for closer military and political association between Britain and Western Europe. He went so far as to suggest that Britain could 'pool our resources with our European allies so that Western Europe as a whole might become a third nuclear power comparable with the United States and the Soviet Union'. This disturbed Lord Salisbury: he doubted whether 'a policy on these lines could be pursued consistently with the maintenance of the Anglo-American alliance which, in his view, offered the best hope of securing the free world from Soviet aggression'.[2] The Macmillan government chose to emphasise the American link.

The Restoration of the Special Relationship

Macmillan was able to report to the Cabinet on 29 January that Eisenhower was prepared to resume friendly relations with Britain, and had suggested a meeting either in Washington or in Bermuda. Macmillan chose to meet under the Union flag in Bermuda: there was to be no image of British supplication to Washington. When Macmillan and Eisenhower met at Bermuda on 21 March, Macmillan was 'frank' about Middle Eastern questions, and warned of the danger of a 'real rift' between London and Washington if Nasser succeeded in imposing his proposed long-term arrangements over the operation of the Suez Canal. Eisenhower spoke of his delight in sitting down with his former comrade-in-arms, and agreed with Macmillan that Anglo-American solidarity was the core of the Western alliance: if the English-speaking peoples could not live and work together there was little hope. The American President thought that nationalism was a stronger spirit than communism. Eisenhower confided to his diary that this was the most successful international meeting he had attended since the end of the Second World War. Macmillan concluded that Eisenhower 'appeared to be genuinely anxious fully to restore the traditional relationship between the two countries'. Indeed Eisenhower's briefing paper for the conference had pointed to the traditional concept of the Anglo-American alliance, and had emphasised that British and American policies were in agreement regarding areas of vital interest to Britain, particularly in the Middle East.[3]

At Bermuda it was confirmed that Britain was to receive sixty intermediate-range ballistic missiles (IRBMs) from the United States. The revival by Eisenhower of the special relationship and with it the provision of American weaponry to Britain, something which led to a British reliance on American technical knowledge and production, and to later debates as to whether this meant that Britain had an independent nuclear deterrent, assisted the evolution of Britain's new defence policy. The Thor missiles were to be operated under a dual-key arrangement controlled by both the British and the Americans.[4]

In April 1957, following the consideration by the Chiefs of Staff of long-term British defence policy, the White Paper on defence which became linked with the name of the Minister of Defence, Duncan Sandys, placed emphasis on the nuclear deterrent for the following five years.[5] This reliance on nuclear weapons meant that it was possible to abolish National Service. The Royal Air Force's V bombers would be supplemented by ballistic missiles. Thermo-nuclear weapons (hydrogen bombs) would be developed. With the ending of conscription in 1962 service manpower would be reduced from 690,000 to 375,000. In May 1957 the British hydrogen bomb was tested on Christmas Island in the Pacific.

But Britain still needed nuclear information from the United States. When the Soviet Union launched Sputnik, its first space satellite, the United States was shaken. Macmillan was immediately invited to Washington, and in talks there between 23 and 25 October, as Lloyd reported to the Cabinet on 28 October, 'as a result of the personal friendship between the Prime Minister and President Eisenhower, we had now succeeded in regaining the special relationship with the United States we had formerly enjoyed'. The relationship between Washington and London was to be one of 'inter-dependence'. Washington agreed to adopt the principle of pooling resources in the development and production of new weapons. Congress was to be asked to amend the Atomic Energy Act to allow greater co-operation with Britain and other friendly countries. This was in effect the end of the McMahon Act of 1946, which restricted such an exchange of information, and which had forced Britain to develop its own bomb. Washington and London would concert a common policy against Soviet encroachment.[6] Sandys hoped to replace the Royal Air Force's V bombers with the British Blue Streak missile. This was, however, vulnerable to Soviet attack. Macmillan negotiated an alternative with Eisenhower in March 1960: in return for being allowed to purchase the American missile Skybolt, Britain would permit the Americans to use Holy Loch in Scotland as a submarine base.[7]

Anglo-American Collaboration over Military Planning

Throughout the late 1950s Washington and London collaborated closely over military planning and the management of alliance security. G. Wyn Rees argues that during the latter part of the 1950s Britain and the United States, although *de facto* members of three major alliances, NATO, CENTO and SEATO, 'subordinated these organisations to their own national security plans because they regarded the alliances as serving only a limited part of their interests'. The main interest of both Washington and London lay in collaboration between themselves. Rees suggests that the regional members of the alliances thought Britain and the United States selfish and intransigent.

But for British and American policymakers the Anglo-American special relationship was special, and the two countries were prepared to co-operate in defence matters 'in both nuclear and conventional fields, to a level that they were unwilling to share with other countries'. Washington thought that London could be useful with its experience and strategically important military bases, but many American leaders considered that the Anglo-American alliance was of more importance to Britain than it was to the United States. London wanted an integrated partnership with Washington in which military planning would be shared between the British Chiefs of Staff and the American Joint Chiefs of Staff. This was difficult to achieve at a time when domestic considerations made defence cuts essential and when the Americans were demanding increased levels of British conventional forces.

It was the NATO alliance that was regarded by Washington and London as the most important, and it was possible to discern a wider community of interest between members of NATO, and Britain and the United States. But there was more friction evident between the two nuclear powers over the management of this alliance than between any of the others. Divided over issues such as the extent to which a nuclear exchange could be expected to be decisive, and the relative utility of conventional versus nuclear weapons, the British often found themselves in a minority, but did not give in and instead tried to change the American perspective. With the development of the Baghdad Pact into the Central Treaty Organisation (CENTO) in August 1959, the political intention of the pact receded and CENTO concentrated more on economic planning. Rees argues that the South East Asia Treaty Organisation (SEATO) was merely a paper tiger because Britain and the United States lacked the will to make the organisation effective: London and Washington 'ensured that the growth of SEATO remained stunted and they insisted that no Western troops were stationed in the region'.[8]

The Transfer of Power in the Middle East

At a time when British and American officials on the higher levels had difficulty in talking to one another in a civil fashion, in the aftermath of the Suez crisis, London and Washington reassessed Middle Eastern policy. On London's part there was perhaps a little more emphasis on the Churchill administration's aim of 'getting the Americans in', and a little less on 'the flexing of British muscles' evidenced by the Eden government. The Americans finally realised, against the background of the Soviet threat, that they would have to assume an increasing responsibility for the defence of the Middle East, and the winning of the 'hearts and minds' in the area in Cold War terms. The State Department, particularly after the visit to the Middle East of the Secretary of State, John Foster Dulles, had warned Eisenhower that Britain could no longer play the role assigned to it for the defence of the Middle East in Western strategy, and that the United States would have to prepare to take over. The Eisenhower Doctrine for the Middle East was a reflection of this.

In British defence policy and global strategy, the Middle East was no longer of cardinal importance. Eden had initiated further assessments of Britain's reduced role in world affairs before the nationalisation of the Suez Canal. Britain's defence and foreign policy had to take account of economic realities. The government of Harold Macmillan implemented the cost-effectiveness principal of Empire, assessed what value associated and dependent countries were to Britain, and who would move in if Britain moved out. The 'wind of change' associated with Africa was evident elsewhere.[9] In the Middle East the British interest shifted increasingly to securing the oil supplies from Kuwait in particular, and the Gulf in more general terms. This effectively constituted a transfer of power.

Alongside this British reassessment, the Americans refined an envisaged Congressional resolution which Dulles had described to Lloyd in Paris on 10 December. Initially drafted by Herman Phleger, the Chief Legal Officer in the State Department, incorporating suggestions made by Dulles, outlined by Eisenhower on 1 January 1957 to leaders from both parties and houses in Congress, the President delivered it on 5 January to a joint session on Capitol Hill. The reasoning behind what became known as the Eisenhower Doctrine for the Middle East was that there was a vacuum in the Middle East, which had to be filled by the United States before it was filled by the Soviet Union. The President outlined a programme to strengthen economically the nations of the Middle East, and asked for flexibility to use funds, and for provision to use the armed forces of the United States. Caccia pointed out that there was nothing in the doctrine that was addressed to Britain or to Washington's other Western allies. This was American unilateral action. Shortly afterwards, Dulles was reported to have said that he would not like to be an American soldier in the Middle East with a Briton on one side and a Frenchman on the other. This 'slip' apparently embarrassed both Dulles and the State Department, and the British decided not to press the matter.[10]

Eisenhower, and many of his officials, could not grasp the importance of the Gulf for Britain. Eisenhower chose King Saud as his man in the Middle East. The President confessed that he knew little about Saud, and in 1958 acknowledged that this policy had been a mistake and that Britain's choice of Nuri had been a wiser one.[11] Although the Eisenhower Doctrine initially seemed like American unilateral action in the Middle East to fill the vacuum left by Britain's withdrawal, what evolved by the time of the Syrian crisis of August 1957 was a willingness on the part of Washington to consult intimately with Britain over policy in the area. And by the time of the crises in Lebanon, Jordan and Iraq in July 1958 the United States had, in effect, acknowledged that it had assumed the leadership of the 'Free World' in the Middle East. Washington's actions during the Anglo-American invasion of Jordan and Lebanon showed the extent to which it had taken over Britain's place in the Middle East, and filled the vacuum left by the British decline in the area, evidenced in the aftermath of the Second World War, particularly with the end of Britain's mandate over Palestine.[12]

In 1958 the British Cabinet and Defence Planning Committees confirmed a policy, already evident in 1956, that Britain's 'great' interest in the Middle East lay in Kuwait with its oil and sterling reserves. Initially this was listed above the only other 'great' interest, Turkey, and later Iran and Aden were added. As Britain moved towards an Anglo-American policy for the Middle East, Kuwait and the Gulf were initially seen as areas of predominant British interest. It was, however, acknowledged that Britain could not act forcibly without American support, and that this support did not have to be military. London could not persuade Washington to embark on joint planning for the protection of Kuwait. When Iraq seemed to threaten the invasion of Kuwait in 1961, however, Washington not only gave diplomatic support, but allowed for the contingency of possible military support as well, and throughout refrained from imposing a policy on London.[13]

The Kuwait crisis of 1961 forced the acceptance on Macmillan and other British officials that there had at least to be the appearance of an Arab solution to an Arab question. This constituted a move away from the methods of the previous century, and an acknowledgement of the value of the policy outlined by Eden for the Cabinet in 1953, of the need to harness the social and economic aspirations of the common people of the Middle East at a time when the tide of nationalism was rising fast. It had also been Eden's government, just before the start of the Suez crisis of 1956, that had initiated the review of British policy in order to transfer effort from military preparations to that of improving Britain's economic and political position.

Britain's policy for the Middle East that evolved throughout the 1950s was, in many ways, initiated with the change in military strategy and the straitened economic circumstances in mind. That policy was also, in effect, helped by Washington's assumption of an increased responsibility in the area. Eisenhower, during his first presidency, had not wanted this. He preferred to leave Britain in the lead there, and had wanted Britain to pay as much as possible for the area's defence. It was, however, Eisenhower's policy during the Suez crisis of 1956 that led, as Henry Kissinger later observed, to the United States having to take over Britain's burdens in the Middle East.[14] This was evident during the Kennedy presidency.

The Offshore Islands Crisis of 1958

The success of the Anglo-American operation in Lebanon and Jordan in 1958, and the Soviet failure to respond by sending troops to the Middle East, convinced the Chinese Communists that they should show the Soviets how to resist imperialists: on 23 August the Chinese Communists unleashed a massive bombardment on the offshore island of Quemoy. Privately Eisenhower had indicated that he was willing to use nuclear weapons if an attack on the offshore islands were actually launched. Macmillan was not well informed about the situation by either the Foreign Office or the Americans. On 3 September he wrote to Eisenhower saying that he wanted a common front with the Americans and would appreciate a private message. That message came from Dulles, and Macmillan responded that Britain could not support the American position wholeheartedly: Taiwan and the offshore islands were 'in different juridical categories'. The crisis was defused by Sino-American ambassadorial talks. Macmillan knew that his suggested solutions were not considered seriously in Washington.[15] Washington did not appreciate London's continued trading with Communist China at a time of the American trade embargo.

The Paris Summit and the U-2

London and Washington also arranged their own summits with Nikita Khrushchev at a time when the Soviet leader was threatening Berlin.

Anglo-American plans for a summit in Paris were thwarted when the Soviets shot down an American U-2 reconnaissance plane on 1 May 1960. Macmillan tried to rescue the summit, and, to demonstrate Anglo-American solidarity, drove around Paris in an open car with Eisenhower.[16]

Personal Relationships

Eisenhower determined to restore the special relationship with Britain. He was helped in this by Macmillan on a personal level. Macmillan in his relations with the President went out of the way to mention his links with the United States, having like Churchill had an American mother, and also reminiscing about his wartime experiences with the President in North Africa. In practice, it was Selwyn Lloyd and Dulles who responded to each other and managed the alliance. On 21 January 1961 John Kennedy, the son of the Irish-American ambassador in London in the early stages of the war, Joseph Kennedy, who had not wanted to help Britain, was inaugurated as President. The ceremony depicted John Kennedy as the symbol of a new vigorous culture. This was at a time when, after South Africa's exclusion from the Commonwealth, Macmillan had decided to move Britain towards Europe. In April 1961, while in Washington, Macmillan learnt from the new administration that Anglo-American relations would be strengthened not weakened if Britain joined the European Common Market.

Perhaps, ironically, it was the visible close relationship that evolved between an establishment leftover from an Edwardian wilderness and the first American President to be born in the 20th century, seen as young and inexperienced, that led to the Anglo-American nuclear alliance and to General Charles de Gaulle's veto of British membership early in 1963.[17] Macmillan described this relationship as being like one between a father and a son. It was founded in the aftermath of Kennedy's first meeting with Khrushchev, where the American President was treated in a scornful way in the light of the failed invasion of Cuba, the Bay of Pigs episode. Kennedy then went to London: on 4 June 1960 Macmillan and he chatted informally over a lunch of sandwiches and whisky. The American President asked for advice and it was the foundation of a trusting friendship: Kennedy later said that he was able to share his loneliness with the British Prime Minister.[18]

The Cuban Missile Crisis

This confiding is what Kennedy did in his conversations with Macmillan over the telephone during the Cuban missile crisis of November 1962, when the placing of missiles by the Soviet Union on the island of Cuba, ninety miles from the American coast, possibly a manoeuvre to threaten the Western presence in Berlin, seemed to place the world on the verge of nuclear holocaust, the sort of scenario described by Nevil Shute in his novel *On the Beach*, the film of which had been rushed to Moscow on its release in 1958.

In 1969 a book by the President's brother, Robert Kennedy attributed a great deal to the influence of the British ambassador in Washington, David Ormsby-Gore (Lord Harlech), related to the Kennedys and a frequent weekend guest at the Kennedy complex at Hyannis Port. This book stated that on matters such as the distance of the blockade, Kennedy took the advice of the British ambassador over that of his own officials. This interpretation of events has been challenged as has the claim that Ormsby-Gore was the only man, outside the closed group of Americans, Kennedy consulted on the issue of whether to mount an airstrike or enforce a blockade. Kennedy had asked for Ormsby-Gore as British ambassador in Washington. This has been seen as an instance of an Anglo-American alliance managed by family relationships.[19]

Recent research suggests that Sir Kenneth Strong of British intelligence was informed of the presence of Soviet missiles on Cuba on 16 October, even before the much recorded apparent deduction by him on 17 October based on beds being carried into the Pentagon. The British were an exception to the edict that no information was to be passed to anyone outside a small trusted circle of Americans. John Dickie has observed: 'That Strong was considered worthy of exemption from this high-security edict is proof that in times of crisis in the Cold War, whatever the cynics said about Britain as a hapless bystander, the British were not left on the outside.' Not only Strong, but Ormsby-Gore was briefed. Kennedy sent a personal message to Macmillan in advance of that to any other Western leader. Macmillan did not let Kennedy know of his personal hesitations about the American handling of the crisis, or what he saw as legal difficulties in the international arena. The Prime Minister and Alec Douglas-Home even considered calling an international conference. But Macmillan did offer to have the British Thor missiles immobilised in Turkey at the same time as the American ones to enable Khrushchev to back down. Every night Kennedy sounded out Macmillan on the telephone: the President found these conversations of 'inestimable value'.[20]

The Nassau Agreement

Although the telephone transcripts show the two men referring to each other as President and Prime Minister, the intimacy and confidence established during the Cuban missile crisis helped Macmillan handle the crisis that burst when the American administration threatened to cancel the Skybolt missile in favour of the submarine-launched Polaris and Minutemen missiles. Macmillan faced domestic turmoil: he had removed six ministers in the 'night of the long knives'; he was struggling to handle the financial crisis with an incomes policy; abroad, the Central African Federation was disintegrating.

At Nassau, in the Bahamas, between 18 and 21 December 1962, Kennedy met the United States's 'obligation to the British'. Macmillan asked for Polaris as a substitute for Skybolt. Despite the opposition of advisers like George Ball, Kennedy gave Britain Polaris at low cost and helped to preserve the British independent nuclear deterrent for the following three decades. It was a financial gift to Britain as well: Britain had to pay only £50,000 for every £1 million worth of rockets. The Polaris missiles were intended for the development of a multilateral NATO force. Macmillan secured the vital proviso: 'The Prime Minister made it clear that, except where Her Majesty's Government may decide that her supreme national interests are at stake, these British forces will be used for the purposes of international defence of the Western alliance in all circumstances.' Macmillan, in writing to the Queen, paid tribute to Kennedy's 'sense of fairness and willingness to be persuaded by argument and over-rule those of his advisers who were not sympathetic to our views'.[21]

The Multilateral Force and the Test Ban Treaty

The United States proposed a Multilateral Force as a means of coping with difficulties in NATO over West Germany. Britain saw a Multilateral Force as a challenge to its independent nuclear deterrent. Later the Conservative government of Sir Alec Douglas Home and the Labour government of Harold Wilson opposed the idea of a Multilateral Force. Britain agreed with the Soviet Union that a Multilateral Force could lead to nuclear proliferation. Britain did support the Americans in their attempt to secure Soviet agreement to an international non-proliferation treaty, as Britain did not want other countries to acquire nuclear weapons.

Faced with public demands at home, reassured by its nuclear relationship with the United States, and worried about the dangers implicit in nuclear testing, the Macmillan government worked for a nuclear test ban. Though London favoured a Comprehensive Test Ban Treaty (CTBT), it urged Washington to accept a Partial Test Ban Treaty (PTBT) and argued that verification was not critical. The governments of Britain, the United States and the Soviet Union signed the Test Ban Treaty on 5 August 1963. John Dickie has observed that 'both Kennedy and Macmillan saw it as a peak in their partnership'. A few months later Macmillan resigned, and Kennedy was murdered in Dallas.[22]

Britain's Role

Over the decades the personal reputations of these men and their wives has been sullied by evidence of adultery and homosexuality.[23] But this has not marred verdicts of what they achieved on the world scene particularly in the handling of the Cuban missile crisis. It is easy to overlook that Macmillan was not always successful in winning the Americans to his point of view, though the British did help to achieve a compromise solution to the situation in Laos, and there was joint Anglo-American action in 1962 to deter China from taking further military action in the Sino-Indian border dispute.[24] This was the time of Dean Acheson's snide remark at West Point Military Academy on 5 December 1962 that:

> Great Britain has lost an empire and has not yet found a role. The attempt to play a separate role – that is apart from Europe, a role based on a 'special relationship' with the United States, a role based on being head of a 'Commonwealth' which has no political structure or unity or strength and enjoys a fragile and precarious relationship by means of the sterling area and preferences in the British market – this role is about played out.

Macmillan regarded this as 'a calculated insult to the British nation'. Kennedy authorised the official American reply:

> US–UK relations are not based only on a power calculus, but also on deep community of purpose and long practice of close cooperation. Examples are legion: nuclear affairs, Sino-Indian crisis, in which Sandys and Harriman missions would have been ineffective without each other, Berlin, and also Cuba, where British Government backed US strongly on short notice and where President and Prime Minister were in daily intimate consultation to a degree not publicly known. 'Special relationship' may not be a perfect phrase, but sneers at Anglo-American reality would be equally foolish.

Much has been made of what Macmillan was supposed to have observed when he was Minister at Algiers in 1942: 'These Americans represent the new Roman Empire and we Britons, like the Greeks of old, must teach them how to make it go.'[25] It was the Attlee administration, and in particular Bevin and the Foreign Office's education of the Americans in overseeing the transition from the *Pax Britannica* to the *Pax Americana*, which reflected this particular attitude. Macmillan and Kennedy were friends: Kennedy at Nassau wanted to help Macmillan when the Prime Minister was confronted by a domestic crisis. To suggest that Macmillan gave the arrogant image of an elder statesman educating a younger politician is to underestimate Macmillan's sophistication in handling the Americans, and to denigrate what appears to have been a sincere friendship which guaranteed the nuclear alliance between Britain and the United States that endured for three decades, on terms immeasurably favourable to Britain. This was a personal achievement, and virtually a personal gift in defiance of a hostile bureaucracy, from an American President to a British Prime Minister. It was perhaps the ultimate vindication of the endorsement by the Attlee government of the recommendation of the Permanent Under-Secretary's Committee in 1949 that the basis of British foreign and alliance policy should be the 'special relationship' with the United States.

8

THE EUROPEAN DIMENSION

Contemporary journalists and academics with the benefit of hindsight have viewed Anglo-American relations between the eras of Macmillan and Kennedy, and of Margaret Thatcher and Ronald Reagan, in a negative light. Variously described as 'the lean years of the almost forgotten friendship', the 'weakening' and 'muted' relationship, the alliance 'depreciated' and 'estranged', this period of what one writer has described as the era of 'the Labour ascendancy'[1] – seemingly implying that the administration of Edward Heath was almost socialist in its approach – is generally regarded as one in which there was no 'special relationship' between London and Washington.[2]

The Redefinition of the Relationship

In the early 1950s it had been the Americans under Eisenhower who had devalued the special relationship. In the 1960s and 1970s it was the British, and in particular Harold Wilson and Edward Heath, who were anxious to demonstrate that London's relations with Washington were not really different from those with its other allies. On his first visit to Washington as Prime Minister in December 1964, Wilson initiated this redefinition at a White House lunch:

> Some of those who talk about the Special Relationship, I think, are looking backwards and not forwards. They talk about the nostalgia of our imperial age. We regard our relationship with you not as a special relationship but as a close relationship governed by the only things that matter, unity of purpose and unity in our objectives.[3]

Edward Heath defied the opinion polls when he became British Prime Minister on 19 June 1970: the BBC had made no provision for this and had to improvise an extension to the Conservative side of the swingometer. Richard Nixon was pleasantly surprised and hoped to work closely with a fellow conservative. But Heath was probably the first British Prime Minister in thirty years without any commitment to the Anglo-American special relationship. He had served as Britain's chief negotiator for entry into the European Economic Community and was a convinced European. He did not want Britain to be refused entry a third time. Although on one level he seemed to give the British public the impression that Britain's entry to Europe was largely equivalent to joining a customs union, and that Britain would act in Europe as Washington's spokesman, Heath discouraged the American connection. As Prime Minister he did not even visit that country until he had been in office for six months, and then although he was photographed playing a symbolic duet with Nixon on the piano, Heath responded to the President's warm references on at least seven occasions to the 'special relationship' with evident embarrassment and another redefinition of it as being a 'happy and natural' relationship.

Henry Kissinger, Nixon's White House assistant and later Secretary of State, observed that Heath viewed the '"special relationship" as an obstacle to the British vocation in Europe'. Not only did Heath want no higher status in Washington than any other European leader, but 'he came close to *insisting* on receiving no preferential treatment'.[4] Britain's emphasis was on being a good European. It was only with the return of Labour, when James Callaghan became first Foreign Secretary, and then Prime Minister that the Atlantic alliance was given a greater prominence.

The Working Relationship

With successive British administrations obsessed with the European dimension it is easy to overlook the sustained operation of the Anglo-American relationship during these fifteen years. Wilson might have publicly espoused the ending of Britain's independent nuclear deterrent, but he did little about this and remained anxious for Britain to remain under the American nuclear umbrella. Indeed it was his Labour successor, Callaghan, who prepared for the replacement of Polaris by the American Trident missile. An everyday close working relationship persisted between the British and American defence establishments: the British Ministry of Defence maintained, in the mid-1970s, seventy-five front-line staff officers in Washington when there were only seven in Bonn and ten in Paris. British and American defence officials frequently visited one another, and the intelligence organisations, despite the impression given in John le Carré's novels, worked in comparative harmony and unity.[5]

On the political front, around the time of Britain's second application for European membership, Robert Hathaway quotes National Security Council adviser, McGeorge Bundy as observing:

> In the very nature of things, British interest[s] and ours intersect in every continent, and usually in rather complicated ways. . . . My own thinking is governed by a conviction that, if we can understand them correctly, our real interests will nearly always turn out to be very close to each other indeed.

American officials in London agreed:

> we need the support and sympathy of the British. If they are unable to go it alone, in their relative weakness, neither can we everywhere. We touch one another at too many points and are still affected by what the other does in too many situations to be able to dispense with mutual support of some kind. We consult together more frequently and extensively than with any third countries. On many matters and in widely different circumstances our policies are made to fit agreed lines of action.[6]

When Moscow made moves towards détente in July and August 1972, Kissinger relied on the Soviet expert in the Foreign Office, Sir Thomas Brimelow, and his small group of British advisers to draft responses to a Soviet proposal for a renunciation of nuclear weapons. Brimelow massaged this into an agreement to renounce the threat of force in diplomacy. Kissinger described Brimelow's role as being an example of the Anglo-American special relationship 'at its best, even at a time when the incumbent Prime Minister was not among its advocates': 'There was no other government which we would have dealt with so openly, exchanged ideas with so freely, or in effect permitted to participate in our deliberations.'[7]

As in the 1940s and 1950s the United States continued to sustain Britain economically. The first Wilson government, faced with a massive balance of payments deficit, hoped for American assistance to support the pound sterling. Some of Johnson's advisers, however, thought it inappropriate to assist Britain financially at a time when there were no official British troops in Vietnam, and when Britain was threatening to withdraw from its responsibilities East of Suez and in Germany. Other counsellors warned that if Britain were not assisted it would be forced to cut its defence commitments even further.

Late in 1964, the Johnson administration arranged $3 billion of credits for Britain of which the American share was $1 billion. In 1965 the Americans helped the British secure a further $925 million in credits from American and European central banks.[8] In November 1968, when faced with the prospect of a British devaluation of the pound from $2.80 to $2.40, according to the Wilson's memoirs, the American treasury took fright, but although the Americans stiffened 'there was no sign that this was backed by anything in the nature of a cheque-book'. When faced by the imminent prospect of a British devaluation, however, Johnson spoke in the warmest terms to the British ambassador in Washington 'and said that "he was putting his stack behind Prime Minister Wilson"'.[9]

With the Sterling crisis of 1976, seen on a popular level in the United States and elsewhere as a result of 'the British disease', the manifestation of which was a corporate state run by the trade unions with a people dulled by three decades of the welfare state into thinking that the state owed them a living rather than their owing anything to the common wealth, Washington again assisted with the arrangement of a standby credit of $5.3 billion, of which it provided $2 billion. Alan Dobson in his account emphasises that this time there were strings attached: credit was only for six months. Dobson insists that neither William Simon, the American Treasury Secretary, not Arthur Burns of the Federal Reserve Bank had much faith in the economic policies of the Labour government. The Americans refused further help until the International Monetary Fund had dictated the terms of Britain's deflation. Hathaway offers a different emphasis: 'Sharing many of the same problems of inflation, unemployment, stagnation, escalating energy prices, budgetary deficits, and international payments imbalances, officials of the two nations assumed an interdependence directly contrary to the attitudes prevalent during the 1930s.' Officials on both sides of the Atlantic saw the need to concert their policies to combat common threats. Hathaway cites the correspondence between Arthur Burns, chairman of the Federal Reserve Board, and Sir Leslie O'Brien, the governor of the

Bank of England, as an instance of this, as well as officials urging President Gerald Ford to authorise the necessary assistance to Britain as its society was irrevocably linked to that of the United States.[10]

Personalities

The managers of the Anglo-American alliance in the period from 1964 to 1979 did not enjoy the same terms of intimacy as had those during periods of the previous decade. But in assessing this it is important to remember that when the special relationship was revived in the aftermath of the Second World War personal relations between those at the top were not particularly good, though there was an understanding and friendship in evidence between many of the officials who worked together from the opposite sides of the Atlantic. It appears that on a working level this was also true of Anglo-American relations during these fifteen years.

During Alec Douglas-Home's brief premiership he antagonised President Johnson on 7 January 1964 with the announcement that London was providing Cuba with credit to buy 400 British buses. In reality British trade with Cuba had been greatly reduced, but Home's resentment over American instructions as to where Britain could sell its goods marred his visit to the White House on 12 February 1964. Johnson saw Britain as aiding Washington's enemy, and the relationship was further soured by Home's television statement that people like Castro were not brought down by economic boycotts and sanctions.

Initially effusive in their reciprocal praise of each other, Wilson and Johnson viewed one another with some suspicion. Johnson thought that Wilson was only too keen to cross the Atlantic to bolster his domestic position. The American President thought that the British Prime Minister was too clever by half. So did his successor. Nixon disliked Wilson's smooth talk. When the two men first met, on Nixon's visit to Britain in February 1979, Wilson suggested early on to Nixon that they call each other by their first names. Kissinger observed that 'a fish-eyed stare from Nixon squelched this idea'.[11] Nixon was excited at the prospect of working with his fellow conservative, Heath, and especially with Home who as Foreign Secretary on 24 September 1971 ordered the expulsion of 105 Russians from Britain claiming that they were spies. But Nixon's overtures of friendship were met with a deliberate and sustained aloofness by the Europe-obsessed Heath. Heath was allowed access by telephone to Nixon at any time, but he did not ring.

Perhaps these relationships were not helped by a British public which viewed Johnson as a crude Texan in comparison with the Camelot image of Kennedy, and did not greet Nixon with any great warmth. The situation was not helped either by a British media, fashionably dominated by what was known at the time as the 'new left', inclined to present both Presidents as manifestations of evil and to treat American Vietnam policy with little sympathy, indeed all too ready to expound the devil theory of American foreign policy at a time when revisionist views of the Cold War had not been seriously challenged and were widely propagated on British television, in the press, and in academic circles. In this regard the British media largely reflected its American counterparts.

When Wilson returned as Prime Minister, against the background of the miners' strike, the three-day week, and frequent electricity blackouts, he confined himself in foreign affairs to Israel and South Africa and left decisions on priorities to the Foreign Secretary, James Callaghan. Callaghan insisted that the special relationship with Washington had supreme importance despite the commitment to Europe, and he told Kissinger that he wanted to stop the 'mutual needling' between Washington and London. But Kissinger thwarted Callaghan and declined to co-ordinate British and American policy over the deposition of Archbishop Makarios in Cyprus. When the Turks invaded, Callaghan objected to Kissinger that Washington was too concerned about Turkey's place in NATO; and he resented an American attitude which saw Cyprus as a little local problem. He thought Kissinger devious. Shortly after becoming Prime Minister, Callaghan was faced with Kissinger's attempts to solve Britain's Rhodesian problem. But Kissinger's shuttle diplomacy in Africa did not match his Middle East ventures and scarred Anglo-American relations.

There were hopes of better relations when Jimmy Carter took over from Ford, and Cyrus Vance succeeded Kissinger as Secretary of State. The British ambassador in Washington, Sir Peter Ramsbottom, had advised London that Carter was likely to be elected and the British had earned Carter's gratitude by taking him seriously. But the new Foreign Secretary, David Owen, replaced Ramsbottom by Peter Jay, Callaghan's son-in-law, a move regarded as blatant nepotism by circles on Capitol Hill. Nevertheless, Owen humoured Carter by giving human rights priority, and Callaghan's first visit to Carter in March 1977 was marked at least by a superficial cordiality between the two men.[12]

Probably this deepened. According to Zbigniew Brzezinski, the National Security Council adviser, Callaghan became Carter's favourite allied leader: 'I was amazed how quickly Callaghan succeeded in establishing himself as Carter's favourite, writing him friendly little notes, calling, talking like a genial older uncle, and lecturing Carter in a pleasant manner on the intricacies of inter-allied politics. Callaghan literally co-opted Carter in the course of a few relatively brief personal encounters.'[13]

Policies

From London's perspective the policies pursued in the fifteen years between Macmillan and Thatcher reflected changing assessments of Britain's role in the world. After the end of the Second World War, Churchill had seen Britain as having three options: pursuing the special relationship with the United States; becoming part of Europe; or developing the Commonwealth connection. Churchill had viewed these three circles as being overlapping and not mutually exclusive. Although the emphasis during the years 1964–79 was on Europe, and limiting Britain's responsibilities signalled by the withdrawal from East of Suez, the pursuit was not single-minded. An examination of British defence policy during this period illustrates this, and the continued importance of the Anglo-American relationship.

Initially Wilson's first Labour government seemed determined to pursue a policy of worldwide influence, to maintain the nuclear deterrent, and to continue a British presence East of Suez. Faced immediately with economic crises, Denis Healey, the Secretary of State for Defence, initiated defence reviews which led to the cancellation of the British aircraft projects, including the TSR2, and of the CVA 01 fleet carrier for the navy, and a British withdrawal East of Suez, to be completed by the mid-1970s, plans for which were accepted by the Cabinet in April 1967. Lord Carrington, as Conservative Secretary of State for Defence in the administration of Edward Heath, extended the life of the carrier fleet, but Britain did not sustain a presence East of Suez.

It was during the premiership of James Callaghan that a report by Professor Ronald Mason, the Chief Scientific Adviser in the Ministry of Defence, and Sir Anthony Duff, Deputy Under-Secretary in the Foreign Office, recommended that Polaris should be replaced with Trident submarines and C4 missiles. In January 1979, on the island of Guadeloupe, Callaghan met Carter, the French Premier Valéry Giscard d'Estaing, and Chancellor Helmut Schmidt of West Germany, to discuss Bonn's concern over the SALT (Strategic Arms Limitation Talks) negotiations and the Soviet deployment of intermediate-range SS-20 missiles, which were targeted on Western Europe from a long way inside the Soviet Union. From this meeting evolved the NATO 'twin track' response to the SS-20 missiles. First, American cruise missiles would be deployed in Western Europe. Secondly, there would be negotiations with Moscow to eliminate all intermediate-range missiles. But, from London's point of view, most important of all, Carter also indicated that he was prepared to offer Britain Trident. The Anglo-American special relationship, despite surface ruffles, still ran deep.[14]

Initially these ruffles were most evident in the differing approach to the war in Vietnam. Against the background of domestic discontent with the United States's Vietnam policy at the time of sixties youth culture and flower power, and pressure from the left wing of the Labour party, Wilson not only refused Johnson the comfort of the commitment of British troops, a commitment the Australians were prepared to make, but took it upon himself to act as a mediator. One of these proposed initiatives of June 1965 using Commonwealth leaders showed Wilson's presidential style of government: not only was it kept from Johnson but his Foreign Secretary, Michael Stewart, did not know of it. Wilson used personal emissaries, and had visions in February 1967 of Britain and the Soviet Union reactivating their roles as co-chairmen of the Geneva Conference on Indo-China. Misunderstandings between Wilson and Johnson were not helped by the lack of warmth in their personal relationship. Johnson and many American officials felt that Britain's refusal to commit even a token force of the Black Watch to the war in Vietnam negated its right to exercise any influence.[15]

Even at this time Washington appreciated the skills of British diplomats, particularly in that area of the world where Britain had exercised suzerainty for almost half a century. At a time of waning enthusiasm for Israel's occupation of Arab lands in the aftermath of the June 1967 (Six Day) War, the United Nations Security Council, on 22 November 1967, passed Resolution 242. This was a triumph for British diplomacy. In the early stages of discussion Britain refrained from supporting an American draft which the Arabs considered too favourable to Israel. George Brown, the British Foreign Secretary, however, did assure Abba Eban, the Israeli representative, that Britain would only advocate Israeli withdrawal if agreed boundaries were secured to establish a permanent peace. Britain devised a resolution the wording of which was ambiguous enough to provide the necessary loopholes for both sides. Resolution 242, which provided for a 'just and lasting peace' within 'secure and recognized boundaries', for Israel to withdraw 'from territories occupied in the recent conflict' and for there to be an acknowledgement of all states' 'sovereignty, territorial integrity and political independence', formed the basis of the subsequent peace process in the Middle East.[16]

But in Washington's eyes British diplomatic skills did little to compensate for the British decision to withdraw from East of Suez. As late as June 1967, Johnson criticised Britain's envisaged withdrawal from the Far East. In that region there had been a certain division of responsibility, with Britain handling confrontation in Malaysia. At a time when Johnson wanted at least a token British force committed to Vietnam, Britain reversed the East of Suez strategy outlined in the Defence Review of February 1966, in which it was stated that Britain would maintain a major military capability outside Europe. The Supplementary Statement on Defence Policy of July 1967 revised commitments and deployment plans in the light of a British policy to encourage indigenous developments so as to enable the withdrawal of British forces from the Far East and the Middle East. Following the devaluation of sterling in November 1967, by the end of that year ten thousand British servicemen and women had returned from the Far East with the conclusion of the 'Confrontation' campaign in Borneo. Britain evacuated Aden on 29 November 1967 and the People's Democratic Republic of Yemen was established. On 16 January 1968 Wilson told the House of Commons that British forces would be withdrawn from the Far East and the Persian Gulf by the end of 1971. The British emphasis was to be on Europe. On 25 January 1968 Healey explained to the House of Commons that with the withdrawal from East of Suez Britain would have more forces in Europe.[17]

During Nixon's presidency the United States hoped for a greater European role in world affairs to ease Washington's international burdens. Kissinger was suspicious of a closed trading system led by members of the European Community, which could exclude the United States. This led to Kissinger's appeal on 23 April 1973 for that year to be called the Year of Europe. With Britain a member of the European Community, Heath refused to be separated from his European partners, and in a letter of July 1973 insisted on a collective European response to Washington: Britain would no longer be involved in bilateral exchanges with the United States. Nixon's reply was unusually cool. The European response countered the American economic arguments and pointed also to the considerable share of defence undertaken by the European nations, particularly towards NATO.[18]

Heath dreamed, in the words of his biographer, of accomplishing 'the irreversible transformation of Britain's foreign policy'. For Heath, membership of a united Europe held out the prospect of Britain in partnership recovering the leading role in world affairs that it could no longer play on its own. Heath increasingly saw American and European interests diverging, and resented what seemed to him an American belief that, so far as Britain was concerned, the American interest should prevail. Heath inclined to the view that if the Americans offered consultation it was only in a cursory fashion. Publicly, in a Guildhall speech in November 1973, Heath proclaimed his vision of a multipolar world: Washington and Moscow had to realise that Peking and Tokyo, Cairo and Tel Aviv, as well as Western Europe, were 'vitally important too'.

With the outbreak of war between the Arab states and Israel on 9 October 1973 Heath clearly aligned Britain with its European partners in avoiding any antagonism of the Arabs. Earlier Heath had moved Britain away from its apparent policy of alignment with Israel, one that had been pursued by a Labour government headed by a Zionist Prime Minister, and had sent Home to ride a camel in Egypt. The Conservative government in November 1970 urged Golda Meir, Israel's Prime Minister, to relinquish the conquered territories.

On 10 October 1973 Washington indicated its annoyance at the British refusal to supply spare parts for Israeli Centurion tanks. Heath, on 17 October, refused American planes facilities in Cyprus for airlifting arms supplies to Israel. Then on 24 October, Washington as a warning to Moscow, placed its army, naval and air forces on a nuclear alert. Britain was the only ally that was informed of this move, and it was not consulted: Kissinger telephoned the British ambassador. Kissinger viewed this as a classic instance of how the special relationship operated: 'We shared our information as a matter of course, despite the fact that the Heath Government was doing its utmost to distance itself from us in Europe and had rather conspicuously underlined its different perspective in the Middle East.' London, however, felt that it had not been given the same amount of consultation as it had experienced during the Cuban missile crisis: Home had been present on both occasions. The Foreign Secretary did, however, secure confirmation from the Soviets that they had no intention of interfering in the war between Egypt and Israel and restrained Britain's European partners from placing Washington on public trial for mounting a nuclear alert on European soil without adequate consultation. Home, unlike Heath, believed in the special relationship and took it upon himself to lecture Kissinger on the need for London to be taken more systematically into Washington's confidence: the Foreign Secretary hoped for the restoration of the old intimacy. Washington, after all, had not apprised Britain of its initiative in ping-pong diplomacy, and the moves towards recognising Communist China.[19]

Callaghan's Foreign Secretary, David Owen, ended Heath's emphasis on Britain's role in the world being that of a member of a European partnership. Owen restored the concept of trying to solve issues by mounting joint Anglo-American ventures. On the Rhodesian issue, where the rebel Prime Minister, Mr Ian Smith, had outlasted his British equivalent at the time of the Unilateral Declaration of Independence, Owen was assisted by Carter and his Secretary of State, Cyrus Vance, but hindered by the American Ambassador to the United Nations, Andrew Young, who some came to think had the priority of representing Black Africa rather than his own country. The Americans seemed to view the Rhodesian problem as one of black civil rights. In the end British proposals were scuppered by an American insistence that the new national army would be based on the 'liberation forces', rather than a combination of all the forces.[20]

In the Middle East, however, the Americans acted on their own. Britain's role was restricted to providing a neutral venue at Leeds Castle in Kent for the talks between Vance and his Egyptian and Israeli counterparts on 18–20 July 1978. Britain was not involved in the negotiations that led to the Camp David accords, and Callaghan refused to accede to Carter's request to undertake, in an emergency, to sell crude oil from the North Sea to the Israelis.

Callaghan did, however, respond to Washington's request for a Big-Four Western summit, which met in the sunshine of the French island of Guadeloupe in the West Indies to consider measures to counter the threat of the Soviet Union's intermediate-range SS-20 missiles. Here Callaghan secured Carter's offer of a new generation of nuclear weapons for Britain, but pictures of him sitting in the sun while Britain endured the 'winter of discontent' and rubbish lay in the streets and bodies were not buried, and his somewhat cavalier treatment of the situation on his return, did not help his election prospects. The electorate chose Britain's first woman Prime Minister.[21]

When he assumed the presidency, Eisenhower had demoted Britain to being just one among a number of allies. After the Suez crisis he revived the special relationship. Heath, when he was Prime Minister, explained to the Americans that Britain had to be part of a collective European response to the Americans: the Anglo-American bilateral relationship was at an end. The realities of politics made Eisenhower conscious of the value of an Anglo-American management of world affairs. From the British perspective, Callaghan tried to mount a similar offensive when he succeeded Heath as Prime Minister. The Labour politician immediately instructed that preference was to be given to the American connection even at a time of difficult negotiations over Britain's accession to Europe. There was a return to an Anglo-American diplomacy in an attempt to secure a settlement of the Rhodesian question. Even before the romance of Margaret Thatcher and Ronald Reagan there was evidence of the deep current of the Anglo-American relationship, with Carter's willingness to provide Britain with a new generation of nuclear weapons. In the end even the 'lean years' defied the detractors of the special relationship and declarations that it was dead. It survived the attempt by Heath to remould British policy in a European framework.

9

THE ATLANTIC PREFERENCE

On 30 June 1997, the eve of the transfer of Hong Kong to Chinese sovereignty, Margaret Thatcher, referring to the decision of the American Secretary of State, Madeleine Albright, to boycott the Chinese ceremony along with her British counterpart, spoke of Britain and the United States always being there for one another. The BBC interviewer recalled still having on her mantelshelf a gold-embossed invitation from the then British Prime Minister to an 'at home' in the Great Hall of the People in Peking, and observed that, of course, Mrs Thatcher had been at home there then.

Margaret Thatcher and Ronald Reagan

During her premiership Mrs Thatcher transformed the image of Britain from being that of the parasitic sick man of Europe to one of an industrious, thriving, patriotic nation, with a seat at the Great Table of world politics, a seat which she personally had earned at the very least through her role in ending the Cold War. From Pretoria to Peking, regimes across the world have followed her belief in the free enterprise economy, if not in the primacy of the individual. Renowned for her abolition of society, and for her conviction that there are only individual men and women and families, Margaret Thatcher, at the end of the twentieth century, probably represents the triumph of John Stuart Mill's nineteenth-Century philosophy of economic and personal liberalism over totalitarianism, socialism and Marxist-Leninism. Regimes which formerly espoused these latter doctrines have become converts to what is widely described as 'Thatcherism'. That Thatcher phenomenon was possible because of her handling of the trans-Atlantic relationship, and of an American President for whom she felt a real warmth and empathy, and her cultivation of the Anglo-American special relationship, after an initial flirtation with Europe had been rebuffed, based on the perception that whatever the surface disagreements might be, the current between Britain and the United States flowed deep, and in the end, the two countries were always there for one another.

Mrs Thatcher was President Ronald Reagan's last guest at a State Banquet in Washington on 16 November 1988. She referred to Reagan's presidency as 'one of the greatest in America's history', and said that she and her great friend had enjoyed the same political dreams and the same way of achieving them. In response President Reagan paid tribute to the Prime Minister's part in achieving an 'extraordinary change' in international relations: 'Yours was the part of courage and resolve and vision. Something sure has happened. We have transformed this decade into a turning point of our age – and for all time.'[1]

Never defeated at the polls, discarded by men in the Conservative Party on the pretext of hostility to the European connection, Mrs Thatcher enjoyed an international reputation and admiration which was not always shared by those at home. Despised by the 'chattering classes', which saw her as a social inferior who had transformed the Conservative party into a working-class party – though that working class was effectively becoming a house-owning middle class with the purchase of its council houses – she was derided by champagne socialists and the intellectual press led by the newly founded broadsheet *The Independent*; in academic circles Mrs Thatcher's reputation has been marred by what was seen as a personal attack by her on the British university system by restricting funding after a vote by the congregation of her old university, Oxford, refused the Prime Minister an honorary doctorate. These sections of British society were also inclined to regard President Reagan as something of a joke. But, on the surface at any rate, the workings of the Anglo-American alliance at this time helped to transform the international system with the ending of the Cold War and the worldwide acceptance of free-enterprise economics.

Mrs Thatcher's approach to world affairs coincided closely with that of the post-1945 Labour Foreign Secretary Ernest Bevin. Bevin opted for the Anglo-American special relationship over a European con- nection or the cultivation of the newly emerging Commonwealth (as distinct from the old 'White' Dominions). Bevin, as he observed on

23 August 1950, thought that the British people were doubtful of
Europe: 'How could he go down to his constituency – Woolwich –
which had been bombed by Germans in the war, and tell his con-
stituents that the Germans would help them in a war against Russia? . . .
Similarly in regard to France, the man in the street, coming back from
a holiday there, was almost invariably struck by the defeatist attitude
of the French.'[2] David Reynolds has observed that Mrs Thatcher's
'suspicion of foreigners was intense and her contempt for the French and
Germans in particular was a matter of common gossip in Whitehall and
Westminster'. Reynolds considers Mrs Thatcher's outlook as one
common to her generation, those who had come of age in the 1940s, and
who remained deeply affected by the memories of the Second World
War and the Cold War: 'This left her hostile to Russia, enthusiastic
about America, sceptical about the continentals and convinced of the
need for a strong defence.'[3] Mrs Thatcher's Cabinet colleagues have
speculated that her deep distrust of the Germans was a gut reaction,
possibly absorbed from the outlook of her husband Denis, who had
served as a major in the Royal Artillery during the Second World War.[4]

Sometimes viewed as prejudiced and dogmatic, Mrs Thatcher, like
Bevin before her, was in reality pragmatic and open to persuasion. At the
start of her record period in office she allowed herself to be convinced by
Lord Carrington and his Foreign Office that Ian Smith's White minority
government in Rhodesia should be forsaken and support given to the
guerrillas (terrorists in many Conservatives' eyes) of the Patriotic Front.
Rhodesia became independent Zimbabwe in April 1980.[5] Similarly,
despite the attempt of the Irish Republican Army to blow her up in
Brighton in October 1984, Mrs Thatcher allowed herself to be persuaded, against her convictions and instincts, to sign the Hillsborough
Agreement with the Republic of Ireland in November 1985, which
eroded British sovereignty and allowed Dublin a say in the affairs of
Ulster, a territory which she personally regarded as an integral part of the
United Kingdom.[6] Similarly she was swayed to give in to China and to
sign an agreement with Peking in December 1984 that Hong Kong would
be returned to China in 1997, and for fifty years after that enjoy the status
of a Special Administrative Region: the 'one nation, two systems' concept.[7]

The Special Relationship with the United States

It was probably Mrs Thatcher's pragmatism which, after an early
thwarted flirtation with Heath's idea that Britain could play a world role

as part of Europe, led her to the calculated conclusion, identical with that of William Strang's Permanent Under-Secretary's Committee in 1949, that the corner-stone of Britain's foreign policy was the special relationship with the United States. Early on she realised that a friendship as well as a working relationship with the American President Ronald Reagan, based on a similar perception of the world's political and economic order, would enable her to sit at the world tables. To say that this was all shrewd calculation, however, is to deny the real warmth Mrs Thatcher felt for someone she regarded as a really nice man.

The two first met in London in April 1975 and established a rapport. Much of this was based on a common hatred of Communism and a suspicion of the Soviet system, dubbed the 'Evil Empire' by Reagan in an address to the National Association of Evangelicals in March 1983. But Mrs Thatcher was harder on the Russians than even Reagan: in January 1976 she warned the West that the Kremlin was after world domination and wanted to consign the democracies to 'the scrap heap of history'. The Soviet army newspaper, *Red Star*, called her the 'Iron Lady'. On her first visit to see Reagan, between 25 and 28 February 1981, Mrs Thatcher assured the President that 'we in Britain stand with you. . . . Your problems will be our problems and when you look for friends we will be there.'[8]

A one-time columnist on *The Times*, Geoffrey Smith, has suggested that both Reagan and Mrs Thatcher were elected to lead countries 'whose self-confidence had been severely damaged and which wanted above all to walk tall in the world again'. He describes Reaganism and Thatcherism as a state of mind, a determination to change all this: though both believed in less government, they believed just as passionately in strong government.[9]

The Defence and Intelligence Relationship

It has been observed that in official circles the Anglo-American special relationship has consistently been taken to mean a defence (particularly in the nuclear field) and intelligence relationship. Mrs Thatcher demonstrated an ability to utilise this. Initially capitalising on Carter's indication at the Guadeloupe meeting with Callaghan that as part of the response to the deployment by the Soviet Union of intermediate-range SS-20 missiles targeted on Western Europe, the United States was prepared to offer Britain Trident C4 missiles to replace Polaris, she signed an agreement on 14 July 1980 under which Britain would only have to pay for 5 per cent of the research and development costs. Early in Reagan's presidency the Americans decided to replace Trident C4 with the much more expensive Trident D5. Caspar Weinberger, the Secretary of State for Defence who was later given an honorary knighthood for his assistance to Britain during the Falklands War, arranged for Britain to obtain the D5 system on bargain basement terms. This implied the indefinite and unquestioned continuance of the Anglo-American nuclear partnership, something that the United States would not share with any other ally. In formalising the arrangement Reagan wrote to Mrs Thatcher on 11 March 1982 about the importance Washington attached to the maintenance by London of an independent nuclear deterrent.[10]

Co-operation between London and Washington in the intelligence field continued, and at this time revelations about leaks in the American services helped an understanding of British difficulties over traitors. There was a special relationship between Britain's Government Communications Headquarters, based at Cheltenham in Gloucestershire, and the American National Security Agency with its headquarters outside Washington. At this time too, London revealed the extent to which its Special Forces had helped the Americans during the Vietnam War. Mrs Thatcher publicly endorsed the arrival of American Cruise missiles on British soil. The first arrived at Greenham Common in 1983 and sparked off years of protest by women's groups outside the base.[11]

Rhetoric and Reality

Some authorities have commented on the difference between the rhetoric and the reality of Mrs Thatcher's support of Washington's position internationally. Although she supported Carter's condemnation of the Soviet invasion of Afghanistan, Britain ignored the American plea to boycott the 1980 Olympics in Moscow.[12] There were also divisions over the Middle East, with the British participation in the European Economic Community Venice Declaration of 1980, which envisaged a greater role for the Palestine Liberation Organisation in Arab-Israeli peace negotiations. Britain had not been consulted about the Camp David accords and seemed reluctant to be involved in any implementation of them. Lord Carrington, as Foreign Secretary, was suspicious of an American policy that seemed dictated by domestic pressure mounted by the American-Israel Public Affairs Committee. The American Secretary of State, Alexander Haig, considered the British policy as pro-Arab. Britain did, however, pursue a policy similar to that of the United States over the Iran-Iraq war.[13]

There was a matching difference between the rhetoric and the reality of the United States's support for Britain. In 1982, when Argentina took over the Falkland Islands by force, as in the late 1930s, it was left again to Britain to uphold a tenuous international system based on the principal that territory could not be seized by force. But this time Britain enjoyed the active support of the United States. At the outset of the crisis, on the surface, the American role was that of neutral mediator: Haig indulged in shuttle diplomacy. Jeane Kirkpatrick, the American Ambassador to the United Nations, publicly endorsed a policy that right-wing regimes could help Washington in its fight against Communism and that the dictatorship of General Leopoldo Galtieri of Argentina should be supported on that basis: if Washington helped London to reclaim the Falkland Islands an ally within the sphere of the Monroe Doctrine could be alienated, as well as Washington's other allies within Latin America.

The American Secretary of Defence, Caspar Weinberger, responded immediately, however, to the request from the British Ministry of Defence in London for particular requirements for the British task force sailing towards the South Atlantic. If a British request were not met within twenty-four hours Weinberger wanted to know why. American Sidewinder air-to-air missiles, Shrike anti-radar missiles, mortar and other hardware were sent. Weinberger was even prepared to supply an American warship to replace possible British losses. He allowed the British to use the American facilities on Ascension Island. Much of Weinberger's support became public knowledge after 29 April 1982 with the passing of a resolution by the Senate aimed at achieving the full withdrawal of Argentinian forces from the Falkland Islands. American intelligence provided London with information as to Argentinian military movements. The procedures for all this were already in place, but, as Dickie has commented: 'Some of the most crucial assistance came clandestinely on the Old Pals network between senior members of the Intelligence Services.' John Lehman, the American Secretary of the Navy, later described what he saw as being the almost automatic support for Britain. The leader of the task force, Admiral Sandy Woodward, in his assessment of the campaign, stated that the outcome would have been different but for the decisiveness of the Sidewinder missile and the use of Ascension Island.[14]

While some analysts emphasise the importance of the operation of the bureaucratic structures-officials on both sides of the Atlantic who liked and understood one another-and the workings of a long standing association when the special relationship came into action during the Falklands War, others have pointed to the importance of the personal connection of those who managed the alliance. Geoffrey Smith points to Reagan's role:

> despite recurring evidence that he never really quite understood why the islands mattered so much to Britain, despite many indications that he certainly did not appreciate the details of the dispute, Reagan never let Thatcher down over the Falklands. . . . Reagan knew how much the issue meant to Thatcher. He realised that her position was hanging in the balance and he delivered.

The British Prime Minister did not consult the President every night over the telephone. Reagan observed that this was not necessary 'because the understanding was there. She knew where we stood with each other.' Records of the telephone calls show a determined Prime Minister, one not prepared to give way to Presidential suggestions of avoiding humiliating the Argentinians. On 31 May 1982, with British troops ready to take Port Stanley, she snapped at her friend Ron: 'I'm not handing over the island now, I didn't lose some of my best ships and some of my finest lives to leave quietly under a ceasefire without the Argentines withdrawing.' Any Presidential argument was cut short until Reagan relented: 'Well, Margaret, I know that I've intruded and I know how . . .'. Afterwards Reagan is believed to have said with admiration: 'That's one hell of a tough lady.'[15]

There is general agreement that the British victory in the Falklands War, against tremendous odds, revealed a deep patriotism within the British people, restored Britain's international prestige, and helped to secure Mrs Thatcher's domestic position and subsequent victories in general elections. It confounded those who had seen Suez as the last imperial war, which had relegated Britain to minor power status, after which the British people had been prepared to turn inwards and leave the upholding of the international system to others. To some extent conscious of what had happened in 1956, in 1982 the United States backed Britain, in the words of President Ronald Reagan, 'its closest ally'.

There were, however, difficulties in the fields of foreign and economic affairs during the Thatcher–Reagan era. Washington was worried by European protectionism. But this was a time of enormous American economic investment in Britain and startling British investment in the United States with famous American names suddenly falling under British ownership. Americans seemed not to resent this in the same way as they had resented the Japanese take-over.[16] When martial law was imposed in Poland in 1981 and the United States imposed sanctions in June 1982 which endangered the Siberian gas pipeline and the economic viability of British firms involved in this venture, faced by the danger of American legal action, Mrs Thatcher threatened to use British legislation to force those firms to honour their contracts. She also publicly criticised the American invasion of the Commonwealth island of Grenada in 1983, to replace a Marxist dictator, and Washington's failure to consult London on this. But in April 1986 she allowed the use of bases in Britain for the American bombing raids on Libya in retaliation for apparent terrorist activities. Although Mrs Thatcher had private doubts about the acceptability of this action and had earlier, in January 1986, condemned 'retaliatory strikes that are against international law', she never betrayed these feelings in public. This loyalty to Reagan and the Atlantic alliance greatly enhanced her reputation in the United States. Similarly the Prime Minister appears to have had hesitations about the sense of Reagan's 'Strategic Defense Initiative' (SDI), a series of space stations and laser beams to protect the United States against nuclear weapons. She publicly supported the President while in private lecturing him, in her role as a chemist, on the implausibility of the project, and at the same time attempting to secure contracts for British industry.[17]

The End of the Cold War

It was the respect with which Mrs Thatcher was held in Washington that meant that credence was given to her insistence in the middle of December 1984, after a meeting at Chequers, that she liked Makhail Gorbachev, seen as the heir to the Kremlin, and felt that 'We can do business together.' Mrs Thatcher encouraged dialogue between Reagan and the new Soviet leader. She inaugurated a new approach to international relations by the principal adversaries in what had been described as the 'Cold War'.[18]

Reagan almost went too far. At the Reykjavik summit meeting with Gorbachev in October 1986 the President nearly accepted the proposal to abolish all nuclear weapons, with obvious ramifications for the British independent deterrent. Mrs Thatcher left immediately for Washington to extract assurances from Reagan that nuclear weapons were still important, and that he would not include British and French nuclear arsenals with the American.

In the events leading to the end of the Cold War, and the tearing down of the Berlin Wall and the dissolution of the Soviet Union, both Gorbachev and Reagan sounded Mrs Thatcher as to how to approach one another. In March 1987, equipped with a wardrobe from Aquascutum, Mrs Thatcher went to Moscow. Geoffrey Smith has observed: 'The respect that she was given established beyond doubt her distinctive role as an interlocutor in the developing East–West dialogue. She was confirmed as a star on the world stage.' George P. Shultz, the American Secretary of State, went to Moscow shortly afterwards, capitalised on Mrs Thatcher's earlier conversations with Gorbachev on arms reductions, and in the end the Prime Minister benefited in electoral terms from a dramatic disarmament agreement.[19] In 1990 the 'Iron Lady' announced that the Cold War was over. By then she was an object of adulation in Russia.

The Preference for the American Connection

Mrs Thatcher had a preference for the American connection: whenever there was a choice 'her heart lay across the Atlantic rather than across the Channel'. In 1986 she preferred that Westland helicopters be rescued by an American company rather than by the European consortium favoured by her Secretary of State for Defence, Michael Heseltine. She continued to support Reagan during the 'Irangate' crisis, despite indications from British intelligence about suspicious circumstances. Moves towards a federal Europe horrified Mrs Thatcher and became personalised in her dislike of the European Commission's President, Jacques Delors. Speaking at Bruges in September 1988 she warned that 'we have not successfully rolled back the frontiers of the state in Britain, only to see them re-imposed at a European level with a European super-state exercising a new domination from Brussels'.[20]

The End of the Special Relationship?

Contemporary observers have noted that the end of the Cold War meant that the defence alliance between Britain and the United States, often seen by Washington as the foundation stone of the special relationship, was not needed any longer. In this new era of optimism there was a new American President, George Bush. Mrs Thatcher was no longer needed as an intermediary between Washington and London. Bush was alienated by her hesitations over German reunification, and changes in the State Department by George Baker, the new Secretary of State, indicated that Washington might favour a special relationship with the European Community as a whole and West Germany in particular. Some resented the extent to which Mrs Thatcher had apparently made American foreign policy, and the way a telephone call from her could lead to Reagan discarding State Department recommendations. In the nuclear discussions with the Russians a 'gulf' opened up between London and Washington: Mrs Thatcher was hesitant over envisaged reductions but, apart from by the Dutch, was not supported by her fellow NATO allies. Baker wanted a united Germany within NATO; Mrs Thatcher feared German aggrandisement. When her Trade and Industry Secretary Nicholas Ridley was forced to resign over an article of 14 July 1990 in which he had observed that monetary union was 'a German racket, designed to take over the whole of Europe', that the French were behaving as Germany's 'poodles', and that as for handing over sovereignty to the European Community, 'you might as well give it to Adolf Hitler', Mrs Thatcher observed: 'Naturally, some people, particularly those who lived through the last war, feel a number of apprehensions and there's nothing unusual about that.' But, pragmatic as always, in October 1990, Mrs Thatcher accepted full British membership of the European Monetary System.[21]

It was not the completion of the agreement on German reunification that ended Washington's aloofness from London, but Mrs Thatcher's enthusiastic endorsement of Bush's stand against Iraq when it invaded Kuwait in August 1990. There was not only her public statement at Aspen Colorado, but also the co-operation of the Anglo-American team which secured the Security Council resolution demanding that Iraq withdraw its troops from Kuwait. Thatcher's unswerving support for the American position again, as Dickie has commented, 'put the British Government in a totally different relationship from that of any other partner of the United States during the Gulf crisis'. It was not just rhetoric: Britain made a huge military commitment.[22]

Mrs Thatcher, however, was discarded by her party. It was the European dimension that led to her demise: in October 1990 she denounced a European Community timetable for monetary union and called sterling 'the most powerful expression of sovereignty you can have'. When she was challenged for the leadership by Michael Heseltine, two leadership ballots led to her resignation and the choice of John Major as her successor.

Margaret Thatcher's view of the Anglo-American alliance was probably encapsulated in her statement at a dinner in Washington in 1985 to celebrate two hundred years of diplomatic relations between Britain and the United States: 'There is a union of mind and purpose between our peoples which is remarkable and which makes our relationship truly a remarkable one. It is special. It just is, and that's that.'

John Dickie has advanced the argument that during the tenure of John Major at Number 10, Anglo-American relations became '"Special" No More': it was the end of the affair. Initially a partnership was evident with the mounting of Operation Desert Storm to liberate Kuwait. But the decision to end the war was one taken by the American President acting on the advice of his military and political staffs, and not one jointly decided by Washington and London. Britain was informed but not consulted. After this, Dickie argues: 'When there was no longer a Communist threat requiring Britain to be the alliance standard-bearer in Europe for the Americans, the principal *raison d'être* of that relationship had gone.' Open divisions were evident between Washington and London on issues such as the Vietnamese boat people, with the Americans being opposed to any forced repatriation. Britain could be said to have been excluded by Washington from the Middle East peace negotiations, but the United States had effectively replaced Britain as the paramount power there several decades earlier. Dickie, however, argues the case that it was with the signing of the Maastricht Treaty by Britain on 10 February 1992 that Britain was committed to a European Union, and that the undertaking to work towards a common foreign policy 'ruled out any prolongation of the Special Relationship on foreign policy co-ordination'.[23]

Born in 1943, Major did not share Mrs Thatcher's generation's view of Europeans, Americans and the Cold War. Bill Clinton, elected President in November 1992, had been born after the end of the Second

World War. Though of the same generation, his relationship with Major was not helped by what was perceived as Conservative Party support for the Republicans during the campaign, though to some extent this was negated by the tactics of the British ambassador in Washington, Sir Robin Renwick, who arranged for one of his First Secretaries to follow the Democrat campaign. Clinton concentrated on American economic problems: Britain was part of a European Community which seemed to threaten American economic interests. Clinton appeared to challenge Britain's formal position as a Great Power, with the American proposal in June 1993 to increase the Permanent Members of the Security Council from five to seven with the addition of Germany and Japan. Washington did not consult London about the 'Gaza-Jericho First' agreement between Israel and the Palestine Liberation Organisation in September 1993, an oil embargo against Libya, and there were major trans-Atlantic differences over the handling of the situation in the former Yugoslavia, particularly evident when Clinton argued that the West had a moral duty to intervene there with force.[24]

In November 1995, however, *The Times* observed that the special relationship had been relaunched: Clinton told both Houses of Parliament that 'the United States will name one of the newest and most powerful of its surface ships, a guided missile destroyer, the *United States Ship Winston Churchill*'. This coincided with the President's insistence that the link with Britain 'stands above the rest; a model for the ties that should bind democracies' and his personal efforts to secure concessions for peace from Sinn Fein and the Ulster Unionists in Northern Ireland.[25]

After Clinton's re-election, and the arrival of the New Labour Prime Minister, Mr Tony Blair, at Number 10, Quentin Letts, *The Times's* American correspondent, recalled that with the return of the Democrats to the White House in 1992 Washington had given up most pretence of listening to London. Though some blamed Conservative Central Office for this, and their clumsy move in sending researchers across the Atlantic to help Bush in his presidential election campaign, there were greater reasons for the fading of the special relationship. Washington's future focus, Letts argues, is likely to be on China or South America rather than Europe. In the Clinton White House, relations with Britain are low on the list of priorities. The President's view of Britain was formed at Oxford in the late 1960s when he had seen 'a class-ridden nation in which people shivered in winter around electric fires and desultory cups of Bovril'.

The Times correspondent goes on to observe that with Clinton expressing his admiration for Blair, Britons might dream of a revival of the special relationship, but the bitter truth is that the American intelligentsia loathes the British. It has become socially acceptable in the United States to depict Britons 'as arrogant, dowdy and (with perhaps a little more justification) hard-drinking freeloaders'. Equivalent depictions of Jews, African-American Americans, Italians, Egyptians or Germans would result in prosecution for racism or at least public disgrace. The British invasion of the American media is resented. Hollywood has sustained the anti-British bias evident earlier in the films of the Irish-descended John Ford, and propaganda items during the Second World War like *Mission to Moscow* (directed by Michael Curtis in 1943), with a box office cinema which portrays most villains with English accents. It has provided a spate of popular films with youth idols cast as Irish Republican Army heroes. Letts insists that this attitude persists 'not only in tough-talking Manhattan but also in administrative circles, in the US judiciary, and in local government'. His message is that Eurosceptics who think that the United States offers Britain an alternative future to Europe should remember that 'America's elite has even less time for us than the Federalists of Brussels.'[26]

After the experience of the Heath years, British policy moved away from an emphasis on the European dimension to a preference for the Atlantic connection. This flowered with the friendship between Mrs Thatcher and President Reagan. Hesitations over the European association prompted the Conservative Party to eject Mrs Thatcher. New Labour became ardent converts to the European cause, while the Conservative Party tore itself apart over the issue. The Commonwealth has faded as one of the three interlocking circles which Churchill saw as the basis of British foreign policy. The choice between Europe and the United States remains. As Churchill observed earlier, they are not necessarily mutually exclusive.

10

CONCLUSIONS

The Myth of Finite History

Few, if any, today would accept the possibility of finite history. In 1961
E. H. Carr in *What is History?*, widely recognised as one of the most
important intellectual works of the post-1945 era,[1] pointed to Lord
Acton's hopes at the height of Victorian optimism that the *Cambridge
Modern History* he was editing would be the opportunity to 'bring home
to every man the last document, and the ripest conclusions of
international research'. Acton anticipated that although 'ultimate
history' would not be possible in his generation, 'we can dispose of
conventional history, and show the point we have reached on the road
from one to the other, now that all information is within reach, and
every problem has become capable of solution'. Carr points to
Professor Sir George Clark's comments sixty years later on the beliefs
Acton expresses in the introduction to the second *Cambridge Modern
History*. Clark points out that historians expect their work to be
superseded again and again: 'They consider that knowledge of the past
has come down through one or more human minds, has been
"processed" by them, and therefore cannot consist of elemental and
impersonal atoms which nothing can alter.' He explains further that
faced with this, scholars have become sceptical and some have accepted
the doctrine that 'since all historical judgements involve persons and
points of view, one is as good as another and there is no "objective"
historical truth'.[2]

In 1993 R. J. B. Bosworth, in a work as challenging and important as
E. H. Carr's *What is History?*, concluded his magisterial study of history
writing and the Second World War with the observation:

If the messages of the People's war are to survive 'the end of history', historians, proudly accepting the burden of their own 'authority', must go on explaining to our societies that our task in exploring the history of the Second World War, and any other issue, is to assess the evidence, find an answer, write it down on a piece of paper, and humbly acknowledge that it is wrong.[3]

Anglo-American Relations in Perspective

Interpretations of the significance of Anglo-American relations for the makers of British foreign policy have changed over the decades. Sometimes the academic interpretations have reflected the political preoccupations of the British leaders. This was particularly evident in the late 1960s and early to mid-1970s when a generation of journalists, academic commentators and British leaders yet again buried the Anglo-American special relationship, only for it to rise again, phoenix-like, in the 1980s. The passing of the Republican administration in the United States in the early 1990s led to further death knells being sounded. The academic perspective has often followed the political fashion. At the time of the Heath government in Britain there was a great deal said about Washington wanting a special relationship with Bonn rather than London; in the 1990s speculation has had it that it would be Berlin, or perhaps, in the future, Peking or even Buenos Aires, that would matter more to Washington. Writings on Anglo-American relations have sometimes reflected the recent obsessions with systems, the rise and fall of empires, and generalisations drawn from the past to apply to the future.[4]

It is not usually the historian's prerogative to generalise from a series of unique events; historiographers, however, do succumb to the temptation to discern trends in scholarship, and often to explain these in terms of sources that have suddenly become available, or present preoccupations that have made certain events in the past seem to be of particular interest.

Crucial for writings in the field of Anglo-American relations was the decision by Harold Wilson to change the fifty-year closure rule for British documents to thirty years, so that, in January 1968, a welter of documentation suddenly became available to researchers. A new generation of young British, or British-trained, scholars, together with some North Americans who seemed to enjoy spending summers in London, discerned from the British documents a rather different story from the one that had often been written from the American documents by American scholars. Old assumptions began to be challenged. Still under the influence of writings on power politics fashionable in the 1950s, much of the initial concentration was on challenging the assumption that the United States, during the 1920s, increased its economic power in relation to that of Britain. This new literature suggested that in the 1920s Washington's emerging economic strength merely meant that the power it exercised on the international scene was 'more potential than real'. Britain's power, however, was 'real': Britain still had a relatively strong economy, overseas wealth, a stable currency, and was able to sustain its status as a Great Power.

Until the opening of the British documents in the Public Record Office, the years leading to the outbreak of the Second World War, and the war itself, were largely viewed through the vision Winston Churchill presented, particularly in his memoirs of the Second World War. Neville Chamberlain was depicted as having thrown away the last chance for preserving peace by rejecting Roosevelt's overture of January 1938. Churchill's memoirs perhaps reflect his ideal of the Anglo-American special relationship at the time that he was writing them – the period of joining the Cold War – rather than the reality of the Second World War. He was only too anxious to stress the cultural unity of the English-speaking peoples as a force for order, and his intimate relationship with Roosevelt, through which he was able to influence Allied policy. The publication of many scholarly works, and of many of the documents, however, has had little impact outside a narrow circle of historians.

The story contained in the documents shows that by October 1937 Roosevelt was aware of the dangers of the international situation and of the need to educate American public opinion. Eden wanted to involve the United States alongside Britain in joint action in the Far East, so that if war came in Europe, the United States would automatically be in-volved alongside Britain there. But Washington understood the Foreign Secretary's intentions and refused to be trapped. The secret staff con-versations between Britain and the United States in January 1938 and May 1939 were indicative of the President's intentions. He was not offended by Chamberlain's reaction to his peace overture of January 1938, and the American documents show that Roosevelt had no intention of taking a strong stand. Eden resigned over this but he was mistaken in his assumptions about American policy. Roosevelt was anxious to help Britain to fight a war by blockade, as he suggested in

September 1938 and again in August 1939. But Roosevelt was hampered by domestic crises, congress and public opinion. He said that he could only go as far as the public would allow him, though he tried to go further. Chamberlain's policy was dictated by a concern for American opinion. Britain did not have to face a war on three fronts: Chamberlain's cautious policy during the Tientsin crisis in 1939, hampered by the attitude of the United States, succeeded. And, on the eve of war, Roosevelt did indicate his willingness to apply pressure on Japan if that country became hostile.

Churchill's account of his intimate collaboration with Roosevelt led to a distortion even in the academic literature on the origins of the Cold War, a literature initially mainly American, or East-European-American, in origin which inclined to the view of American-Soviet confrontation as having been started by the Americans during the Second World War. But the documentary research has shown Roosevelt and Stalin working together and leaving Churchill in the cold throughout the wartime conferences, as well as the United States and the Soviet Union collaborating together for the postwar world to the exclusion of Britain. There was also a literature, popular at a time when American students were anxious to find an intellectual justification for refusing to fight in Vietnam, which depicted the events of these years as mainly American imperialism threatening a peaceful non-expansionist Soviet Union. As the British documents became available, a group of historians has increasingly challenged this 'Americocentric' view of the origins of the Cold War, and has seen Britain as the original Cold War warrior, one determined to educate the United States to the realities of what it perceived as the Soviet threat. But this interpretation has been resisted or ignored by many establishment American historians.

Those proponents of the devil theory of American foreign policy have consistently upbraided Truman for precipitating Chinese intervention in the Korean War. The documents have, however, revealed that it was a British initiative to change the original intention of the Korean operation from merely repelling the 'aggressor' north of the 38th parallel, to the original United Nations objective of establishing a unified and democratic Korea. When the Communist Chinese entered the war and there were reverses, the British Cabinet was told that whatever might be said in the House of Commons, Britain was just as responsible as the United States.

A great deal of the established literature assumes that when Churchill became Prime Minister and Eisenhower President the so-called old wartime special relationship was revived, and that Eden's policy during the Suez crisis endangered this. The record shows that there was no special relationship during the Suez crisis: Eisenhower demoted Britain to being merely one among a number of allies as soon as he came into office. If anything, it was his Secretary of State, John Foster Dulles, who implemented American foreign policy as if London were still the special ally. Recently released documents show that Dulles was offered Britain's military plans by Eden, that Macmillan understood the significance of waiting until after the American presidential election before mounting the invasion of the Suez canal but did not make this clear to the British Cabinet, that Eisenhower was not particularly upset by the Anglo-French invasion until the election results started coming through and it was clear that his party had lost in both houses of Congress, and that Macmillan's allegations of the heavy selling of sterling in New York that led to the British withdrawal from the Suez Canal have no foundation. Eisenhower later regretted his Suez policy, and his overall Middle East policy, which supported Saudi Arabia rather than the British choice of Iraq. The President acknowledged that Britain had been right. He revived the special relationship. Britain, in any case, even before the Suez crisis, against the background of a new limited defence policy and an emphasis on domestic expenditure, had decided to limit its role in the world and hoped that the United States would assume some of its responsibilities in the Middle East.

The documents could be said to show the mounting of an Anglo-American operation in Lebanon and Jordan in 1958, Washington's willingness to assist Britain during the Kuwait crisis of 1961, and the intimacy between Macmillan and Kennedy during the Cuban missile crisis. But some historians have read them in a different way, and imply that even during the era of Anglo-American mutual interdependence, the special relationship was a shadow and not a reality.[5] But that is the nature of historical debate. The thirty-year rule, and the delayed publication of the American documents, restricts the exercise of setting accepted assumptions against the historical record for the later period.

But it is still possible to examine the validity of the recommendations of William Strang's Permanent Under-Secretary's Committee, which in 1949 outlined the basis of British foreign policy, and pointed out that Britain had no option other than to rely on the United States. The Commonwealth and the nations of Western Europe between them were not strong enough to deter the Soviet Union. There were risks inherent in this policy: in the United States hyphenate pressure groups could dictate a policy inimical to the United States and its allies. There was a pragmatic calculation as to how Britain could best utilise the special relationship in its own interests. It was this calculation which formed the basis of Britain's Cold War foreign policy. Margaret Thatcher, for instance, mounted a foreign policy centred on the special relationship, but based ultimately on what she saw as Britain's best interests. There is little evidence of sentimentality in the attitude of British policymakers in their understanding and operation of the relationship with the United States. Apart from the era of Wilson and Heath, British leaders have consistently tried to capitalise on what they have commonly described as the special relationship.

Looking back, Margaret Thatcher has observed:

The North Atlantic Alliance, the I[nterntional] M[onetary] F[und], the World Bank, splitting the atom, victory in two World Wars and in Korea and the Gulf, the defeat of fascism and of communism and the triumph of freedom – these are the fruits of the Anglo-American alliance through this century. This is the story of that remarkable achievement and the enduring friendship between two great peoples.[6]

NOTES

1 Rapprochement

1. S. E. Morison, H. S. Commager and W. E. Leuchtenburg, *A Concise History of the American Republic* (New York, 1977), pp. 83–97; H. G. Nicholas, *The United States and Britain* (Chicago, IL, 1975), pp. 8–10.
2. B. Perkins, *The First Rapprochement: England and the United States, 1795–1805* (Berkeley, CA, 1967).
3. Nicholas, op. cit., pp. 14–20.
4. H. Jones, *To the Webster–Ashburton Treaty: A Study in Anglo-American Relations, 1783–1843* (Chapel Hill, NC, 1977); W. D. Jones, *The American Problem in British Diplomacy, 1841–1861* (London, 1974), pp. 29–54, 209.
5. W. D. Jones, op. cit., p. 185.
6. M. Crawford, *The Anglo-American Crisis of the Mid-Nineteenth Century: 'The Times' and America, 1850–1862* (Athens, GA, 1987), p. 11.
7. Nicholas, op. cit., pp. 33–51; S. F. Bemis, *A Diplomatic History of the United States* (New York, 1936), p. 381; A. P. Dobson, *Anglo-American Relations in the Twentieth Century: Of Friendship, Conflict and the Rise and Decline of Superpowers* (London, 1995), p. 11.
8. H. C. Allen, *Great Britain and the United States* (New York, 1955), p. 614.
9. J. B. Brebner, *The North Atlantic Triangle* (New Haven, CT, 1945), p. 251; quoted by B. M. Russett, *Community and Contention: Britain and America in the Twentieth Century* (Cambridge, MA., 1963), p. 5.
10. A. C. Turner, *The Unique Partnership: Britain and the United States* (New York, 1971), pp. 50–2.
11. Classic accounts of this period include: L. M. Gelber, *The Rise of Anglo-American Friendship: A Study in World Politics, 1891–1906* (London, 1938); B. Perkins, *The Great Rapprochement: England and the United States, 1895–1914* (New York, 1968). For an analysis of the Anglo-Japanese Alliance see I. H. Nish, *The Anglo-Japanese Alliance: The Diplomacy of Two Island Empires, 1894–1907*, 2nd edn (London, 1985).
12. C. Bell, *The Debatable Alliance: An Essay in Anglo-American Relations* (London, 1964), pp. 11, 14.
13. M. Beloff, 'The Special Relationship: An Anglo-American Myth', in M. Gilbert (ed.), *A Century of Conflict, 1850–1950: Essays for A. J. P. Taylor* (London, 1966), pp. 148–71 at p. 154.
14. R. G. Neale, *Britain and American Imperialism, 1898–1900* (St Lucia, Brisbane, 1965), p. 174.
15. S. Anderson, *Race and Rapprochement: Anglo-Saxonism and Anglo-American Relations, 1895–1904* (London, 1981).

16. Turner, op. cit., p. 55.
17. A. Orde, *The Eclipse of Great Britain: The United States and British Imperial Decline, 1895–1956* (London, 1996), pp. 34–5.
18. Turner, op. cit., pp. 56–7; Dobson, op. cit., p. 28.
19. Russett, op. cit., pp. 7–8.
20. Orde, op. cit., pp. 41–2.
21. Nicholas, op. cit., p. 62.
22. E. May, *The World War and American Isolation, 1914–1917* (Cambridge, MA,1959); A. Link, *Wilson*, 5 vols (Princeton, NJ, 1947–65); R. Gregory, *The Origins of American Intervention in the First World War* (New York, 1971); P. Devlin, *Too Proud to Fight* (New York, 1975).
23. J. W. Coogan, *The End of Neutrality: The United States, Britain, and Maritime Rights, 1899–1915* (Ithaca, NY, 1981), pp. 14–16.
24. Morison *et al.*, op. cit., pp. 541–9.
25. D. R. Woodward, *Trial by Friendship: Anglo-American Relations, 1917–1918* (Lexington, 1993).
26. Nicholas, op. cit., pp. 68–73; S. P. Tillman, *Anglo-American Relations at the Paris Peace Conference of 1919* (Princeton, NJ, 1961), esp. pp. 401–8; Orde, op. cit., p. 61.
27. A. J. Ward, *Ireland and Anglo-American Relations, 1899–1921* (London, 1969), p. 258.
28. Nicholas, op. cit., p. 73.

2 Isolationism and Appeasement

1. D. Cameron Watt, 'Foreword'; B. J. C. McKercher, 'Introduction', in B. J. C. McKercher (ed.), *Anglo-American Relations in the 1920s: The Struggle for Supremacy* (London, 1991), pp. x-xiii; 1–16.
2. G. W. Egerton, 'Ideology, Diplomacy, and International Organisation: Wilsonism and the League of Nations in Anglo-American Relations, 1918–1920', in McKercher (ed.), op. cit., pp. 17–54.
3. H. G. Nicholas, *The United States and Britain* (Chicago, IL, 1975), pp. 74–7.
4. Ibid., pp. 81–5.
5. M. J. Hogan, *Informal Entente: The Private Structure of Cooperation in Anglo-American Economic Diplomacy, 1918–1929* (Columbia, MO, 1977); K. Burk, 'The House of Morgan in Financial Diplomacy, 1920–1930', in McKercher (ed.), op. cit., pp. 125–57.
6. R. A. Dayer, 'Anglo-American Monetary Policy and Rivalry in Europe and the Far East, 1919–1931', in McKercher (ed.), op. cit., pp. 158–86.
7. A. P. Dobson, *Anglo-American Relations in the Twentieth Century: Of Friendship, Conflict and the Rise and Decline of Superpowers* (London, 1995), pp. 51–2.
8. J. R. Ferris, 'The Symbol and the Substance of Seapower: Great Britain, the United States and the One-Power Standard, 1919–1921', in McKercher (ed.), op. cit., pp. 55–80.
9. Nicholas, op. cit., pp. 79–80; B. J. C. McKercher, 'Between Two Giants: Canada, the Coolidge Conference, and Anglo-American Relations in 1927', in McKercher (ed.), op. cit., pp. 81–124; I. H. Nish, *Alliance in Decline: A Study in Anglo-Japanese Relations, 1908–23* (London, 1972), pp. 368–82.

10. See D. Richardson, 'The Geneva Disarmament Conference, 1932–34', in D. Richardson and G. Stone (eds), *Decisions and Diplomacy: Essays in Twentieth-Century International History* (London, 1995), pp. 60–82.

11. A. Orde, *The Eclipse of Great Britain: The United States and British Imperial Decline, 1895–1956* (London, 1996), pp. 102–5. Important monograph studies include: C. Thorne, *The Limits of Foreign Policy: The West, the League and the Far Eastern Crisis of 1931–1933* (London, 1972); E. M. Andrews, *The Writing on the Wall: The British Commonwealth and Aggression in the East, 1931–1935* (Sydney, 1987); I. Nish, *Japan's Struggle with Internationalism: Japan, China and the League of Nations, 1931–3* (London, 1993).

12. R. Ovendale, *The Origins of the Arab–Israeli Wars*, 2nd edn (London, 1992), p. 67.

13. F. Costigliola, *Awkward Dominion: American Political, Economic and Cultural Relations with Europe, 1919–1933* (Ithaca, NY, 1984), p. 131; see also F. Costigliola, 'Anglo-American Financial Rivalry in the 1920s', *Journal of Economic History*, XXXVII (1977), pp. 911–34; Dobson, op. cit., pp. 58–67.

14. Public Record Office, London, CAB 23/78, fos 330–7, CM12(34)1, Secret, 22 March 1934.

15. See A. Trotter, *Britain and East Asia, 1933–1937* (London, 1975); S. L. Endicott, *Diplomacy and Enterprise: British China Policy 1933–1937* (Manchester, 1975).

16. For an account of the contemporary as well as academic literature on American isolationism see R. Ovendale, *'Appeasement' and the English Speaking World: Britain, the United States, the Dominions, and the Policy of 'Appeasement', 1937–1939* (Cardiff, 1975), pp. 9–16.

17. W. S. Churchill, *The Gathering Storm* (London, 1948), p. 199; see W. R. Rock, *Appeasement on Trial: British Foreign Policy and its Critics, 1938–1939* (New York, 1966), pp. 23–4, for a bibliography of accounts of Roosevelt's overture and historians' verdicts on it.

18. See W. R. Rock, *Chamberlain and Roosevelt: British Foreign Policy and the United States, 1937–1940* (Columbus, OH, 1988); contra R. A. C. Parker, *Chamberlain and Appeasement: British Policy and the Coming of the Second World War* (London, 1993), pp. 297–306. See also A. Offner, *American Appeasement: United States Foreign Policy and Germany, 1933–1938* (Cambridge, MA, 1969); C. A. MacDonald, *The United States, Britain and Appeasement, 1936–1939* (London, 1981); D. Reynolds, *The Creation of the Anglo-American Alliance, 1937–41: A Study in Competitive Co-operation* (London, 1981), pp. 7–62.

19. *Foreign Relations of the United States* (hereafter FRUS), 1937(1), pp. 131–2, Chamberlain to Roosevelt, 28 September 1937.

20. Ovendale, *'Appeasement' and the English-Speaking World*, pp. 38–63.

21. FO 371/20954, F5683/9/10, Lindsay to Foreign Office, Telegram, 24 August 1937; Minute by Ronald, 25 August 1937.

22. FO 371/20663, A7441/228/45, Mallet to Foreign Office, Telegram no. 344, 13 October 1937.

23. FO 371/21017, F9736/6799/10, Eden to Lindsay, Telegram no. 2, Lock and Key, 10 November 1937.

24. Ovendale, *'Appeasement' and the English-Speaking World*, pp. 66–91.

25. Ibid., pp. 88–91, 253–5.

26. FO 371/21526, fos 196–8, Chamberlain to Lindsay, Telegram no. 35, Most Secret, 13 January 1938; Telegram no. 36, Most Secret, 13 January 1938.

27. FO 371/21526, fos 163–5, A2127/64/45, Roosevelt to Chamberlain, Telegram, Most Secret, 17 January 1938 received 18 January 1938.

28. FO 371/21526, fos 153–5, A2127/64/45, Eden to Chamberlain, 18 January 1938 (draft, revise); fos 156–9, Eden to Chamberlain, 18 January 1938 (not sent, for oral communication to Chamberlain).

29. CAB 23/92, fos 1–23, CM7(38), Secret, 20 February 1938.

30. W. L. Langer and S. E. Gleason, *The Challenge to Isolation, 1937–1940* (London, 1952), p. 32.

31. Ovendale, *'Appeasement' and the English-Speaking World*, p. 113.

32. CAB 24/277, fos 1–7, CP161(38), Annexed Memorandum by F. Ashton-Gwatkin.

33. See Ovendale, *'Appeasement' and the English-Speaking World*, pp. 13–17, 20, 35, 84, 139–40, 196–9.

34. FO 371/21527, A7504/64/45, Lindsay to Foreign Office, Telegram no. 349, Most Secret and Important, 19 September 1938.

35. FO 371/22815, fos 203–5, A5899/98/45, Lothian to Halifax, Telegram no. 391, 30 August 1939; *Documents on British Foreign Policy, 1919–1939*, 3rd Series, VII, p. 429, no. 569, Lothian to Halifax, Telegram no. 392, 31 August 1939.

36. CAB 27/625, fos 6–8, FP(6)53rd Mtg, Lock and Key, 20 June 1939.

37. CAB 23/100, fos 8–14, CM33(39)3, Secret, 21 June 1939; CAB 2/9, fos 28–30, Committee of Imperial Defence Minutes of 362nd Meeting DP(P), Lock and Key, 26 June 1939.

38. CAB 24/288, fos 211–12, CP178(39), Memorandum by Halifax on the situation in the Far East, Lock and Key, 21 August 1939.

39. FO 371/28815, fos 203–5, A5899/98/45, Lothian to Halifax, Telegram no. 391, 30 August 1939.

40. See Ovendale, *'Appeasement' and the English-Speaking World*, pp. 240–63.

41. Public Record Office, London, PREM 1/229, Chamberlain to Tweedsmuir, 19 November 1937.

42. See Ovendale, *'Appeasement' and the English-Speaking World*, p. 284 note 80.

43. I. Macleod, *Neville Chamberlain* (London, 1961), pp. 255–6.

3   The Second World War

1. W. S. Churchill, *The Second World War*, 6 vols (London, 1948–54); D. Cameron Watt, 'Foreword', in B. J. C. McKercher (ed.), *Anglo-American Relations in the 1920s: The Struggle for Supremacy* (London, 1991), pp. x–xiii at p. x; D. Reynolds, 'Roosevelt, Churchill, and the Wartime Anglo-American Alliance, 1939–1945: Towards a New Synthesis', in W. R. Louis and H. Bull (eds), *The 'Special Relationship': Anglo-American Relations since 1945* (Oxford, 1986), pp. 17–41 at pp. 17–18; W. F. Kimball (ed.), *Churchill and Roosevelt: The Complete Correspondence*, 3 vols (London, 1984); J. Charmley, 'Churchill's Roosevelt', in A. Lane and H. Temperley (eds), *The Rise and Fall of the Grand Alliance, 1941–45* (London, 1995), pp. 90–107.

2. J. L. Gaddis, 'The Emerging Post-revisionist Synthesis on the Origins of the Cold War', *Diplomatic History*, VII (1983), pp. 171–204; R. Ovendale, *The English-Speaking Alliance: Britain, the United States, the Dominions and the Cold War, 1945–1951* (London, 1985), pp. 86–7, for a survey of this literature.

3. R. J. Maddox, *The New Left and the Origins of the Cold War* (Princeton, NJ, 1973) exposed methodological aberrations in the revisionist writings. W. F. Kimball, though critical of Maddox in 'The Cold War Warmed Over', *American Historical Review*, vol. 79 (1974), pp. 1119–36, conceded that most revisionist writings had been eliminated from university reading lists.

4. J. Irving, *A Prayer for Owen Meany* (London, 1989).

5. See, for example, M. Howard, 'Frozen Postures', *Sunday Times*, 24 September 1972.

6. For a survey of this literature see M. A. Stoler, 'A Half-Century of Conflict: Interpretations of US World War II Diplomacy', in M. J. Hogan (ed.), *The Historiography of American Foreign Relations since 1941* (Cambridge, 1995), pp. 166–205; H. Jones and R. B. Woods, 'Origins of the Cold War and the Near East: Recent Historiography and the National Security Imperative', in Hogan (ed.), op. cit., pp. 234–69.

7. For a discussion of this literature see F. M. Carroll, 'Anglo-American Relations and the Origins of the Cold War: the New Perspective', *Canadian Journal of History*, XXIV (1989), pp. 191–208.

8. D. Reynolds, *The Creation of the Anglo-American Alliance, 1937–41: A Study in Competitive Co-operation* (London, 1981), pp. 63–92.

9. J. P. Lash, *Roosevelt and Churchill, 1939–1941: The Partnership that Saved the West* (New York, 1976), p. 128.

10. R. Ovendale, *'Appeasement' and the English-Speaking World: Britain, the United States, the Dominions, and the Policy of 'Appeasement', 1937–1939* (Cardiff, 1975), pp. 199–200.

11. See D. Reynolds, *Lord Lothian and Anglo-American Relations, 1939–1940* (Philadelphia, PA, 1983).

12. See W. F. Kimball, *The Most Unsordid Act: Lend-Lease, 1939–1941* (Baltimore, MD, 1969).

13. K. Burk, 'American Foreign Economic Policy and Lend-Lease', in Lane and Temperley (eds), op. cit., pp. 43–68 at p. 64.

14. *The Times*, 19 November 1987, editorial; W. Carr, *Poland to Pearl Harbor: The Making of the Second World War* (London, 1985), p. 141.

15. See R. B. Woods, *A Changing of the Guard: Anglo-American Relations, 1941–1946* (Chapel Hill, NC, 1990), pp. 51–4.

16. J. Baylis, *Anglo-American Defence Relations, 1939–1984: The Special Relationship*, 2nd edn (London, 1984), pp. 4–7.

17. P. Lowe, *Great Britain and the Origins of the Pacific War: A Study of British Policy in East Asia, 1937–1941* (Oxford, 1977), p. 232; A. Best, *Britain, Japan and Pearl Harbor: Avoiding War in East Asia, 1936–41* (London, 1995), esp. pp. 160–92.

18. Excerpts from these works can be found in R. Dallek (ed.), *The Roosevelt Diplomacy and World War II* (New York, 1970); G. M. Waller (ed.), *Pearl Harbor: Roosevelt and the Coming of the War*, rev. edn (Lexington, MA, 1976); G. W. Prange, *At Dawn We Slept: The Untold Story of Pearl Harbor* (London, 1982); J. Costello, *The Pacific War* (London, 1982).

19. J. Rushbridger and E. Nave, *Betrayal at Pearl Harbor: How Churchill Lured Roosevelt into War* (London, 1991); *The Independent*, 9 March 1989; *Guardian Weekly*, 21 July 1991; *The Times*, 12 July 1993, 26 November 1993; R. Aldrich, 'Conspiracy or Confusion? Churchill, Roosevelt and Pearl Harbor', *Intelligence and National*

Security, VII (1992), pp. 335–46; D. Kahn, 'The Intelligence Failure of Pearl Harbor', *Foreign Affairs*, vol. 70(5) (1991), pp. 136–52; L. W. Tordella and E. C. Fishel, 'A New Pearl Harbor Villain', *Intelligence and Counterintelligence*, VI, pp. 363–88; D. Kaiser, 'Conspiracy or Cock-up? Pearl Harbor Revisited', D. C. S. Sissons, 'More on Pearl Harbor', *Intelligence and National Security*, IX (1994), pp. 354–72, 373–9.

20. H. D. Hall and C. C. Wrigley, *Studies of Overseas Supply* (London, 1956); W. H. McNeill, *America, Britain and Russia: Their Cooperation and Conflict, 1941–1946* (London, 1953), p. 17.

21. R. Ovendale, *Britain, the United States, and the End of the Palestine Mandate, 1942–1948* (Woodbridge, Suffolk, 1989), pp. 6–7.

22. See Woods, op. cit., esp. p. 399; R. N. Gardner, *Sterling–Dollar Diplomacy in Current Perspective*, 3rd edn (New York, 1980); R. Clarke and A. Cairncross (eds), *Anglo-American Economic Collaboration in War and Peace, 1942–1949* (Oxford, 1982); A. P. Dobson, *US Wartime Aid to Britain, 1940–1946* (New York, 1986).

23. C. Barnett, 'Anglo-American Strategy in Europe', in Lane and Temperley (eds), op. cit., pp. 174–89; K. Sainsbury, *Churchill and Roosevelt at War: The War They Fought and the Peace they Hoped to Make* (London, 1994); D. Reynolds, *Rich Relations: The American Occupation of Britain, 1942–1945* (London, 1995); A. Danchev, *Very Special Relationship: Field-Marshal Sir John Dill and the Anglo-American Alliance, 1941–44* (London, 1986).

24. Public Record Office, London, FO 800/452, fol. 34, Def/48/5A, COS(48) 16th Mtg, Confidential Annex, 2 February 1948.

25. E. Barker, *The British between the Superpowers, 1945–50* (London, 1983), p. 4.

26. J. Wheeler-Bennett, and A. Nicholls, *The Semblance of Peace* (London, 1972), p. 290; J. M. Burns, *Roosevelt: The Soldier of Freedom, 1940–1945* (London, 1971), pp. 103, 569. A critique of Burns is offered by R. Dallek: see R. Dallek, 'Franklin D. Roosevelt as World Leader', *American Historical Review*, vol. 76 (1971), pp. 1503–15; *Franklin D. Roosevelt and American Foreign Policy, 1932–1945* (New York, 1979); see also J. Bishop, *FDR's Last Year, April 1944–April 1945* (London, 1974); W. F. Kimball, *The Juggler: Franklin Roosevelt as Wartime Statesman* (Princeton, NJ, 1991); F. Harbutt, *The Iron Curtain: Churchill, America, and the Origins of the Cold War* (New York, 1986); Ovendale, *The English-Speaking Alliance*, pp. 3–25; H. B. Ryan, *The Vision of Anglo-America: The US–UK Alliance and the Emerging Cold War, 1943–1946* (Cambridge, 1987). T. H. Anderson argues that during his last few days Roosevelt was being moved towards a tougher stand against the Russians. See T. H. Anderson, *The United States, Great Britain, and the Cold War, 1944–1947* (Columbia, MO, 1981), pp. 49–51.

27. S. Wells, *The Time for Decision* (London, 1944), pp. 66–117, McNeill, op. cit., pp. 164–5; W. R. Louis, *Imperialism at Bay: The United States and the Decolonization of the British Empire, 1941–1945* (London, 1978); C. J. Bartlett, 'Inter-allied Relations in the Second World War', *History*, vol. 63 (1978), pp. 390–5; G. R. Hess, *America Encounters India, 1941–1947* (Baltimore, MD, 1971); R. Callahan, *Churchill: Retreat from Empire* (Wilmington, DE, 1984); R. Nadeau, *Stalin, Churchill, and Roosevelt Divide Europe* (London, 1990); J. Charmley, *Churchill's Grand Alliance: The Anglo-American Special Relationship 1940–57* (London, 1995), pp. 356–7; W. F. Kimball, 'Wheel within a Wheel: Churchill, Roosevelt, and the Special Relationship', in R. Blake and W. R. Louis (eds), *Churchill* (Oxford, 1994), pp. 291–307.

28. C. M. W. Moran, *Winston Churchill: The Struggle for Survival, 1940–1965* (London, 1966), pp. 132–44; Wheeler-Bennett and Nicholls, op. cit., pp. 142–67; V. H. Rothwell, *Britain and the Cold War, 1941–1947* (London, 1982), pp. 107–23.

29. E. Barker, *Churchill and Eden at War* (London, 1978); G. Warner, 'From Teheran to Yalta: Reflections on F. D. R.'s Foreign Policy', *International Affairs*, vol. 43 (1967), pp. 530–6; G. Ross (ed.), *The Foreign Office and the Kremlin: British Documents on Anglo-Soviet Relations 1941–45* (Cambridge, 1984), pp. 41–51.

30. A. Eden, *The Reckoning* (London, 1964), pp. 460–7; T. Higgins, *Soft Underbelly: The Anglo-American Controversy over the Italian Campaign, 1939–1945* (New York, 1968); Public Record Office, London, FO 381/43335, Foreign Office paper on postwar Soviet policy, 29 April 1944.

31. Public Record Office, London, CAB 65/45, fol. 21, WM(44)11, Most Secret, 25 January 1944; CAB 65/46, fol. 41, WM(44)63, Top Secret, 11 May 1944; E. Barker, *British Policy in South-East Europe in the Second World War* (London, 1976); Rothwell, op. cit., pp. 128–36.

32. Moran, pp. 232–7; CAB 65/51, fos 78–9, WM(45)22, Top Secret, 19 February 1945; R. M. Hathaway, *Ambiguous Partnerships: Britain and America, 1944–47* (New York, 1981), pp. 112–31.

33. D. Cameron Watt, *Succeeding John Bull: America in Britain's Place, 1900–1975* (Cambridge, 1984), pp. 194–219; D. Halberstam, *The Best and the Brightest* (London, 1974), pp. 102–3.

34. George C. Marshall Library, Lexington, VA, Joint Chiefs of Staff White House Records of Fleet Admiral William D. Leahy 1942–1949, Folder 88, Research and Analysis Branch of OSS: Problems and Objectives of United States Policy, 2 April 1945.

35. S. A. Ambrose, *Eisenhower and Berlin, 1945: The Decision to Halt at the Elbe* (New York, 1967); W. Ullmann, *The United States in Prague, 1945–1948* (New York, 1978); L. Woodward, *British Foreign Policy in the Second World War*, vol. 3 (London, 1971), pp. 490–578.

36. G. Kolko, *The Politics of War* (New York, 1968), pp. 280–313, 488–91; see also the critique of Kolko in Maddox, *The New Left and the Origins of the Cold War*, pp. 103–22; H. S. Truman, *Years of Trial and Hope* (London, 1956), p. 108; *United Kingdom Parliamentary Debates, House of Lords*, 5th Series, 138, cols 777–8, 18 December 1945; G. C. Herring Jr, 'The United States and British Bankruptcy, 1944–1945: Responsibilities Deferred', *Political Science Quarterly*, vol. 86 (1971), pp. 260–80; Woods, op. cit., pp. 312–23.

37. D. Yergin, *Shattered Peace* (Boston, MA, 1977), pp. 79–86; Wheeler-Bennett and Nicholls, op. cit., pp. 311–14, 547–51; J. Tillapaugh, 'Closed Hemisphere and Open World? The Dispute over Regional Security at the U.N. Conference, 1945', *Diplomatic History*, II (1978), pp. 25–42; Wilson D. Miscamble, 'Anthony Eden and the Truman–Molotov Conversations, April 1945', *Diplomatic History*, II (1978), pp. 167–80.

38. C. L. Mee Jr, *Meeting at Potsdam* (London, 1975); F. Williams, *A Prime Minister Remembers* (London, 1961), p. 5; CAB 65/54, fos 23–5, CM(45)10, Top Secret, 20 June 1945; Moran, op. cit., pp. 279–82.

39 G. Alperowitz, *Atomic Diplomacy: Hiroshima and Potsdam* (London, 1966), pp. 14, 236–42; *The Decision to Use the Atomic Bomb and the Architecture of an American Myth* (London, 1995); C. Thorne, *Allies of a Kind: The United States, Britain and the War*

against Japan, 1941–1945 (London, 1978), pp. 678–80; P. Lowe, 'The War against Japan and Allied Relations', in Lane and Temperley (eds), op. cit., pp. 190–206.

4 The Cold War: Educating the Americans

1. For a survey of this literature see J. S. Walker, 'Historians and Cold War Origins: The New Consensus', in G. K. Haines and J. S. Walker (eds), *American Foreign Relations: A Historiographical Review* (Westport, CT, 1981), pp. 207–36.
2. B. Perkins, 'Unequal Partners: The Truman Administration and Great Britain', in W. R. Louis and H. Bull (eds), *The 'Special Relationship': Anglo-American Relations since 1945* (Oxford, 1986), pp. 43–64 at p. 64.
3. F. M. Carroll, 'Anglo-American Relations and the Origins of the Cold War: The New Perspective', *Canadian Journal of History*, XXIV (1989), pp. 191–208 at p. 206.
4. R. Ovendale, 'Britain, the USA, and the European Cold War, 1945–8', *History*, vol. 67 (1982), pp. 217–35; A. Bullock, *Ernest Bevin, Foreign Secretary, 1945–1951* (London, 1983); R. Smith and J. Zametica, 'The Cold Warrior: Clement Attlee Reconsidered, 1945–7', *International Affairs*, vol. 61 (1985), pp. 237–52.
5. See R. Ovendale, *The English-Speaking Alliance: Britain, the United States, the Dominions and the Cold War, 1945–1951* (London, 1985).
6. For an account of Bevin's consideration of the creation of a West European bloc in 1945, see D. Cameron Watt, *Succeeding John Bull: America in Britain's Place, 1900–1975* (Cambridge, 1984), p. 106; see also R. Edmonds, *Setting the Mould: The United States and Britain, 1945–1950* (Oxford, 1986), pp. 171–4.
7. See Ovendale, *The English-Speaking Alliance*, pp. 245–70.
8. For the case that Bevin, between about August 1947 and April 1948, showed considerable interest in the idea of a 'third force' balancing the power of the United States and the Soviet Union, see J. Young, *Britain and European Unity, 1945–1992* (London, 1993), pp. 14–18; more extreme interpretations can be found in J. Kent, *British Imperial Strategy and the Origins of the Cold War, 1944–49* (Leicester, 1993); and S. Croft, *The End of Superpower: British Foreign Office Conceptions of a Changing World, 1945–51* (Aldershot, Hants, 1994).
9. R. Ovendale, 'William Strang and the Permanent Under-Secretary's Committee', in J. Zametica (ed.), *British Officials and British Foreign Policy, 1945–50* (Leicester, 1990), pp. 212–27.
10. Public Record Office, London, FO 800/512, fol. 8, US457, Attlee to Truman, Telegram no. 8463, Personal and Top Secret, 17 August 1945.
11. Ovendale, *The English-Speaking Alliance*, pp. 31–3; J. L. Gormley, 'The Washington Declaration and the "Poor Relation": Anglo-American Atomic Diplomacy, 1945–46', *Diplomatic History*, VIII (1984), pp. 125–43; J. Baylis, *Ambiguity and Deterrence: British Nuclear Strategy* (Oxford, 1995), pp. 52–60; M. Gowing, 'Nuclear Weapons and the "Special Relationship"', in Louis and Bull (eds), op. cit., pp. 118–28; *Independence and Deterrence: Britain and Atomic Energy, 1945–52*, 2 vols (London, 1974); H. Macmillan, *Riding the Storm* (London, 1971), pp. 313–41.
12. B. J. Bernstein, 'American Foreign Policy and the Origins of the Cold War', in

B. J. Bernstein (ed.), *Politics and Policies of the Truman Administration* (Chicago, IL, 1970), pp. 15–77.

13. Public Record Office, London, FO 371/5830, Roberts to Bevin, no. 797, 16 January 1946; see J. Zametica, 'Three Letters to Bevin: Frank Roberts at the Moscow Embassy, 1945–46', in Zametica (ed.), op. cit., p. 39–97.

14. B. R. Kuniholm, *The Origins of the Cold War in the Near East: Great Power Conflict and Diplomacy in Iran, Turkey and Greece* (Princeton, NJ, 1980); B. Rubin, *The Great Powers in the Middle East, 1941–1947: The Road to the Cold War* (London, 1980); W. R. Louis, *The British Empire in the Middle East, 1945–1951: Arab Nationalism, the United States, and Postwar Imperialism* (Oxford, 1984), pp. 65–8.

15. See T. Sharp, *The Wartime Alliance and the Zonal Division of Germany* (Oxford, 1975); A. Deighton, *The Impossible Peace: Britain, the Division of Germany and the Origins of the Cold War* (Oxford, 1990).

16. FO 800/451, fol. 44, Def/46/3, Bevin to Attlee, 13 February 1946.

17. For a discussion as to whether Bevin agreed to end British aid to Greece as a way of bringing the Americans back into international affairs, see R. Frazier, *Anglo-American Relations with Greece: The Coming of the Cold War, 1942–47* (London, 1991), p. 175.

18. Princeton University Library, George Kennan Papers, Box 17, The National War College Strategy, Policy and Planning Course, National Security Problems, 17–28 March 1947, Revised.

19. See Ovendale, *The English-Speaking Alliance*, pp. 29–58.

20. Georgetown University Library, Washington DC, Robert F. Wagner Papers, Box 3, File 47, Confidential Memorandum, 13 March 1947; Wagner to Vandenberg, 19 March 1947.

21. Some of the basic ideas could have developed from conversations between Roberts and Kennan. See S. Jackson, 'Prologue to the Marshall Plan: The Origins of the American Commitment to a European Recovery Program', *Journal of American History*, vol. 65 (1979), pp. 1043–68; for accounts of the Marshall Plan see M. J. Hogan, *The Marshall Plan: America, Britain, and the Reconstruction of Western Europe, 1947–1952* (Cambridge, 1987); H. Pelling, *Britain and the Marshall Plan* (London, 1988).

22. R. Ovendale (ed.), *British Defence Policy since 1945: Documents in Contemporary History* (Manchester, 1994), pp. 18–41.

23. R. Ovendale, *Britain, the United States, and the End of the Palestine Mandate, 1942–1948* (Woodbridge, Suffolk, 1989); 'Britain and the End of the Palestine Mandate, 1945–48', in R. J. Aldrich and M. F. Hopkins (eds), *Intelligence, Defence and Diplomacy: British Policy in the Post-War World* (London, 1994), pp. 133–48; see also M. Jones, *Failure in Palestine: British and United States Policy after the Second World War* (London, 1986); M. J. Cohen, *Palestine and the Great Powers, 1945–1948* (Princeton, NJ, 1982).

24. *Foreign Relations of the United States (FRUS) 1947* (2), pp. 815–16, Anglo-French conversations, British memorandum of conversation, Top Secret, Undated.

25. FO 800/452, fos 32–41, Def/48/5A, COS(48)16, Confidential Annex, 2 February 1948.

26. See C. Wiebes and B. Zeeman, 'The Pentagon Negotiations March 1948: The Launching of the North Atlantic Treaty', *International Affairs*, vol. 59 (1983), pp. 351–63.

27. FO 800/453, fos 83–6, Def/48/40, British Embassy Washington to Foreign Office, Top Secret, 13 July 1948.
28. FO 800/483, fol. 2, NA481, Roberts to Wright and Jebb, 1 June 1948.
29. Ovendale, *Britain, the United States, and the End of the Palestine Mandate, 1942–1948*, pp. 217–307.
30. See A. Shlaim, 'Britain, the Berlin blockade and the Cold War', *International Affairs*, vol. 60 (1984), pp. 1–14; *The United States and the Berlin Blockade, 1948–1949: A Study in Crisis Decision-Making* (Berkeley, CA, 1983).
31. See S. Duke, 'U. S. Basing in Britain, 1945–1960', in S. W. Duke and W. Krieger (eds), *US Military Forces in Europe: The Early Years, 1945–1970* (Boulder, CO, 1993), pp. 117–52.
32. FO 800/460, fos 200–1, Eur/48/48, extract of a conversation between Bevin and Marshall on 4 October 1948.
33. Australian Archives, Canberra, A5954, Box 1970, PMM(48)9, Secret, 19 October 1948.
34. Australian Archives, Canberra, A5799, 4815, Attlee to J. B. Chifley, Top Secret, 29 December 1948.
35. See Ovendale, *The English-Speaking Alliance*, pp. 245–72.
36. R. Ovendale, 'Great Britain and the Atlantic Pact', in E. Di Nolfo, *The Atlantic Pact Forty Years Later: A Historical Reappraisal* (Berlin, 1991), pp. 72–8; *The English-Speaking Alliance*, pp. 59–87; E. Reid, *Time of Fear and Hope: The Making of the North Atlantic Treaty, 1947–1949* (Toronto, 1979); T. P. Ireland, *Creating the Entangling Alliance: The Origins of the North Atlantic Treaty Organization* (London, 1981); N. Henderson, *The Birth of NATO* (London, 1982); J. Baylis, *The Diplomacy of Pragmatism: Britain and the Formation of NATO, 1942–1949* (London, 1993); R. H. Ferrell, 'The Formation of the Alliance, 1948–1949', in L. S. Kaplan, (ed.), *American Historians and the Atlantic Alliance* (Kent, OH, 1991), pp. 11–32; G. Warner, 'Britain and Europe in 1948: the View from the Cabinet', in J. Becker and F. Knipping (eds), *Power in Europe? Great Britain, France, Italy and Germany in a Postwar World, 1945–1950* (Berlin, 1986), pp. 27–46.

5 The Cold War: Global Strategy

1. Public Record Office, London, FO 371/76386, W5573/3/500G, Makins to Bevin, 9 November 1949; Minute, 23 November 1949; FO 371/76385, W4707/3/500g, Strang to Bevin, 24 August 1949; PUSC(51) Final, Anglo-American relations: present and future, 24 August 1949; PUSC(51) Final, second revise, Anglo-American relations: present and future. See R. Ovendale, 'William Strang and the Permanent Under-Secretary's Committee', in J. Zametica (ed.), *British Officials and British Foreign Policy, 1945–50* (Leicester, 1990), pp. 212–27 at pp. 222–4.
2. R. Ovendale, *The English-Speaking Alliance: Britain, the United States, the Dominions and the Cold War, 1945–1951* (London, 1985), pp. 245–70.
3. R. Ovendale, *Britain, the United States, and the Transfer of Power in the Middle East* (London, 1996), pp. 24–33; G. McGhee, *Envoy to the Middle East: Adventures in Diplomacy* (New York, 1969); D. Silverfarb, *The Twilight of British Ascendancy in the*

Middle East: A Case Study of Iraq, 1941–1950 (New York, 1994); I. H. Anderson, *ARAMCO: The United States and Saudi Arabia: A Study of the Dynamics of Foreign Oil Policy, 1933–1950* (Princeton, NJ, 1981), pp. 185–6.

4. R. Ovendale, *The Origins of the Arab–Israeli Wars*, 2nd edn (London, 1992), pp. 137–8; I. Pappé, *Britain and the Arab–Israeli Conflict, 1948–51* (London, 1988); A. Ilan, *The Origin of the Arab–Israeli Arms Race: Arms, Embargo, Military Power and Decision in the 1948 Palestine War* (New York, 1996).

5. Ovendale, *Britain, the United States, and the Transfer of Power in the Middle East*, pp. 30–1.

6. FO 371/124968, ZP242, Some notes on British Foreign Policy by Roger Makins, Confidential, 11 August 1951.

7. Ovendale, *Britain, the United States, and the Transfer of Power in the Middle East*, pp. 31–48; J. Cable, *Intervention at Abadan: Plan Buccaneer* (London, 1991); D. R. Devereux, *The Formulation of British Defence Policy towards the Middle East, 1948–56* (London, 1990); J. A. Bill, 'America, Iran, and the Politics of Intervention, 1951–1953', in J. A. Bill and W. R. Louis (eds), *Mussadiq, Iranian Nationalism, and Oil* (London, 1988), pp. 261–95.

8. FO 371/91185, fos 150–6, E1024/36, Record of meeting at Foreign Office on 29 June 1951, Top Secret.

9. Ovendale, *Britain, the United States, and the Transfer of Power in the Middle East*, pp. 48–53; *The English-Speaking Alliance*, pp. 118–42; for an analysis of the British Middle East Office see P. W. T. Kingston, *Britain and the Politics of Modernization in the Middle East, 1945–1958* (Cambridge, 1996).

10. See H. Leigh-Phippard, *Congress and US Military Aid to Britain: Interdependence and Dependence, 1949–56* (London, 1995) for an account of the defence assistance relationship between Britain and the United States.

11. Ovendale, *The English-Speaking Alliance*, pp. 114–84; R. J. McMahon, 'The Cold War in Asia: The Elusive Synthesis', in M. J. Hogan (ed.), *America in the World: The Historiography of American Foreign Relations since 1941* (Cambridge, 1995), pp. 501–35.

12. Australian Archives, Canberra, A1838, 383/5/1 Pt 1, JIC(FE)(49)9 (Final), Communism in the Far East covering the period 1 October 1948 to 31 March 1949; 383/5/1 Pt 1, JIC(FE)(49)42 (Final), Report by Joint Intelligence Committee Far East for period 1 April to 30 September 1949, Secret, 3 December 1949.

13. FO 371/75771, F14604/1015/10, Minute by Burgess, 29 September 1949.

14. FO 371/75816, F14878/1023/10, Foreign Office to British Representatives Abroad, Telegram no. 371, Confidential, 7 October 1949; Minutes by P. D. Coates, 5 October 1949; W. Strang, 6 October 1949; W. E. Beckett, 6 October 1949; Foreign Office to Paris, Telegram no. 2700, Immediate and Confidential, 10 October 1949. For details see Ovendale, *The English-Speaking Alliance*, pp. 193–5.

15. Ovendale, *The English-Speaking Alliance*, pp. 185–210; Q. Zhai, *The Dragon, the Lion, and the Eagle: Chinese–British–American Relations, 1949–1958* (Kent, OH, 1994), pp. 28–45.

16. Public Record Office, London, FO 800517, fos 106–9, Franks to Bevin, Telegram no. 2233, Particular Secrecy, 16 August 1950.

17. Ovendale, *The English-Speaking Alliance*, pp. 211–24; W. Stueck, 'The Limits of

Influence: British Policy and the American Expansion of the War in Korea',
Pacific Historical Review, vol. 55 (1986), pp. 65–96; P. Lowe, 'The Significance of
the Korean War in Anglo-American relations, 1950–3', in M. Dockrill and J. W.
Young (eds), *British Foreign Policy, 1945–56* (London, 1989), pp. 173–96; R. J.
Foot, 'Anglo-American Relations in the Korean Crisis: The British Effort to
Avert an Expanded War, December 1950–January 1951', *Diplomatic History*, X
(1986), pp. 43–57.
18. Ovendale, *The English-Speaking Alliance*, pp. 220–38.
19. Public Record Office, London, CAB 129/45, fos 317–27, CP(51)64, Note by
Attlee on Pacific defence and appendices, Secret, 27 February 1951; R. J.
O'Neill, 'The Korean War and the Origins of ANZUS', in C. Bridge (ed.),
Munich to Vietnam: Australia's Relations with Britain and the United States since the 1930s
(Carlton, Victoria, 1991), pp. 99–113.
20. CAB 129/46, fos 89–96, CP(51)166, Memorandum by Morrison on Japanese
peace treaty, Secret, 19 June 1951; C. Hosoya, 'Japan, China, the United States
and the United Kingdom, 1951–2: The Case of the "Yoshida Letter"',
International Affairs, vol. 60 (1984), pp. 247–59.
21. See G. Warner, 'the Labour Governments and the Unity of Western Europe,
1945–51', in R. Ovendale (ed.), *The Foreign Policy of the British Labour Governments,
1945–1951* (Leicester, 1984), pp. 61–82.
22. Ovendale, *The English-Speaking Alliance*, pp. 284–5; J. W. Young, *Britain, France,
and the Unity of Europe, 1945–1951* (Leicester, 1984); *Britain and European Unity,
1945–1992* (London, 1993), pp. 14–8.
23. R. Ovendale (ed.), *British Defence Policy since 1945: Documents in Contemporary History*
(Manchester, 1994), pp. 58–84; R. Bullen and M. E. Pelly assisted by H. J.
Yasamee and G. Bennett, *Documents on British Policy Overseas*, series II, vol. III
(London, 1989), esp. pp. vii-xxiii.
24. Ovendale, *The English-Speaking Alliance*, p. 283.
25. J. Dickie, *'Special' No More - Anglo-American Relations: Rhetoric and Reality* (London,
1994), pp. 59–60.

6 One among a Number of Allies

1. See S. G. Rabe, 'Eisenhower Revisionism: The Scholarly Debate', in M.
J. Hogan (ed.), *America in the World: The Historiography of American Foreign Relations
since 1941* (Cambridge, 1995), pp. 300–25; the traditional analysis of Dulles as a
strong Secretary of State is in H. Finer, *Dulles over Suez* (London, 1964); this
interpretation is examined in T. Hoopes, *The Devil and John Foster Dulles* (Boston,
1973); F. W. Marks, *Power and Peace: The Diplomacy of John Foster Dulles* (Westport,
CT, 1993).
2. L. Mosley, *Dulles: A Biography of Eleanor, Allen, and John Foster Dulles and their Family
Network* (London, 1978); see R. Ovendale, *Britain, the United States, and the Transfer
of Power in the Middle East, 1945–1962* (London, 1996), pp. 59–177.
3. R. Ovendale (ed.), *British Defence Policy since 1945: Documents in Contemporary History*
(Manchester, 1994), pp. 89–90.
4. For an account of Britain's position in the world economy at this time, see D.

Reynolds, *Britannia Overruled: British Policy and World Power in the 20th Century* (London, 1991), pp. 206–10.

5. Ovendale (ed.) *British Defence Policy*, pp. 97–109; Public Record Office, London, CAB 131/12, Annex 1, D(52)26, Report by the Chiefs of Staff for the Defence Committee of the Cabinet on Defence Policy and Global Strategy, Top Secret, 17 June 1952; W. Jackson and Lord Bramall, *The Chiefs: The Story of the United Kingdom Chiefs of Staff* (London, 1992), pp. 281–93.

6. CAB 128/27 Pt 2, CC62(54)1, Secret, 1 October 1954.

7. See A. I. Singh, *The Limits of British Influence: South Asia and the Anglo-American Relationship, 1947–56* (London, 1993), pp. 157–92.

8. Public Record Office, London, PREM 11/392, Churchill to Eden, 6 January 1953.

9. PREM 11/486, Churchill to Eden, 4 April 1953; see P. Boyle, 'The "Special Relationship" with Washington', in J. W. Young (ed.), *The Foreign Policy of Churchill's Peacetime Administration, 1951–1955* (Leicester, 1988), pp. 29–54; M. F. Hopkins, 'The Washington Embassy: The Role of an Institution in Anglo-American Relations, 1944–55', in R. J. Aldrich and M. F. Hopkins (eds), *Intelligence, Defence and Diplomacy: British Policy in the Post-war World* (London, 1994), pp. 79–99.

10. R. Ovendale, *'Appeasement' and the English-Speaking World: Britain, the United States, the Dominions, and the Policy of 'Appeasement', 1937–1939* (Cardiff, 1975); *The English-Speaking Alliance: Britain, the United States, the Dominions and the Cold War 1945–1951* (London, 1985).

11. Reynolds, *Britannia Overruled*, p. 195.

12. PREM 11/208, fol. 6, M16(C)51, Churchill to Lord Cherwell, 10 November 1951.

13. PREM 11/49, fos 180–3, M190/52, Churchill to Alexander, Top Secret, 3 April 1952.

14. CAB 128/27 Pt 1, fos 31–2, CC1(54)2, Secret, 7 January 1954.

15. R. Ovendale, *The Origins of the Arab–Israeli Wars*, 2nd edn (London, 1992), pp. 153–4; W. R. Louis, 'Musaddiq and the dilemmas of British imperialism', in J. A. Bill and W. R. Louis (eds), *Musaddiq, Iranian Nationalism, and Oil* (London, 1988), pp. 228–60; CAB 128/26 Pt 2, fol. 388, CC50(53)4, Secret, 25 August 1953.

16. Ovendale, *The Origins of the Arab–Israeli Wars*, p. 154; *Britain and the Transfer of Power in the Middle East*, pp. 87, 90, 125–30.

17. PREM 11/465, fol. 18, PM/MS/53/48; fol. 16, M94/53, Churchill to Selwyn Lloyd and Sir William Strang on draft aide memoire to Israel: Churchill failed to understand that Bevin was not anti-Semitic, but opposed Zionism. See R. Ovendale, *Britain, the United States, and the End of the Palestine Mandate, 1942–1948* (Woodbridge, Suffolk, 1989), p. 133.

18. R. Ovendale, 'Churchill and the Middle East, 1945–55', in R. A. C. Parker (ed.), *Sir Winston Churchill: Studies in Statesmanship* (London, 1995), pp. 150–61.

19. CAB 127/27 Pt 1, fos 320–2, CC43(54)1, Secret, 22 June 1954; fos 350–1, CC47(54)2, Secret, 7 July 1954; R. Ovendale, 'Egypt and the Suez Base Agreement', in Young (ed.), *The Foreign Policy of Churchill's Peacetime Administration*, pp. 134–55; T. H. A. Owen, 'Britain and the Revision of the Anglo-Egyptian Treaty, 1949–1954' (PhD dissertation, University of Wales, Aberystwyth, 1991).

20. *Foreign Relations of the United States* (hereafter cited as FRUS), 1952–4(9), pp. 394–8, Memorandum of Meeting of National Security Council on 9 July 1953.
21. V. Bator, *Vietnam: A Diplomatic Tragedy* (London, 1967), pp. 17–125; G. Warner, 'The Settlement of the Indo-China War', in Young (ed.), op. cit., pp. 233–59.
22. Ovendale, *The English-Speaking Alliance*, pp. 183–241; Q. Zhai, *The Dragon, the Lion, and the Eagle: Chinese–British–American Relations, 1949–1958* (Kent, OH, 1994); M. Dockrill, 'Britain and the First Offshore Islands Crisis, 1945–55', in M. Dockrill and J. W. Young (eds), *British Foreign Policy, 1945–56* (London, 1989), pp. 173–96.
23. J. W. Young, *Britain and European Unity, 1945–1992* (London, 1993), pp. 35–43; S. Dockrill, *Britain's Policy for West German Rearmament 1950–1955* (Cambridge, 1991); N. Wiggershaus, 'The Decision for a West German Defence Contribution', in O. Riste (ed.), *Western Security: The Formative Years, European and Atlantic Defence, 1947–1953* (Oslo, 1985), pp. 198–214; G. M. Shepherd, 'Britain, Germany and the Cold War, 1951–1955' (D.Phil dissertation: University of Oxford, 1992), pp. 11–234.
24. J. W. Young, 'Cold War and Detente with Moscow', in Young (ed.), *The Foreign Policy of Churchill's Peacetime Administration*, pp. 55–80; *Winston Churchill's Last Campaign: Britain and the Cold War, 1951–5* (Oxford, 1996), pp. 290–314; M. Gilbert, *Winston S. Churchill*, vol. VIII, *'Never Despair', 1945–1965* (London, 1988), pp. 827–45.
25. Reynolds, *Britannia Overruled*, p. 185.
26. Young, *Britain and European Unity*, pp. 43–52.
27. CAB 128/29, fos 136–7, CM15(55)6, Secret, 16 June 1955; S. Shamir, 'The Collapse of Project Alpha', in W. R. Louis and R. Owen (eds), *Suez: 1956: The Crisis and its Consequences* (Oxford, 1989), pp. 73–100.
28. CAB 128/29, fol. 210, CM23(55)9, Secret, 14 July 1955; B. H. Reid, 'The "Northern Tier" and the Baghdad Pact', in Young (ed.), *The Foreign Policy of Churchill's Peacetime Administration*, pp. 159–79; W. R. Louis and R. Robinson, 'The Imperialism of Decolonization', *Journal of Imperial and Commonwealth History*, XXII (1994), pp. 462–511 at p. 478; Ovendale, *Britain, the United States, and the Transfer of Power in the Middle East*, pp. 108–39.
29. Ovendale, 'Egypt and the Suez Base Agreement', pp. 152–3; CAB 128/29, fos 364–5, CM34(55)8, Secret, 4 October 1955.
30. CAB 128/30, fos 112–13, CM10(56)1, Secret, 9 February 1956.
31. CAB 128/30, fol. 178, CM19(56)1, Secret, 6 March 1956.
32. CAB 129/30, fos 225–7, CM23(56)5, Confidential Annex, 15 March 1956.
33. CAB 128/30 Pt 2, fol. 405, CM46(56)9, Secret, 28 June 1956.
34. See Ovendale (ed.), *British Defence Policy*, pp. 110–11.
35. CAB 128/30 Pt 2, fos 525–8, CM62(56)2, Confidential Annex, 28 August 1956.
36. CAB 128/30 Pt 2, fol. 563, CM67(56)6, Secret, 26 September 1956.
37. Eisenhower Library, Abilene, Ann Whitman File, Dulles-Herter Series, Box no. 7, File John Foster Dulles, July 1956, Dulles to Eisenhower, 16 July 1956; Ann Whitman Diary Series, Box no. 8, File September 1956, Diary ACW, Diary 17 September 1956; Ovendale, *The Origins of the Arab–Israeli Wars*, pp. 161–72; CAB 134/1217, EC(56)12, Top Secret, 8 August 1956; CAB 128/30 Pt 2, fos 469–72, CM54(56), Confidential Annex, 27 July 1956; fos 481–3, CM56(56), Confidential Annex, 1 August 1956; fos 525–8, CM62(56)2, Confidential

Annex, 2 August 1956; L. Mosley, *Dulles: A Biography of Eleanor, Allen, and John Foster Dulles and their Family Network* (London, 1978), pp. 409–11; PREM 11/1176, EC(56) 22nd Meeting, Secret, 27 August 1956; Foreign Office to Washington, Secret, 1 September 1956; FO 800/726, Foreign Office to Washington, Telegram no. 3568, Secret, 5 August 1956; PREM 11/3431, JE14211/368G, Lloyd to Westlake, no. 133, Secret, 8 August 1956; Eden to Lloyd, 10 August 1956.

38. *FRUS*, 1955–7(16), pp. 382–91, Special National Intelligence Estimate, 5 September 1956; FO 800/726, Foreign Office to Washington, Telegram no. 4061, Emergency, 6 September 1956; K. Kyle, *Suez* (London, 1992), p. 224; CAB 128/30 Pt 2, fol. 531, CM63(56), Confidential Annex, 6 September 1956; FO 800/726, Makins to Foreign Office, Telegram no. 1939, Secret, 8 September 1956, despatched received 9 September 1956; Ovendale, *The Origins of the Arab–Israeli Wars*, pp. 172–3.

39. Eisenhower Library, Abilene, John Foster Dulles Papers, 1951–9, General Correspondence and Memoranda Series, Box no. 1, File Memoranda of Conversations - General L through M (2), Memorandum of Conversation with Macmillan, Personal and Private, shown to Hoover but no further distribution, Personal and Private, 25 September 1956; Ovendale, *The Origins of the Arab–Israeli Wars*, p. 173; FO 800/726, Foreign Office to Washington, Telegram no. 4540, Top Secret, 1 October 1956.

40. CAB 128/30 Pt 2, fos 625–6, CM74(56)1, Confidential Annex, 25 October 1956; see, generally, Ovendale, *The Origins of the Arab–Israeli Wars*, pp. 168–87; S. W. Lucas, *Divided We Stand: Britain, the United States and the Suez Crisis* (London, 1991); Kyle, *Suez*; G. Warner, 'The United States and the Suez Crisis', *International Affairs*, vol. 67 (1991), pp. 303–17.

41. Eisenhower Library, Abilene, John Foster Dulles Papers, 1951–9, General Correspondence and Memoranda Series, Box no. 2, File Strictly Confidential E-H(2) Gruenther to Dulles, 29 October 1956; Ann Whitman File, Ann Whitman Diary Series, Box no. 8, File November 1956, Diary ACW(2), Diary 3 November 1956; *FRUS* 1955–7(16), pp. 745–6, Editorial note; CAB 128/30 Pt 2, fol. 641A, CM77(56), Confidential Annex, 2 November 1956; Geoffrey Warner, 'Review Article the United States and the Suez Crisis', *International Affairs*, vol. 67 (1991), pp. 303–17.

42. FO 115/4545, VR1091/960G, Record of conversation between Lloyd and Elliot at Washington on 18 November 1956; Ovendale, *The Origins of the Arab–Israeli Wars*, p. 181; for a critique of Allen Dulles's later claims before the Senate that he had offered forewarnings see R. J. Aldrich, 'Intelligence, Anglo-American Relations and the Suez Crisis, 1956', *Intelligence and National Security*, IX (July 1994), pp. 544–54 at p. 550; P. L. Hahn, *The United States, Great Britain and Egypt, 1945–1956* (Chapel Hill, NC, 1991).

43. Eisenhower Library, Abilene, Ann Whitman File, Ann Whitman Diary Series, Box no. 8, File October 1956, Diary ACW(2), Diary 30 October 1956; DDE Diary Series, Box no. 20, File November 1956, Miscellaneous (4), Eisenhower to Gruenther, Personal, 2 November 1956; Eisenhower to Lew W. Douglas, Personal, 3 November 1956; FO 800/726, Foreign Office to Washington, Telegram no. 5181, Secret, 5 November 1956; *FRUS*, 1955–7(16), pp. 1025–7, Telephone conversation between Eisenhower and Eden, 6 November 1956,

Whitman File, Eisenhower Library; FO 371/121274, V1075/13/G, Eden to Eisenhower, Telegram no. 5254, Top Secret, 7 November 1956; Eisenhower Library, Abilene, Ann Whitman File, Ann Whitman Diary Series, Box no. 8, File November 1956, Diary ACW(2), Diary 6–8 November 1956.

44. *FRUS*, 1955–7(16), pp. 1012–13, Editorial note; Ovendale, *The Origins of the Arab–Israeli Wars*, pp. 182, 186; D. B. Kunz, *The Economic Diplomacy of the Suez Crisis* (Chapel Hill, NC, 1991); L. Johnman, 'Defending the Pound: The Economics of the Suez Crisis, 1956', in A. Gorst, L. Johnman and W. S. Lucas (eds), *Post-war Britain, 1945–64: Themes and Perspectives* (London, 1989), pp. 172–81.

45. J. Aitken, *Nixon: A Life* (London, 1993), p. 244.

46. CAB 128/30 Pt 2, fos 652–3, CM81(56), Secret, 7 November 1956; fol. 693, CM89(56)2, Secret, 27 November 1956; fol. 707, CM93(56), Secret, 30 November 1956.

47. *FRUS*, 1955–7(12), pp. 376–82, Memorandum from Rountree to Dulles, 5 December 1956; CAB 12830 Pt 2, fos 728–9, CM97(56)2, Secret, 7 December 1956.

48. See Ovendale, *Britain, the United States, and the Transfer of Power in the Middle East*, pp. 140–77.

7 Mutual Interdependence

1. Public Record Office, London, FO 371/126682, AU1051/15, 1040/4/56, Minute by A. Windham, 16 January 1957; Public Record Office, London, CAB 128/30 Pt 2, fol. 793, CM4(57), Secret, 9 January 1957; CAB 128/31 Pt 1, fol. 24, CC1(57)2, Secret, January 1957.

2. CAB 128/30 Pt 2, CM3(57), Secret, 8 January 1957.

3. *Foreign Relations of the United States* (hereafter cited as *FRUS*) 1955–7(17), pp. 452–8, Memorandum of a conversation at Bermuda, 21 March 1957; pp. 461–2, Eisenhower Diaries, 21 March 1957, Secret, Whitman Files, Eisenhower Library; CAB 128/30 Pt 1, fol. 171, CC22(57)3, Secret, 22 March 1957; Eisenhower Library, Abilene, Ann Whitman File, International Series, Box no. 3, File Bermuda Conference 20–4 March 1957(1), Summary Briefing Paper, Secret.

4. See I. Clark, *Nuclear Diplomacy and the Special Relationship: Britain's Deterrent and America, 1957–1962* (Oxford, 1994), pp. 38–76; J. Melissen, *The Struggle for Nuclear Partnership: Britain, the United States and the Making of an Ambiguous Alliance, 1952–1959* (Groningen, 1993), pp. 63–92.

5. *Cmnd 124, Defence Outline of Future Policy* (London, April 1957).

6. CAB 128/31 Pt 2, fos 525–6, CC76(57)2, Secret, 28 October 1957; M. Dockrill, 'Restoring the "Special Relationship": the Bermuda and Washington Conferences, 1957', in M. Dockrill and G. Stone (eds), *Decisions and Diplomacy: Essays in Twentieth-Century International History* (London, 1995), pp. 205–23.

7. Clark, op. cit., pp. 157–89.

8. G. W. Rees, *Anglo-American Approaches to Alliance Security, 1955–60* (London, 1996), esp. pp. 164, 135, 133.

9. R. Ovendale, 'Macmillan and the Wind of Change in Africa, 1957–60', *Historical Journal*, vol. 38 (1995), pp. 455–77.

10. *FRUS*, 1955–7(12), pp. 410–12, Memorandum from Murphy to Dulles, 15 December 1956; D. D. Eisenhower, *The White House Years: Waging Peace, 1956–1961* (London, 1966), pp. 178–81; Eisenhower Library, Abilene, Ann Whitman File, DDE Diary Series, Box no. 20, File December 1956, Diary– Staff Memoranda, Memorandum of Conference with Eisenhower, Top Secret, 20 December 1956; FO 371/127739, V10345/2, Caccia to Foreign Office, Telegram no. 30, Secret, 5 January 1957 despatched received 6 January 1957: FO 371/127753, V10731, J. E. Coulson to H. Beeley, Secret and Guard, 19 January 1957.

11. Eisenhower Library, Abilene, Ann Whitman File, Ann Whitman Diary Series, Box no. 8, File June 1958, Diary ACW (2), Diary 15 June 1958.

12. R. Ovendale, *Britain, the United States, and the Transfer of Power in the Middle East, 1945–1962* (London, 1996), pp. 198–215.

13. Ibid., pp. 216–41.

14. Henry Kissinger, 'Suez Weakened Europe', *The Listener*, 20 May 1982, pp. 9–11.

15. R. MacFarquhar, *Sino-American Relations, 1949–1971* (New York, 1972), pp. 101–81; H. Macmillan, *Riding the Storm, 1956–1959* (London, 1971), pp. 538–56; R. K. Betts, *Nuclear Blackmail and Nuclear Balance* (Washington, 1987), pp. 68–76; D. A. Rosenberg, 'The Origins of Overkill: Nuclear Weapons and American Strategy', in N. Graebner (ed.), *The National Security: Its Theory and Practice, 1945–1960* (New York, 1986), pp. 123–95.

16. H. Macmillan, *Pointing the Way, 1959–1961* (London, 1972), pp. 61–92.

17. M. Camps, *Britain and the European Community, 1955–1963* (London, 1964); D. Reynolds, *Britannia Overruled: British Policy and World Power in the Twentieth Century* (London, 1991), pp. 216–21.

18. A. Horne, *Macmillan, 1957–1986* (London, 1989), pp. 300–5.

19. R. F. Kennedy, *13 Days: The Cuban Missile Crisis* (London, 1969); R. Reeves, *President Kennedy: Profile of Power* (London, 1994), p. 291; G. D. Rawnsley, 'How Special is Special? The Anglo-American Alliance during the Cuban Missile Crisis', *Contemporary Record*, IX (1995), pp. 586–601; P. G. Boyle, 'The British Government's View of the Cuban Missile Crisis', *Contemporary Record*, X (1966), pp. 22–38.

20. E. Abel, *The Missiles of October: The Story of the Cuban Missile Crisis, 1962* (London, 1969), p. 64; R. S. Thompson, *The Missiles of October: The Declassified Story of John F. Kennedy and the Cuban Missile Crisis* (New York, 1992), pp. 300–3; J. Dickie, *'Special' No More – Anglo-American Relations: Rhetoric and Reality* (London, 1994), pp. 105–21.

21. G. W. Ball, *The Discipline of Power: Essentials of a Modern World Structure* (London, 1968), pp. 90–117; T. C. Sorensen, *Kennedy* (London, 1966), pp. 627–9; A. M. Schlesinger Jr, *A Thousand Days: John F. Kennedy in the White House* (Boston, 1965), pp. 862–6; Horne, op. cit., pp. 437–43; Clark, op. cit., pp. 409–21.

22. See J. P. G. Freeman, *Britain's Nuclear Arms Control Policy in the Context of Anglo-American Relations, 1957–68* (London, 1986); G. T. Seaborg, *Kennedy, Khrushchev and the Test Ban* (Berkeley, CA, 1981); D. Nunnerley, *President Kennedy and Britain* (London, 1972), pp. 91–110; Dickie, op. cit., pp. 125–9.

23. See Reeves, op. cit., p. 781, for a guide to Kennedy's sexual liaisons.

24. C. J. Bartlett, *'The Special Relationship': A Political History of Anglo-American Relations since 1945* (London, 1992), pp. 95–6.

25. Quoted by Dickie, op. cit., pp. 130–1; D. Reynolds, 'Rethinking Anglo-American Relations', *International Affairs*, vol. 65 (1988–9), pp. 89–111 at p. 109.

8 The European Dimension

1. J. W. Young, *Cold War Europe, 1945–1991: A Political History*, 2nd edn (London, 1996), pp. 136–43.
2. See J. Dickie, *'Special' No More – Anglo-American Relations: Rhetoric and Reality* (London, 1994), pp. 133–71; C. J. Bartlett, *'The Special Relationship': A Political History of Anglo-American Relations since 1945* (London, 1992), pp. 107–47; R. M. Hathaway, *Great Britain and the United States: Special Relations since World War II* (Boston, 1990), pp. 74–117.
3. Quoted by Dickie, op. cit., p. 135.
4. H. Kissinger, *The White House Years* (Boston, 1979), pp. 932–8.
5. Hathaway, op. cit., p. 110.
6. Quoted by Hathaway, ibid., pp. 86–7.
7. H. Kissinger, *Years of Upheaval* (London, 1982), pp. 281–2.
8. Hathaway, op. cit., pp. 79–80; A. P. Dobson, *Anglo-American Relations in the Twentieth Century: Of Friendship, Conflict and the Rise and Decline of Superpowers* (London, 1995), pp. 131–5.
9. H. Wilson, *The Labour Government 1964–1970: A Personal Record* (London, 1971), pp. 455–7.
10. Dobson, op. cit., pp. 144–5; Hathaway, op. cit., pp. 106–7.
11. Kissinger, *The White House Years*, p. 92; Nixon offers a more sanguine version of the meeting, see R. Nixon, *The Memoirs of Richard Nixon* (New York, 1978), pp. 370–1.
12. See Dickie, op. cit., pp. 144–60.
13. Z. Brzezinski, *Power and Principle: Memoirs of the National Security Adviser, 1977–1981* (New York, 1983), p. 291.
14. See R. Ovendale (ed.), *British Defence Policy since 1945: Documents in Contemporary History* (Manchester, 1994), pp. 131–57.
15. Wilson, op. cit., pp. 96–8, 213–14, 254–5, 345–66, 496–503; L. B. Johnson, *The Vantage Point: Perspectives of the Presidency, 1963–1969* (New York, 1971), p. 255; B. Pimlott, *Harold Wilson* (London, 1992), pp. 387–92, 459–65.
16. R. Ovendale, *The Origins of the Arab–Israeli Wars*, 2nd edn (London, 1992), pp. 209–10; G. Brown, *In My Way* (London, 1972), pp. 225–7; W. B. Quandt, *Decade of Decisions: American Policy towards the Arab–Israeli Conflict, 1967–1976* (Berkeley, CA, 1977), pp. 65–6.
17. Ovendale (ed.), *British Defence Policy since 1945*, pp. 136–46; D. Healey, *The Time of My Life* (London, 1990), pp. 278–300.
18. J. Campbell, *Edward Heath: A Biography* (London, 1993), pp. 343–5.
19. Kissinger, *Years of Upheaval*, p. 590; Dickie, op. cit., pp. 145–54; Campbell, pp. 348–51.
20. D. Owen, *Time to Declare* (London, 1991), pp. 291–318; C. Vance, *Hard Choices* (New York, 1983), pp. 284–301; Brzezinski, *Power and Principle*, p. 141.
21. W. B. Quandt, *Camp David: Peacemaking and Politics* (Washington, 1986);

J. Callaghan, *Time and Chance* (London, 1987), pp. 552–7; Dickie, op. cit., pp. 164–71.

9 The Atlantic Preference

1. J. Dickie, *'Special' No More – Anglo-American Relations: Rhetoric and Reality* (London, 1994), p. 205.
2. Public Record Office, London, FO 800/517, fos 114–19, Minute by Dixon of conversation between Bevin and Charles Spofford and Mr Justice Holmes, Secret, 23 August 1950.
3. D. Reynolds, *Britannia Overruled: British Policy and World Power in the Twentieth Century* (London, 1991), p. 258.
4. Dickie, op. cit., p. 210.
5. Lord Carrington, *Reflect on Things Past: The Memoirs of Lord Carrington* (London, 1988), pp. 287–307.
6. M. Thatcher, *The Downing Street Years* (London, 1993), pp. 379–415.
7. Reynolds, *Britannia Overruled*, pp. 262–3.
8. Dickie, op. cit., pp. 174–5.
9. G. Smith, *Reagan and Thatcher* (London, 1990), pp. 23–37.
10. R. Ovendale (ed.), *British Defence Policy since 1945: Documents in Contemporary History* (Manchester 1994), pp. 131, 158–61; Dickie, op. cit., pp. 176–7.
11. See J. Bamford, *The Puzzle Palace: America's National Security Agency and its Special Relationship with Britain's GCHQ* (London, 1982); C. Grayling and C. Langdon, *Just Another Star: Anglo-American Relations since 1945* (London, 1988), pp. 65–106.
12. R. M. Hathaway, *Great Britain and the United States: Special Relations since World War II* (Boston, 1990), pp. 116–17.
13. R. Ovendale, *The Origins of the Arab–Israeli Wars*, 2nd edn (London, 1992), pp. 226–47.
14. Dickie, op. cit., pp. 1–9; C. Weinberger, *Fighting for Peace: Seven Critical Years at the Pentagon* (London, 1990), pp. 143–52; L. Richardson, *When Allies Differ: Anglo-American Relations during the Suez and Falklands Crises* (London, 1996), pp. 111–60; D. Dimbleby and D. Reynolds, *An Ocean Apart* (London, 1988), pp. 314–15.
15. Smith, op. cit., pp. 92–4; Dickie, op. cit., pp. 181–2.
16. See Grayling and Langdon, op. cit., pp. 176–85.
17. Reynolds, *Britannia Overruled*, pp. 275–83; Hathaway, op. cit., pp. 120–5; Smith, op. cit., pp. 125–35, 189–203.
18. Smith, op. cit., pp. 146–60.
19. Ibid., p. 230; G. P. Shultz, *Turmoil and Triumph: My Years as Secretary of State* (New York, 1993), pp. 879–900.
20. Smith, op. cit., p. 227; Thatcher, op. cit., pp. 745–6.
21. C. J. Bartlett, *'The Special Relationship': A Political History of Anglo-American Relations since 1945* (London, 1992), pp. 170–4; Reynolds, *Britannia Overruled*, pp. 283–9; Dickie, op. cit., pp. 207–22.
22. Bartlett, op. cit., pp. 174–8; Dickie, op. cit., pp. 222–5; D. Mervin, *George Bush and the Guardian Presidency* (London, 1996), pp. 180–3.
23. Dickie, op. cit., pp. xiv, 230–42.

24. Ibid., pp. 245–55.
25. *The Times*, 30 November 1995.
26. *Evening Standard*, 13 May 1997.

10 Conclusions

1. See R. J. B. Bosworth, *Explaining Auschwitz and Hiroshima: History Writing and the Second World War 1945–1990* (London, 1993), pp. 23, 27–30, 45, 107, 137.
2. E. H. Carr, *What is History?* (London, 1961), pp. 7–8.
3. Bosworth, *Explaining Auschwitz and Hiroshima*, p. 198.
4. P. Kennedy, *The Rise and Fall of the Great Powers: Economic Change and Military Conflict from 1500 to 2000* (London, 1988); G. Martel, 'The Meaning of Power: Rethinking the Decline and Fall of Great Britain', *International History Review*, XIII (1991), pp. 662–94.
5. N. J. Ashton, *Eisenhower, Macmillan and the Problem of Nasser: Anglo-American Relations and Arab Nationalism, 1955–59* (London, 1996); G. D. Rawnsley, 'How Special is Special? The Anglo-American Alliance during the Cuban Missile Crisis', *Contemporary Record*, IX (1995), pp. 568–601.
6. R. Renwick, *Fighting with Allies: America and Britain in Peace and War* (London, 1996), dustjacket.

SELECT BIBLIOGRAPHY

An outstanding bibliographical essay on the literature in the field of Anglo-American relations can be found in R. M. Hathaway, *Great Britain and the United States: Special Relations since World War II* (Boston, MA, 1990), pp. 157–65.

Abel, E., *The Missiles of October: The Story of the Cuban Missile Crisis 1962* (London, 1969).

Aitken, J., *Nixon: A Life* (London, 1993).

Aldrich, R. J. and M. F. Hopkins (eds), *Intelligence, Defence and Diplomacy: British Policy in the Post-War World* (London, 1994).

Allen, H. C., *Great Britain and the United States* (New York, 1955).

Alperowitz, G., *Atomic Diplomacy: Hiroshima and Potsdam* (London, 1966).

——, *The Decision to Use the Atomic Bomb and the Architecture of an American Myth* (London, 1995).

Ambrose, S. A., *Eisenhower and Berlin, 1945: The Decision to Halt at the Elbe* (New York, 1967).

Anderson, I. H., *ARAMCO: The United States and Saudi Arabia – A Study in the Dynamics of Foreign Oil Policy, 1933–1950* (Princeton, NJ, 1981).

Anderson, S., *Race and Rapprochement: Anglo-Saxonism and Anglo-American Relations, 1895–1904 (London, 1981)*.

Anderson, T. H., *The United States, Great Britain, and the Cold War 1944–1947* (Columbia, MO, 1981).

Andrews, E. M., *The Writing on the Wall: The British Commonwealth and Aggression in the East, 1931–1935* (Sydney, 1987).

Ashton, N. J., *Eisenhower, Macmillan and the Problem of Nasser: Anglo-American Relations and Arab Nationalism, 1955–59* (London, 1996).

Ball, G. W., *The Discipline of Power: Essentials of a Modern World Structure* (London, 1968).

Bamford, J., *The Puzzle Palace: America's National Security Agency and its Special Relationship with Britain's GCHQ* (London, 1982).

Barker, E., *British Policy in South-East Europe in the Second World War* (London, 1976).

——, *Churchill and Eden at War* (London, 1978).

——, *The British between the Superpowers, 1945–50* (London, 1983).

Bartlett, C. J., *'The Special Relationship': A Political History of Anglo-American Relations since 1945* (London, 1992).

Bator, V., *Vietnam: A Diplomatic Tragedy* (London, 1967).

Baylis, J., *Ambiguity and Deterrence: British Nuclear Strategy* (Oxford, 1995).

183

Baylis, J., *Anglo-American Defence Relations, 1939–1984: The Special Relationship*, 2nd edn (London, 1984).

—— (ed.), *Anglo-American Relations since 1939: The Enduring Alliance – Documents in Contemporary History* (Manchester, 1997).

——, *The Diplomacy of Pragmatism: Britain and the Formation of NATO, 1942–1949* (London, 1993).

Becker, J. and F. Knipping (eds), *Power in Europe? Great Britain, France, Italy and Germany in a Postwar World, 1945–1950* (Berlin, 1986).

Bell, C., *The Debatable Alliance: An Essay in Anglo-American Relations* (London, 1964).

Bemis, S. F., *A Diplomatic History of the United States* (New York, 1936).

Bernstein, B. J. (ed.), *Politics and Policies of the Truman Administration* (Chicago, 1970).

Best, A., *Britain, Japan and Pearl Harbor: Avoiding the War in East Asia, 1936–41* (London, 1995).

Betts. R. K., *Nuclear Blackmail and Nuclear Balance* (Washington, 1987).

Bill, J. A. and W. R. Louis (eds), *Mussadiq, Iranian Nationalism, and Oil* (London, 1988).

Bishop, J., *FDR' s Last Year, April 1944–April 1945* (London, 1974).

Blake, R. and W. R. Louis (eds), *Churchill* (Oxford, 1994).

Brebner, J. B., *The North Atlantic Triangle* (New Haven, CT, 1945).

Bridge, C. (ed.), *Munich to Vietnam: Australia's Relations with Britain and the United States since the 1930s* (Carlton, Victoria, 1991).

Brown, G., *In My Way* (London, 1972).

Brzezinski, Z., *Power and Principle: Memoirs of the National Security Adviser, 1977–1981* (New York, 1983).

Bullock, A., *Ernest Bevin, Foreign Secretary, 1945–1951* (London, 1983).

Burk, K., *Britain, America and the Sinews of War, 1914–1918* (Boston, 1985).

Burns, J. M., *Roosevelt: The Soldier of Freedom 1940–1945* (London, 1971).

Cable, J., *Intervention at Abadan: Plan Buccaneer* (London, 1991).

Callaghan, J., *Time and Chance* (London, 1987).

Callahan, R., *Churchill: Retreat from Empire* (Wilmington, DE, 1984).

Campbell, J., *Edward Heath: A Biography* (London, 1993).

Camps, M., *Britain and the European Community, 1955–1963* (London, 1964).

Carr, W., *Poland to Pearl Harbor: The Making of the Second World War* (London, 1985).

Carrington, Lord, *Reflect on Things Past: The Memoirs of Lord Carrington* (London, 1988).

Charmley, J., *Churchill's Grand Alliance: The Anglo-American Special Relationship, 1940–57* (London, 1995).

Churchill, W. S., *The Second World War*, 6 vols (London, 1948–54).

Clark, I., *Nuclear Diplomacy and the Special Relationship: Britain's Deterrent and America, 1957–1962* (Oxford, 1994).

Clarke, R. and A. Cairncross (eds), *Anglo-American Economic Collaboration in War and Peace, 1942–1949* (Oxford, 1982).

Coogan, J. W., *The End of Neutrality: The United States, Britain, and Maritime Rights, 1899–1915* (Ithaca, NY, 1981).

Costello, J., *The Pacific War* (London, 1982).

Costigliola, F., *Awkward Dominion: American Political, Economic and Cultural Relations with Europe, 1919–1933* (Ithaca, NY, 1984).

Crawford, M., *The Anglo-American Crisis of the Mid-Nineteenth Century: 'The Times' and America, 1850–1862* (Athens, GA, 1987).

Croft, S., *The End of Superpower: British Foreign Office Conceptions of a Changing World, 1945–51* (Aldershot, Hants, 1994).

Dallek, R., *Franklin D. Roosevelt and American Foreign Policy, 1932–1945* (New York, 1979).

Dallek, R. (ed.), *The Roosevelt Diplomacy and World War II* (New York, 1970).

Danchev, A., *Very Special Relationship: Field-Marshal Sir John Dill and the Anglo-American Alliance, 1941–44* (London, 1986).

Deighton, A., *The Impossible Peace: Britain, the Division of Germany and the Origins of the Cold War* (Oxford, 1990).

Dickie, J., ' *Special' No More – Anglo-American Relations: Rhetoric and Reality* (London, 1994).

Dimbleby, D. and D. Reynolds, *An Ocean Apart* (London, 1988).

Dockrill, M. and J. W. Young (eds), *British Foreign Policy, 1945–56* (London, 1989).

Dockrill, M. and G. Stone (eds), *Decisions and Diplomacy: Essays in Twentieth-Century International History* (London, 1995).

Dockrill, S., *Britain's Policy for West German Rearmament, 1950–1955* (Cambridge, 1991).

Devereux, D. R., *The Formulation of British Defence Policy towards the Middle East, 1948–56* (London, 1990).

Devlin, P., *Too Proud to Fight* (New York, 1975).

Di Nolfo, E., *The Atlantic Pact Forty Years Later: A Historical Reappraisal* (Berlin, 1991).

Dobson, A. P., *Anglo-American Relations in the Twentieth Century: Of Friendship, Conflict and the Rise and Decline of Superpowers* (London, 1995).

——, *US Wartime Aid to Britain, 1940–1946* (New York, 1986).

Duke, S. W. and W. Krieger (eds), *US Military Forces in Europe: The Early Years, 1945–1970* (Boulder, CO, 1993).

Eden, A., *The Reckoning* (London, 1964).

Edmonds, R., *Setting the Mould: The United States and Britain, 1945–1950* (Oxford, 1986).

Eisenhower, D. D., *The White House Years: Waging Peace 1956–1961* (London, 1966).

Endicott, S. L., *Diplomacy and Enterprise: British China Policy, 1933–1937* (Manchester, 1975).

Finer, H., *Dulles over Suez* (London, 1964).

Frazier, R., *Anglo-American Relations with Greece: The Coming of the Cold War, 1942–47* (London, 1991).

Freeman, J. P. G., *Britain's Nuclear Arms Control Policy in the Context of Anglo-American Relations, 1957–68* (London, 1986).

Gardner, R. N., *Sterling-Dollar Diplomacy in Current Perspective*, 3rd edn (New York, 1980).

Gelber, L. M., *The Rise of Anglo-American Friendship: A Study in World Politics, 1891–1906* (London, 1938).

Gilbert, M. (ed.), *A Century of Conflict, 1850–1950: Essays for A. J. P. Taylor* (London, 1966).

Gilbert, M., *Winston S. Churchill*, vol. VIII, *'Never Despair', 1945–1965* (London, 1988).

Gorst, A., L. Johnman and W. S. Lucas (eds), *Post-war Britain, 1945–64: Themes and Perspectives* (London, 1989).

Gowing, M., *Independence and Deterrence: Britain and Atomic Energy, 1945–52*, 2 vols (London, 1974).

Graebner, H. (ed.), *The National Security: Its Theory and Practice, 1945–1960* (New York, 1986).

Grayling, C. and C. Langdon, *Just Another Star: Anglo-American Relations since 1945* (London, 1988).

Gregory, R., *The Origins of American Intervention in the First World War* (New York, 1971).

Hahn, P. L., *The United States, Great Britain and Egypt, 1945–1956* (Chapel Hill, NC, 1991).

Haines, G. K. and J. S. Walker (eds), *American Foreign Relations: A Historiographical Review* (Westport, CT, 1981).

Halberstam, D., *The Best and the Brightest* (London, 1974).

Hall, H. D. and C. C. Wrigley, *Studies of Overseas Supply* (London, 1956).

Harbutt, F., *The Iron Curtain: Churchill, America, and the Origins of the Cold War* (New York, 1986).

Hathaway, R. M., *Ambiguous Partnership: Britain and America, 1944–1947* (New York, 1981).

——, *Great Britain and the United States: Special Relations since World War II* (Boston, 1990).

Healey, D., *The Time of My Life* (London, 1990).

Henderson, N., *The Birth of NATO* (London, 1982).

Hess, G. R., *America Encounters India, 1941–1947* (Baltimore, 1971).

Higgins, T., *Soft Underbelly: The Anglo-American Controversy over the Italian Campaign, 1939–1945* (New York, 1968).

Hogan, M. J. (ed.), *The Historiography of American Foreign Relations since 1941* (Cambridge, 1995).

——, *Informal Entente: The Private Structure of Cooperation in Anglo-American Economic Diplomacy, 1918–1929* (Columbia, MO, 1977).

——, *The Marshall Plan: America, Britain, and the Reconstruction of Western Europe, 1947–1952* (Cambridge, 1987).

Hoopes, T., *The Devil and John Foster Dulles* (Boston, 1973).

Horne, A., *Macmillan, 1957–1986* (London, 1989).

Ilan, A., *The Origin of the Arab-Israeli Arms Race: Arms, Embargo, Military Power and Decision in the 1948 Palestine War* (New York, 1996).

Ireland, T. P., *Creating the Entangling Alliance: The Origins of the North Atlantic Treaty Organization* (London, 1981).

Jackson, W. and Lord Bramall, *The Chiefs: The Story of the United Kingdom Chiefs of Staff* (London, 1992).

Johnson, L. B., *The Vantage Point: Perspectives of the Presidency, 1963–1969* (New York, 1971).

Jones, H., *To the Webster–Ashburton Treaty: A Study in Anglo-American Relations, 1783–1843* (Chapel Hill, NC, 1977).

Jones, M., *Failure in Palestine: British and United States Policy after the Second World War* (London, 1986).

Jones, W. D., *The American Problem in British Diplomacy, 1841–1861* (London, 1974).

Kaplan, L. S. (ed.), *American Historians and the Atlantic Alliance* (Kent, OH, 1991).

Kennedy, R. F., *13 Days: The Cuban Missile Crisis* (London, 1969).

Kent, J., *British Imperial Strategy and the Origins of the Cold War, 1944–49* (Leicester, 1993).

Kimball, W. F. (ed.), *Churchill and Roosevelt: The Complete Correspondence*, 3 vols (London, 1984).

——, *The Juggler: Franklin Roosevelt as Wartime Statesman* (Princeton, NJ, 1991).

——, *The Most Unsordid Act: Lend-Lease, 1939–1941* (Baltimore, MD, 1969).

Kingston, P. W. T., *Britain and the Politics of Modernization in the Middle East, 1945–1958* (Cambridge, 1996).

Kissinger, H., *The White House Years* (Boston, 1979).

——, *Years of Upheaval* (London, 1982).

Kolko, G., *The Politics of War* (New York, 1968).

Kuniholm, B. R., *The Origins of the Cold War in the Near East: Great Power Conflict and Diplomacy in Iran, Turkey and Greece* (Princeton, NJ, 1980).

Kunz, D. B., *The Economic Diplomacy of the Suez Crisis* (Chapel Hill, NC, 1991).

Kyle, K., *Suez* (London, 1992).

Lane, A. and H. Temperley (eds), *The Rise and Fall of the Grand Alliance, 1941–45* (London, 1995).

Langer, W. L. and S. E. Gleason, *The Challenge to Isolation, 1937–1940* (London, 1952).

Lash, J. P., *Roosevelt and Churchill, 1939–1941: The Partnership that Saved the West* (New York, 1976).

Leigh-Phippard, H., *Congress and US Military Aid to Britain: Interdependence and Dependence, 1949–56* (London, 1995).

Link, A., *Wilson*, 5 vols (Princeton, NJ, 1947–65).

Louis, W. R., *The British Empire in the Middle East, 1945–1951: Arab Nationalism, the United States, and Postwar Imperialism* (Oxford, 1984).

——, *Imperialism at Bay: The United States and the Decolonization of the British Empire, 1941–1945* (London, 1978).

——, and H. Bull (eds), *The 'Special Relationship': Anglo-American Relations since 1945* (Oxford, 1986).

—— and R. Owen (eds), *Suez 1956: The Crisis and its Consequences* (Oxford, 1989).

Lowe, P., *Great Britain and the Origins of the Pacific War: A Study of British Policy in East Asia, 1937–1941* (Oxford, 1977).

Lucas, S. W., *Divided We Stand: Britain, the United States and the Suez Crisis* (London, 1991).

Maddox, R. J., *The New Left and the Origins of the Cold War* (Princeton, NJ, 1973).

Marks, F. W., *Power and Peace: The Diplomacy of John Foster Dulles* (Westport, CT, 1993).

May, E., *The World War and American Isolation, 1914–1917* (Cambridge, MA, 1959).

MacDonald, C. A., *The United States, Britain and Appeasement, 1936–1939* (London, 1981).

MacFarquhar, R., *Sino-American Relations, 1949–1971* (New York, 1972).

Macleod, I., *Neville Chamberlain* (London, 1961).

Macmillan, H., *Pointing the Way, 1959–1961* (London, 1972).

——, *Riding the Storm, 1956–1959* (London, 1971).

McDonald, I. S. (ed.), *Anglo-American Relations since the Second World War* (London, 1974).

McGhee, G., *Envoy to the Middle East: Adventures in Diplomacy* (New York, 1969).

McKercher, B. J. C. (ed.), *Anglo-American Relations in the 1920s: The Struggle for Supremacy* (London, 1991).

McNeill, W. H., *America, Britain and Russia: Their Cooperation and Conflict, 1941–1946* (London, 1953).

Mee, C. L. Jr, *Meeting at Potsdam* (London, 1975).

Melissen, J., *The Struggle for Nuclear Partnership: Britain, the United States and the Making of an Ambiguous Alliance, 1952–1959* (Groningen, 1993).

Mervin, D., *George Bush and the Guardian Presidency* (London, 1996).

Moran, C. M. W., *Winston Churchill: The Struggle for Survival, 1940–1965* (London, 1966).

Morison, S. E., H. S. Commager and W. E. Leuchtenburg, *A Concise History of the American Republic* (New York, 1977).

Mosley, L., *Dulles: A Biography of Eleanor, Allen, and John Foster Dulles and their Family Network* (London, 1978).

Nadeau, R., *Stalin, Churchill, and Roosevelt Divide Europe* (London, 1990).

Neale. R. G., *Britain and American Imperialism, 1898–1900* (St Lucia, Brisbane, 1965).

Nicholas, H. G., *The United States and Britain* (Chicago, IL, 1975).

Nish, I. H., *Alliance in Decline: A Study in Anglo-Japanese Relations 1908–23* (London, 1972).

Nish, I. H., *The Anglo-Japanese Alliance: The Diplomacy of Two Island Empires, 1894–1907*, 2nd edn (London, 1985).

——, *Japan's Struggle with Internationalism: Japan, China and the League of Nations, 1931–3* (London, 1993).

Nixon, R., *The Memoirs of Richard Nixon* (New York, 1978).

Nunnerley, D., *President Kennedy and Britain* (London, 1972).

Offner, A., *American Appeasement: United States Foreign Policy and Germany, 1933–1938* (Cambridge, MA, 1969).

Orde, A., *The Eclipse of Great Britain: The United States and British Imperial Decline, 1895–1956* (London, 1996).

Ovendale, R., *'Appeasement' and the English Speaking World: Britain, the United States, the Dominions, and the Policy of 'Appeasement', 1937–1939* (Cardiff, 1975).

——, *Britain, the United States, and the End of the Palestine Mandate, 1942–1948* (Woodbridge, Suffolk, 1989).

——, *Britain, the United States, and the Transfer of Power in the Middle East* (London, 1996).

—— (ed.), *British Defence Policy since 1945: Documents in Contemporary History* (Manchester, 1994).

——, *The English-Speaking Alliance: Britain, the United States, the Dominions and the Cold War, 1945–1951* (London, 1985).

—— (ed.), *The Foreign Policy of the British Labour Governments, 1945–1951* (Leicester, 1984).

——, *The Origins of the Arab–Israeli Wars*, 2nd edn (London, 1992).

Owen, D., *Time to Declare* (London, 1991).

Pappé, I., *Britain and the Arab–Israeli Conflict, 1948–51* (London, 1988).

Parker, R. A. C., *Chamberlain and Appeasement: British Policy and the Coming of the Second World War* (London, 1993).

—— (ed.), *Sir Winston Churchill: Studies in Statesmanship* (London, 1995).

Pelling, H., *Britain and the Marshall Plan* (London, 1988).

Perkins, B., *The First Rapprochement: England and the United States, 1795–1805* (Berkeley, CA, 1967).

——, *The Great Rapprochement: England and the United States, 1895–1914* (New York, 1968).

Pimlott, B., *Harold Wilson* (London, 1992).

Prange, G. W., *At Dawn We Slept: The Untold Story of Pearl Harbor* (London, 1982).

Quandt, W. B., *Camp David: Peacemaking and Politics* (Washington, 1986).
——, *Decade of Decisions: American Policy towards the Arab–Israeli Conflict, 1967–1976* (Berkeley, CA, 1977).
Rees, G. W., *Anglo-American Approaches to Alliance Security, 1955–60* (London, 1996).
Reeves, R., *President Kennedy: Profile of Power* (London, 1994).
Reid, E., *Time of Fear and Hope: The Making of the North Atlantic Treaty, 1947–1949* (Toronto, 1979).
Renwick, R., *Fighting with Allies: America and Britain in Peace and War* (London, 1996).
Reynolds, D., *The Creation of the Anglo-American Alliance, 1937–41: A Study in Competitive Co-operation* (London, 1981).
——, *Lord Lothian and Anglo-American Relations, 1939–1940* (Philadelphia, PA, 1983).
——, *Britannia Overruled: British Policy and World Power in the 20th Century* (London, 1991).
——, *Rich Relations: The American Occupation of Britain, 1942–1945* (London, 1995).
Richardson, D. and G. Stone (eds), *Decisions and Diplomacy: Essays in Twentieth-Century International History* (London, 1995).
Richardson, L., *When Allies Differ: Anglo-American Relations during the Suez and Falkland Crises* (London, 1996).
Riste, O. (ed.), *Western Security: The Formative Years – European and Atlantic Defence, 1947–1953* (Oslo, 1985).
Rock, W. R., *Appeasement on Trial: British Foreign Policy and its Critics, 1938–1939* (New York, 1966).
——, *Chamberlain and Roosevelt: British Foreign Policy and the United States, 1937–1940* (Columbus, OH, 1988).
Ross, G. (ed.), *The Foreign Office and the Kremlin: British Documents on Anglo-Soviet Relations, 1941–45* (Cambridge, 1984).
Rothwell, V. H., *Britain and the Cold War, 1941–1947* (London, 1982).
Rubin, B., *The Great Powers in the Middle East, 1941–1947: The Road to the Cold War* (London, 1980).
Rushbridger, J. and E. Nave, *Betrayal at Pearl Harbor: How Churchill Lured Roosevelt into War* (London, 1991).
Russett, B. M., *Community and Contention: Britain and America in the Twentieth Century* (Cambridge, MA, 1963).
Ryan, H. B., *The Vision of Anglo-America: The US–UK Alliance and the Emerging Cold War, 1943–1946* (Cambridge, 1987).
Sainsbury, K., *Churchill and Roosevelt at War: The War They Fought and the Peace They Hoped to Make* (London, 1994).
Schlesinger, A. M. Jr, *A Thousand Days: John F. Kennedy in the White House* (Boston, 1965).
Seaborg, G. T., *Kennedy, Khrushchev and the Test Ban* (Berkeley, CA, 1981).
Sharp, T., *The Wartime Alliance and the Zonal Division of Germany* (Oxford, 1975).
Shlaim, A., *The United States and the Berlin Blockade, 1948–1949: A Study in Crisis Decision-Making* (Berkeley, CA, 1983).
Shultz, G. P., *Turmoil and Triumph: My Years as Secretary of State* (New York, 1993).
Silverfarb, D., *The Twilight of British Ascendancy in the Middle East: A Case Study of Iraq, 1941–1950* (New York, 1994).
Singh, A. I., *The Limits of British Influence: South Asia and the Anglo-American Relationship, 1947–56* (London, 1993).

Smith, G., *Reagan and Thatcher* (London, 1990).

Sorensen, T. C., *Kennedy* (London, 1966).

Thatcher, M., *The Downing Street Years* (London, 1993).

Thompson, R. S., *The Missiles of October: The Declassified Story of John F. Kennedy and the Cuban Missile Crisis* (New York, 1992).

Thorne, C., *Allies of a Kind: the United States, Britain and the War against Japan, 1941–1945* (London, 1978).

——, *The Limits of Foreign Policy: The West, the League and the Far Eastern Crisis of 1931–1933* (London, 1972).

Tillman, S. P., *Anglo-American Relations at the Paris Peace Conference of 1919* (Princeton, NJ, 1961).

Trotter, A., *Britain and East Asia, 1933–1937* (London, 1975).

Truman. H. S., *Years of Trial and Hope* (London, 1956).

Turner, A. C., *The Unique Partnership: Britain and the United States* (New York, 1971).

Ullmann, W., *The United States in Prague, 1945–1948* (New York, 1978).

Vance, C., *Hard Choices* (New York, 1983).

Waller, G. M. (ed.), *Pearl Harbor: Roosevelt and the Coming of the War*, rev. edn (Lexington, MA, 1976).

Ward, A. J., *Ireland and Anglo-American Relations, 1899–1921* (London, 1969).

Watt, D. Cameron, *Succeeding John Bull: America in Britain's Place, 1900–1975* (Cambridge, 1984).

Weinberger, C., *Fighting for Peace: Seven Critical Years at the Pentagon* (London, 1990).

Wells, S., *The Time for Decision* (London, 1944).

Wheeler-Bennett, J. and A. Nicholls, *The Semblance of Peace* (London, 1971).

Williams, F., *A Prime Minister Remembers* (London, 1961).

Wilson, H., *The Labour Government, 1964–1970: A Personal Record* (London, 1971).

Woods, R. B., *A Changing of the Guard: Anglo-American Relations, 1941–1946* (Chapel Hill, NC, 1990).

Woodward, D. R., *Trial by Friendship: Anglo-American Relations 1917–1918* (Lexington, KY, 1993).

Woodward, L., *British Foreign Policy in the Second World War*, vol. 3 (London, 1971).

Yergin, D., *Shattered Peace* (Boston, 1977).

Young, J. W., *Britain and European Unity, 1945–1992* (London, 1993).

——, *Britain, France, and the Unity of Europe, 1945–1951* (Leicester, 1993).

——, *Cold War Europe, 1945–1991: a Political History*, 2nd edn (London, 1996).

—— (ed.), *The Foreign Policy of Churchill's Peacetime Administration, 1951–1955* (Leicester, 1988).

——, *Winston Churchill's Last Campaign: Britain and the Cold War, 1951–5* (Oxford, 1996).

Zametica, J. (ed.), *British Officials and British Foreign Policy, 1945–50* (Leicester, 1990).

Zhai, Q., *The Dragon, the Lion, and the Eagle: Chinese–British–American Relations, 1949–1958* (Kent, OH, 1994).

INDEX